Long Way Home

Long Way Home

On the Trail of Steinbeck's America

BILL BARICH

Skyhorse Publishing

Skyhorse Publishing books may be purchased in bulk at special discounts for sales promotion, corporate gifts, fund-raising, or educational purposes. Special editions can also be created to specifications. For details, contact the Special Sales Department, Skyhorse Publishing, 307 West 36th Street, 11th Floor, New York, NY 10018 or info@skyhorsepublishing.com.

Skyhorse® and Skyhorse Publishing® are registered trademarks of Skyhorse Publishing, Inc.®, a Delaware corporation.

Visit our website at www.skyhorsepublishing.com.

10 9 8 7 6 5 4 3 2 1

Library of Congress Cataloging-in-Publication Data is available on file.

Cover design by Tom Lau
Cover photo credit: iStockphoto

Print ISBN: 978-1-5107-3247-6
Ebook ISBN: 978-1-5107-3248-3

Printed in the United States of America

"We do not take a trip; a trip takes us."

— JOHN STEINBECK

Part One

W<small>HEN I WAS</small> in my late teens and hungry for the road, ready to sign on as an angelheaded hipster if only I knew how or where, I bought a copy of John Steinbeck's *Travels with Charley* and whipped through it in a couple of days. The idea of rambling around America carefree and independent, with no particular destination in mind, appealed to my deepest fantasies. Like Steinbeck, I'd drink applejack with fruit pickers, tour the Badlands, and crest the Rockies, perfectly content to survive on cowboy coffee and corned-beef hash and sleep by a fast-flowing stream.

That never happened, of course. More than forty years went by before *Travels* entered my life again when I stumbled on an old paperback edition at a thrift shop in Dublin. The cover illustration showed a rugged-looking Steinbeck sitting on a grassy hillside next to a French poodle tinted an odd shade of purple. In the distance, you can see the camper he called Rocinante after Don Quixote's horse, along with a vineyard and some mountains that resemble the Gabilans near his birthplace in Salinas, California.

"The #1 National Bestseller Now Only 75 Cents," cried a banner over the title. I paid two euros myself, eager to share Steinbeck's adventures again after almost a decade in Ireland, but the book let me down. It bore no relation to my youthful memory of it, except for the affectionate portrait of Charley. The colorful characters I'd enjoyed seemed cut from cardboard, and their dialogue sounded wooden. *Travels* was melancholy rather than merry, steeped in loneliness and fatigue.

Puzzled, I consulted a biography of Steinbeck and a volume of his letters. He'd deliberately intended to distract his readers, I discovered. His wit and warmth were manufactured, a product of his skillful sleight of hand, or so he confided to his editor, Pascal Covici. At the core of *Travels* is a bleak vision of America's decline that he chose to mitigate by telling jokes and anecdotes.

In reality, the United States suffered from "a sickness, a kind of wasting disease," he warned Covici in private, and Americans, overly invested in material toys and saddled with debt, were bored, anguished, discontented, and no longer capable of the heroism that had rescued them from the terrifying poverty of the Depression.

"And underneath it all building energies like gasses in a corpse," he mourned. "When that explodes, I tremble to think what will be the result."

His words had the ring of prophecy when I came across them in August 2008. With the economy in free fall, it appeared as if the gasses had exploded, leaving the survivors to wander haphazardly through the aftermath with no leadership or sense of direction. That was the impression the media created, at any rate, but I couldn't vouch for its accuracy. I had lost touch with my own country during my time abroad, the same reason Steinbeck gave for taking his trip.

He'd been living in New York and England and felt cut off from his subject matter, so he devised a plan to explore the heartland and refresh himself. He once referred to it as Operation Windmills, another reference to its quixotic essence. In September 1960, right after Labor Day, he'd set out from his home in Sag Harbor, the historic whaling village on Long Island, to rediscover America. Initially, his morale was high.

"I'll avoid cities and hit small towns and farms and ranches, sit in bars and hamburger stands and on Sunday go to church," he enthused to some friends. "I am very excited about this. It will be a kind of rebirth."

For a man of fifty-eight, the wish to be reborn suggests a deep unrest, and that was true of Steinbeck. He was more frank with his agent, Elizabeth Otis, dropping the jolly pretense as his departure drew near.

"Between us—what I am proposing is no little trip or reporting," he admitted, "but a frantic last attempt to save my life and the integrity of my creative pulse."

According to his biographer Jay Parini, he was depressed, spiritually adrift, and fearful his best work had all been done. His health was fragile, too. Normally robust, he'd been rattled by a pair of minor strokes that were never properly diagnosed, his wife, Elaine, said. Already the dark thoughts were brewing, but Steinbeck tried valiantly to conquer them. As Americans will do, he looked to the road for a cure.

In spite of its flaws, *Travels* ignited my old fantasies, and I began to think about making a similar trip almost half a century later. As a voluntarily displaced Californian, I understood Steinbeck's craving for some contact with the heartland. Along with rediscovering America myself, I could put his prophecy to the test. If the nation hovered on the edge of ruin, I'd record it faithfully, but I hoped to prove him wrong. In an election year, with the fabled winds of change trying hard to blow, the future was up for grabs.

Steinbeck spent about eleven weeks on the road, while I'd have to settle for six on a tight budget. I considered renting a camper, naturally, but the cost proved astronomical, especially after I factored in the soaring price of gas, so I'd go by car instead and swallow the bitter pill of motel living. In fact, Elizabeth Otis had advised her client to do the same, concerned that Rocinante would isolate him from others and compromise his intention.

For my primary route from coast to coast, I settled on U.S. 50. The highway, lightly traveled in many stretches, runs for about thirty-two hundred miles from Maryland to the Pacific through the middle of America. The back roads would grant me access to plenty of small towns— Coolville, Ohio, say, or Peabody, Kansas—as well as farms and hamburger stands. There'd be no shortage of churches, either. When I saw that Chesapeake Bay, the Missouri River, the Santa Fe Trail, and the Great Basin Desert were all on my itinerary, I nearly broke into a ballad from the Pete Seeger songbook.

With those decisions made, I had just one more issue to address. What about a dog to act as Charley's stand-in? I must have fielded the question fifty times at least. Most people were joking—I don't have a dog—but a few diehard literalists meant business. One woman even offered to loan me her hairless terrier Beanie, an amusing little guy who wears clothes outdoors to protect his sensitive skin from the sun.

As much as I appreciated her generosity, the chance to play valet to a terrier over thirty-two hundred miles struck me as absolutely no fun. Although I'd seized on Steinbeck as a model and an inspiration—I explained this to the kind woman—I did not feel compelled to duplicate his trip in every detail, a dull exercise in comparing and contrasting. What intrigued me was the relative validity of his prophecy.

Travels with Beanie? No way. I'd go it alone.

IN EARLY SEPTEMBER, I booked a ticket to New York on Aer Lingus and a humble Ford Focus with Budget Rent A Car at JFK. For my first night's lodging, I reserved a motel room in Dover, Delaware, perilously close to a harness track and casino I'd already begun to steel myself against. If I hoped to be in San Francisco in time for the presidential election, I'd have to be steadfast. A taste for low entertainment has derailed many an expedition, after all.

A trip spawns advisers in schools, Steinbeck observed, and he was dead right. Without having to ask, I collected tips on hot springs, fishing holes, scenic drives, geological oddities, topless bars, and obscure museums devoted to eccentric pursuits. There were roadside attractions I dared not miss—the UFO Watchtower in Hooper, Colorado, say, just a fifty-two-mile detour from U.S. 50. My pals recommended both fine restaurants and greasy spoons, including the best spots for five-way chili around Cincinnati.

Avoid Indiana on a Sunday, someone counseled me. It's against the law to buy any beer to take home.

On my own, I tried to get up to speed on the America I'd left behind. At times I felt baffled as I trawled the Internet, reading about TiVo digital recorders and Kobayashi, the hot dog eating champ. *American Idol* had passed me by entirely, although for that I was grateful. I'd never visited at an Applebee's, either, where about two million of my fellow citizens chow down every day, nor had I seen a Prius, shopped at Costco, or watched a cage fight. I'd been deprived. Or maybe spared.

In my rare moments of anxiety, which I hated with a passion and refused to ascribe to advancing age, I wondered if Steinbeck's "monster land" would overwhelm me just as it did him. The country he went searching for, a figment based on his nostalgic childhood memories, scarcely existed anymore. The open space of his beloved San Joaquin Valley was rapidly disappearing, for instance. About 1.5 million farms in the United States had gone under since 1950.

Our cities also had been transformed beyond recognition. Of the fifteen largest metro areas, only Los Angeles had gained rather than lost residents over the same period of time. By 1960, Americans had decamped to the suburbs, and one in every four families occupied a house that had been built in the previous decade.

They were in hock to the banks now for their mortgages, auto loans, and such material toys as a television set. Eighty-eight percent of all households owned a TV, as opposed to just 11 percent in the 1950 census. In exchange for their comforts, though, they'd sacrificed a degree of independence. They labored, more and more, for corporations, while the ranks of blue-collar workers and the self-employed were at an all-time low.

For Steinbeck, a self-reliant type, it must have been galling to see the soft underbelly of the nation exposed.

"Over and over I thought we lack the pressures that make men strong and the anguish that makes men great," he griped to Pascal Covici.

He longed for the America of his youth, I believe, and the integrity of Franklin Delano Roosevelt, whose values he shared. In his inaugural address of March 1933, Roosevelt had the audacity to urge his often destitute constituents to keep their financial losses in perspective. A plague of locusts hadn't descended on them, he chided, nor had they endured the hardships of the forefathers.

"Our common difficulties concern, thank God, only material things," FDR intoned. Happiness doesn't lie in the mere possession of money, he added. It lies instead in the joy of achievement and the thrill of creative effort. The unscrupulous money changers "have no vision, and when there is no vision the people perish."

Roosevelt's speech captured the excellence Americans once aspired to, so I packed a copy for my traveling library. FDR joined such old favorites as Emerson, Thoreau, and Melville, but I gave Walt Whitman a break, figuring he must be tired after riding shotgun with so many pilgrims before me. I brought along some Henry Miller, too, and also Sinclair

Lewis's George F. Babbitt, who'd have been knee-deep in the subprime mortgage scandal.

"He made nothing in particular, neither butter nor shoes nor poetry," said Lewis, "but he was nimble in the calling of selling houses for more than people could afford to pay for them."

Steinbeck loaded his camper with tons of junk he never used— padded subzero underwear, for example—so I stuck to the basics. I took a flyrod, a sleeping bag, some hiking boots, binoculars, and a first-aid kit, as well as my laptop, a cell phone, notebooks, and a thick Rand McNally road atlas. Though Steinbeck stocked enough booze to float a fraternity party, I knew the treachery of lonely nights in one-horse towns and exercised caution in that regard.

IF I HAD any doubts about the universal appeal of a road trip, the cabbie who drove me to the Dublin airport put them to rest. When he heard my accent, he regaled me with an account of his recent family holiday at Disney World in Orlando, where the "actual amount of sunshine"—his very words—stunned him and, needless to say, burned him to a crisp. He sighed and wished he could go with me, although that would mean deserting the wife and kids in Ballybrack.

"In a big Cadillac convertible, that'd be the way to do it," he chirped. I didn't have the heart to puncture his daydream by mentioning the Focus.

In New York, my cabbie wore a turban and spoke not at all. He dropped me on the Upper West Side, where I'd stay with friends for a brief while before picking up the car. After the dismal news reports, I expected to see evidence of the apocalypse in the streets, but the miracle of everyday life still went on. The mailman completed his rounds, a little girl fell off her bike and skinned a knee, a furtive couple slipped into a seedy hotel, and so on. I found this somehow comforting.

In sunny Central Park, the ice-cream vendors were doing just fine despite the plunging value of 401(k)s. My friends opened a bottle of wine, and we moved to a terrace and watched dozens of joggers circle the reservoir, trying to outrun any phantoms pursuing them. The talk was of politics, not economics, and how Sarah Palin had lately been meeting with world leaders, among them Asif Ali Zardari, Pakistan's flirtatious new president, who called her "gorgeous."

In *Travels*, Steinbeck used the Spanish term *vacilando* to describe a peculiar kind of wandering. "If one is vacilando, he is going somewhere but doesn't greatly care whether or not he gets there, although he has direction."

I became an expert *vacilador* in Manhattan, visiting museums and galleries and treating myself to lunch at the Grand Central Oyster Bar, where every table was occupied. Shoppers were still splurging on Pescatore's lobster at the station's market, too, and Queso del Tietar from Murray's Cheese at thirty bucks a pound. The prime aged beef at Gallagher's nearby, displayed in all its marbled splendor, had lost none of its allure.

Maybe New Yorkers were in denial, but that was true only in the bastions of privilege. A long line of youths, mostly African American and Hispanic, stood outside a Circuit City on Broadway one morning, clutching their résumés beneath a "Now Hiring" banner. The lucky few to land a job would lose it a few months later when Circuit City went belly-up, a symptom of the nation's woes.

On my last day in Manhattan, I boarded a train at Penn Station for Westbury, off to see the America of my childhood. I'd grown up in one of those instant suburbs of the 1950s, in a tract slapped up on a Long Island potato field. Our Levitt house looked much the same as it did when Mickey Mantle played center field for the Yankees, with its postage-stamp front yard, droopy rhododendrons, and aluminum siding. In the pigskin weather of late September, footballs should have been flying through the air, but the kids must have been indoors tapping at their computers.

I walked to a nearby luncheonette where the senior citizens, dinosaurs of the print era, still reported like clockwork for their papers. Perched on a stool, I drank a cup of coffee strong enough to peel the rust off a bumper and ate an old-fashioned grilled cheese sandwich. The headlines were strictly contemporary, though. NEW YORK COPS TASER NUDE BROOKLYN MAN, shouted the *Post*. FATE OF BAIL-OUT PLAN UNRESOLVED, countered the *Times*.

At our old Little League field, I sat alone in the bleachers and defied

Satchel Paige's advice by looking back to recall my first trip across the country. After college and a Peace Corps stint, I wheeled away from Mellow Lane in 1969, ready to help the hippies in San Francisco save the world. My mother worried that some rednecks like those in *Easy Rider* would shoot me on account of my hair, not yet as long as any of the Beatles', but a balky Corvair did the only damage.

As I climbed Stanyan Street toward the Haight-Ashbury, high on flower-powered dreams, the clutch cable snapped, and I managed to roll back to a Chevron station on Geary Boulevard. I still remembered the station owner's name: Irwin Ching. When he gave me a bill for the repairs, he signed it at the bottom *I. Ching.* I was young enough to interpret this as a positive sign.

OMENS. THEY STILL had me at their mercy. A storm to match Steinbeck's hurricane dumped five inches of rain on New York the night before my departure. The wind howled so wickedly I couldn't sleep, and the road that once beckoned now seemed like a dead end.

"My warm bed and comfortable house grew increasingly desireable and my wife incalculably precious," Steinbeck wrote on the brink of departing, and I identified with him, already pining for my dear Imelda in faraway Dublin.

At breakfast, I dawdled over newspaper stories I'd ordinarily skip, such as the one about Tomoji Tanabe of Japan, reputedly the world's oldest man. On his 112th birthday, Tanabe had expressed a desire to live for "infinity," but at 113 he changed his mind and wanted only five more years—another omen, perhaps. I'd never studied the box scores so religiously, either, but the jig was up when I caught myself lingering over a Bergdorf Goodman ad for the fall line.

Limbs and branches littered Central Park West outside, and filthy water stood ankle-deep at the curb. Only gypsy sharks in black limos swept by, prepared to escort me anywhere at all for triple the standard fare. At last I flagged a yellow cab and took off for the airport to claim the Focus. People huddled under bus shelters, trying but failing to stay dry. We passed housing projects named for Washington and Jefferson, and a bank named for Ponce de Leon. What *this* portended, if anything, I couldn't tell.

At Budget Rent A Car, I encountered a delay. Two clerks were explaining the concept of liability insurance to a German couple, who spoke very little English and were beholden to a weepy blond toddler clinging to his mother's leg and wailing like a troubled infant from the Brothers Grimm.

"If I have accident," the man kept repeating, "but not my cause, I pay?" and the clerks would shake their heads in unison, fold their arms, and spout more confusing legalese with the practiced air of thespians.

Finally, I lost patience and decided to step outside, where the rain had dwindled to a fine mist. I sat on my duffel bag and thumbed through the dog-eared copy of *Travels with Charley* that had started it all. "Well, John, here we go," I muttered. "I hope America doesn't disappoint me as much as it did you."

The omens were definitely improving, in fact. The toddler's crying jag had ended, and the Germans dragged away their luggage and the exhausted lad, freeing the clerks to deal with other customers. A ray of sunshine peeked through the clouds, unaware or unafraid of being a cliché. Ride toward the radiance—that was the order of the day. If I met with no other obstacles, I'd be in Dover well before dark.

Part Two

....

OPTIMISM COMES NATURALLY to most travelers, both a blessing and a curse. As I drove away from the airport, I worked up some excitement again, but the route to Dover hardly qualified as scenic. Stuck on crowded expressways and parkways, I fought boredom to a draw until I reached the Verrazano-Narrows Bridge and woke to a superb view of New York Harbor. When you cross a broad expanse of water, it creates a sense of voyaging. I truly felt under way now, sailing into the great unknown.

In spite of the bruising ten-dollar toll, I was glad I'd chosen not to leave from midtown Manhattan. That was Henry Miller's mistake on his American odyssey in 1944. Fresh off the boat from Paris, Miller bought the first car he looked at without even kicking the tires. He'd taken only half a dozen driving lessons, but he still felt confident of his skills. He could steer, shift gears, and apply the brakes. What else was necessary? He hadn't counted on the Holland Tunnel, his gateway to New Jersey.

"I had never been in the damned hole before, except once in a taxi," he complained. "It was a nightmare. The beginning of an endless nightmare, I should say."

For Miller, the tunnel became an emblem of the country's irritants, and he discovered something new to dislike around every bend. He was terrific at loathing, really, but he never sounded unhappy. Like most optimists, he had a blind spot.

"I always expect the angels to pee in my beer," he said, explaining how disappointed he was when his publisher only coughed up a five-hundred-dollar advance for his travel book instead of the five thousand he anticipated. Briefly knocked off balance, he rebounded in an instant and started ranting.

I sank a bit myself when the horrors of the New Jersey Turnpike loomed ahead. Scholarly tomes have been written about the turnpike's ugliness. Smokestacks, refineries, junkyards, vacant lots, spooky compounds fenced off with concertina wire, there's no end to the ongoing assault on your brain. Miller could have squeezed fifty pages of bile from the first twelve miles alone.

The Walt Whitman Rest Area near Cherry Hill seemed too ripe to make much of as material. The turnpike has thirteen such stops honoring former Jersey residents such as Joyce Kilmer, Thomas Edison, James Fenimore Cooper, and Vince Lombardi. A plaque with the Good Gray Poet's visage and eight lines from "Song of Myself" hangs inside, but it attracted scant attention. Folks were too busy packing it in at Roy Rogers and Nathan's Famous—mostly large folks, it must be noted.

Soon I was back on the turnpike and enjoying another watery vista from the Delaware Memorial Bridge. The Delaware River emptied into the ocean below, the same river Washington crossed on Christmas Day in 1776 to defeat the Hessian troops in Trenton. In Emmanuel Leutze's famous painting, once tacked up in my third-grade classroom, Washington poses in a rowboat whose oarsmen nimbly dodge the ice floes.

On Route One, I turned south and lost the heavy traffic. I was in Delaware now, a state I'd never visited. Only Rhode Island is smaller, I knew that much, but I wanted some physical contact, a tactile sensation of arrival, and pulled over in Odessa, population roughly 350.

Odessa could have been on the Natchez Trace, so sultry was the weather that afternoon. Thunderstorms were brewing. You only had to glance at the mottled sky to confirm it. The crew at the fire department sprawled languidly over some benches out front, fanning themselves with newspapers. The buzz of cicadas was almost deafening. There was no breeze, nor any hint of one to come.

This was a day that advised you to move slowly, think carefully, and calibrate your life in inches. Two gents in ballcaps by the post office were obviously past masters of the strategy, as unhurried as a pair of leaves drifting idly down a stream.

They were discussing whether the Phillies could steal the pennant from the Mets, a subject I felt ready to tackle in detail after my devoted study of the box scores, and when we finished our deliberations and wound up predictably on opposite sides of the fence, I admired an elegant white colonial house nearby that suggested order and decorum and said, "Nice town you've got here."

"We like it okay," one gent replied. "They called it Cantwell's Bridge before they changed the name."

Odessa people are proud of their history to judge by these men. The town, on the Appoquinimink River, was once surrounded by wheat farms, they told me, with six granaries to store the crop before it was shipped to Boston, Philadelphia, and other cities on the East Coast. The name change, effected in 1855, linked the new Odessa to the other one on the Black Sea in Russia, also a major port for grain.

During the Civil War, Odessa acted as a station on the Underground Railroad, another point of pride. If a runaway slave from Maryland or elsewhere made it to the Quaker Meeting House, he or she was considered safe.

"Any fish in that river?" I asked.

"Some bluegills. Carp. Some bass."

"They go to any size?"

"Not that you could prove by us."

The Appoquinimink, more than sixteen miles long, flows into Delaware Bay. Corn and soybeans grow along its banks now. The beautiful marshes constitute the last such undisturbed system in the state. Hidden in the grasses are meadow jumping mice, who thrive on the humidity. The mice will leap as far as three feet if you take them by surprise, but I failed to roust any on my watch, although I would have liked to.

FIELDSBORO, PINE TREE CORNERS, Blackbird, the road rolled on toward Dover. The thunderstorm I'd been promised broke with a fury and brought a welcome freshness to the thick, swampy air.

Though I was eager to get settled at my motel in time to watch the first debate between John McCain and Barack Obama that night, I couldn't resist a fast stop at the You'll Come Back Flea Market because (a) its worn-out merchandise was strewn over a weedy lot the size of a football field and (b) the woman in charge sat in a lawn chair ten feet from the highway with two ham sandwiches on her lap.

She didn't lift her eyes from the traffic or raise a hand to wave when I began to browse, so involved in her own eccentric pursuits that the big picture didn't affect her at all. If Wall Street crumbled to dust tomorrow, she'd still show up for work with her ham sandwiches, or maybe tunafish for variety's sake. She had the inner calm of the Buddha, an enviable state of grace. A talent for living in the moment is a wonderful gift.

If you ever need a refrigerator coil for your 1948 Kelvinator, the You'll Come Back Flea Market probably can oblige. At first glance, the place appeared to be a randomly accumulated mess, but it had a crude organizing principle. Grouped on a wobbly table, for instance, were three dented cyclists' helmets. A cardboard carton was home to many plastic baby dolls often hairless or missing a limb. A gallery of Crock-Pots and microwaves rested on another table, as if several embattled couples had hastily cashed in their wedding presents before they divorced.

Cables and wires coiled like snakes in the grass. A bin of rusty kitchen knives, a metal bed frame, broken appliances, fishing rods, mismatched hubcaps, the inventory went on and on. Oddly, no books were for sale, though, not even a copy of *The Da Vinci Code*.

The woman kept staring at the traffic, oblivious of her only potential customer. When I walked toward her, she took a bite of her sandwich and nodded cordially. It was good to know that I existed.

"Amazing market," I ventured.

She dabbed at her mouth with a paper napkin. "Find what you're looking for?"

"I wasn't looking for anything in particular. Where do you get all this stuff, anyway?"

"My boss, he's real good at it. He goes to backyard sales and garage sales. He loves to collect things."

No lie, I thought. "I'll come back," I joked as I left, but the joke flew right over her head.

THE GUIDEBOOKS TELL how William Penn laid out the Green on State Street in Dover in 1772, so I'd formed an image of the capital as a quiet backwater with quaint historical buildings like those in Odessa, but as I approached Dover, U.S. 13 shed any trace of its rural character and mutated into Dupont Highway, a congested strip of franchises, outlet stores, and gigantic malls.

The phrase "blight on the landscape" doesn't do Dupont Highway justice, but there's no use in carping. Steinbeck railed about it, Miller protested, and yet the march of commerce goes on. Our ability to tolerate trashiness in the service of making money is amply documented. Perhaps the only truly contented Americans at present are those who feel a spring in their step at the sight of a Wal-Mart or a Kmart.

Still, it rankled. To locate my motel in the welter, I called it twice and covered the strip three times before the logo popped out. On a letterboard below the logo was a message, GOD BLESS OUR TROOPS. Almost four thousand soldiers were on active duty at Dover Air Force Base and might welcome such a blessing.

As I checked in, I asked the desk clerk, "Where's Dover?"

"This is Dover."

"The other Dover. William Penn? The Green?"

He caught my drift. Old Dover lay just around the corner. Its outskirts were pretty, too, with mature trees and houses often fitted with screened porches to keep out the fleet of bugs that the humidity encouraged to hatch. The sultriness, along with the madly electrical cicadas, again recalled the Deep South.

A large park with a lake was deserted in the late afternoon. The grand home across from it—the grandest around by far—boasted a MCCAIN FOR PRESIDENT sign on the lawn, next to some ceramic Canada geese. This was the neighborhood's only partisan gesture, a Republican volley fired on Democratic turf. In 2004, John Kerry had carried Delaware by a wide margin.

On Loockerman Street, a man stood in his driveway, playing with a brilliantly colored parrot. He nudged it with his shoe, and the parrot danced away. He wore a dreamy smile, the kind that results from indulging in a favorite pastime. *Unguarded*, that was the word for it. In the simplest terms, he was just enjoying himself and not afraid to let the light shine through. Why should he care what the neighbors thought? He was enjoying himself.

"Won't he fly away?" I wondered.

"Nah, his wings been clipped."

"Where'd you get him?"

"He's from the Amazon."

"Long way to go for a bird."

He laughed at that—joke on target. "There's a guy down that street over there, he's got an even more spectacular one."

Old Dover just limped along, barely surviving. The historic buildings were splendid to see, but the malls and the franchises had killed off most of the businesses. On every block, stores were vacant, boarded up, or for rent. The shoppers had voted with their feet, or rather with their cars, trucks, and SUVs.

Only an army-navy surplus store was thriving. Its windows featured dummies in camouflage uniforms, underage soldiers that might have been acquired from a boys' clothier gone the way of William Penn. One boy soldier waved a flag, while the other held a .22. Hunting season opened soon, so firearms and ammo were selling briskly, although not as briskly as watermelons.

A woman in a Chevy pickup delivered the melons fresh from the farm. They were stacked in the truck's bed, and she'd park or double-park, lift one from the pile, cradle it to her chest, and dash to someone's door. Her melons were the familiar type—green skin, red pulp—but you also can buy Delaware "sugar babies" with black skins and orange bellies, as they say in the trade.

You don't need much land to farm watermelons. Five acres or so will suffice, although the harvesting, still done by hand, is tough enough to exhaust your average Mr. Universe, with the trophy specimens weighing as much as forty pounds.

...

A STRONG ODOR of cooking oil and fried food hung over Dupont High-way that evening. It did not whet my appetite. For dinner, I skipped Boston Market, Denny's, Bob Evans, IHOP, Olive Garden, Applebee's, Pizza Hut, and TGI Friday's, all radiating a cheerfulness I distrusted, for a bowl of pho at a tiny Vietnamese café—rich beef broth, thinly sliced flank steak, crisp bean sprouts, and Thai basil. The price was $7.99, and I had the place to myself.

I thought I'd watch the McCain-Obama debate at a corner bar, the better to sample opinions. Like everyone of my generation, I remem-bered the first televised debate between John F. Kennedy, tanned and confident, and the shifty-looking Richard Nixon with his telltale five-o'clock shadow. The program had scored the highest Nielsen rating up to that point, breaking a record set by the last game of the '59 World Series, between the White Sox and the Dodgers.

The parallels between the Kennedy-Nixon election and the current one were obvious, of course. The Grand Old Party had been on its knees in 1960, as it was in 2008. The Republicans controlled only seven state legislatures and fourteen gubernatorial seats, causing a weary, des-perate Nixon to grasp at straws. Eisenhower's popularity hadn't rubbed off on him at all.

"He has a magic," Nixon grumbled about Ike. "He makes people happy."

Nixon attacked Kennedy for being a bad citizen who refused to sup-port the team because he couldn't be its captain. Moreover, Kennedy had given America an inferiority complex, he said, by implying that our international prestige was tarnished. The Democrats were spendthrifts, Nixon also charged. Their economic policies were guaranteed to in-crease the cost of "everything the housewife buys" by 25 percent.

As for the *good* citizens, they couldn't afford to put their faith in a young, untried leader who hadn't been tested by fire when an arsenal of Soviet warheads was purportedly aimed at the United States. Nixon ratcheted up the fear factor, casting Nikita Khrushchev as a coeval of Emperor Ming, the nemesis of Flash Gordon.

"Incidentally, I have talked with Khrushchev," he bragged, an expe-rienced statesman lording it over the "inexperienced" Kennedy. "He is a cold, hard, ruthless man who feeds on weakness and doubt." His words would find an echo in Republican depictions of Osama bin Laden.

Kennedy's media corps put Nixon's to shame, though, and turned a gaffe of Eisenhower's into a debilitating TV ad. Asked at a press conference to list some helpful suggestions his vice president had supplied, Ike quipped, "If you give me a week, I might think of one." In other ads, Jackie Kennedy addressed some Latino voters in Spanish, while Harry Belafonte, speaking as "a Negro and an American," touted JFK as the next FDR. If elected, Kennedy vowed not to take any orders from the pope.

Even race played a significant role in '60, when Dr. Martin Luther King Jr. was arrested during a sit-in at an Atlanta department store about three weeks before the balloting. A cracker judge sentenced King to four months of hard labor on a technicality, and dispatched him in secret to a Georgia penitentiary, where his supporters feared he'd be lynched.

When Kennedy heard about the situation, he called King's wife to offer his support, and asked his brother Bobby to step in. With the intervention of a New York judge, Bobby managed to free King on bail, and Dr. Martin Luther King Sr. switched parties in gratitude, thanking Kennedy for wiping the tears from his daughter-in-law's eyes.

"I've got a suitcase full of votes," he said, "and I'm going to take them to Mr. Kennedy and dump them in his lap." Some historians credit those votes with deciding the election, the closest of the twentieth century.

Moths fluttered around the screened porches of old Dover as I set out to find a bar. At Irish Mike's Old Towne Pub, the crowd had chosen a football game over McCain-Obama, so I ducked into McGlynns Pub across the way, only to find a reality show on the tube. J.W.'s Sports Bar lived up to its name, and the Lobby House, the last saloon within walking distance of the motel, had opted for music videos.

In the end, I watched the debate in my room. I felt frustrated, but maybe I shouldn't have. John Steinbeck had insisted that strangers wouldn't discuss politics openly, and maybe I should have heeded him. Americans only talked about such harmless topics as baseball and hunting, he argued, but it could also be that Doverites needed no further prodding. With a black population of almost 20 percent and Joe Biden, a native son, on the ticket, Delaware might already have cast its lot with the Democrats.

ON SATURDAY MORNING, the parking lots at Dover's malls began to fill up shortly after nine o'clock, but the Office Depot where I needed to buy a memory stick wouldn't open until ten, so I sat in the car and listened to callers chew over the debate on the radio. America may have a budget deficit, but there's no shortage of hot air.

Apparently Barack Obama was a Muslim and a socialist who intended to redistribute the wealth by stealing from the rich to aid the poor, or so the cranks insisted. Robin Hood wouldn't stand a chance with this bunch. They'd have praised the sheriff of Nottingham for being a fiscal conservative.

Talk radio was inescapable wherever I traveled. All across the country, the same absurdities were recycled daily. Preaching to the converted had become a lucrative industry, and the most successful hosts, whether on the left or the right, often played fast and loose with the facts. In an earlier century, they'd have been selling snake oil. Bald-faced liars earned seven-figure salaries by perversely stirring the pot of discontent.

When the callers grew too nasty to be funny, I killed some time at Dover Downs, the very casino I meant to avoid. I needn't have worried. I have no taste for the slots, and the virtual blackjack dealers failed to seduce me—alien beings born of computer graphics and physically perfect, too, above all the women showing off their creamy cleavage. In the wee hours, broken-hearted losers had fallen for them. I knew it in my bones.

From Dover, my mission accomplished, I drove west through Rising Sun and Canterbury toward Denton and U.S. 50. The cloud cover was thick again, with more rain in the forecast. At the aptly named Marydel, a mere speck, I bid farewell to Delaware and crossed into Caroline County, where the residents have the lowest per capita income in Maryland. The farmers scratch out a living on corn, strawberries, and chickens.

This was sleepy territory, a landscape of flags and churches, manufactured homes and battered pickups. At a convenience store in Henderson, burly guys carried out twelve-packs of Bud Light and Coors Light, although they clearly weren't watching their weight. The smattering of signs around supported John McCain.

Somebody with a sense of humor once christened Goldsboro the "Hub of the Universe," because three highways converge there. It's actually a poor little town with a feed store, a hardware store, and not much else except religion.

Faith seems to sink its roots readily into the fertile soil of such spots, where the promise of an afterlife may carry the sweet balm of relief for people enduring the trials of the present. One house—broken shingles, tarpaper backing exposed, paint flaking from the windowsills—advertised a business called Heaven Sent Books.

Another sign, this for Christian Park in Greensboro. The biblical fervor was so heated in Caroline County I thought it might be a theme park with David slaying Goliath on the hour, but it was a plain old municipal facility on the Choptank River, a major tributary of Chesapeake Bay.

As I followed a dirt road into the woods, a white-tailed doe darted in front of the car, with four fawns bounding along behind her. Sleek, elegant, and so graceful their hooves scarcely touched the ground, you could almost imagine the deer taking flight. The road guttered out in a clearing by the Choptank, not yet tidal in its upper reaches and quite shallow in early autumn, flowing over a pebbly streambed. From the trees came the trilling of birds.

Joe and Paula Talley, a middle-aged couple, stood in the river fully clothed. They wore T-shirts and sneakers, although Joe favored jeans instead of shorts. He sported a beard and a ballcap and held a long white instrument that resembled a weed whacker, gliding it over the Choptank an inch or so above the water. Paula bent to sift through the pebbles, grabbing a handful and then dropping them back.

The Talleys might have been prospecting for gold if Maryland had any, but that wasn't far wrong. They were on a treasure hunt, so intent and focused I tried not to disturb them. Instead I studied the river, very happy in the moment as I always am beside a stream. The Choptank ran swiftly enough to hold trout, although it might be too warm or a tiny bit brackish, so when Joe Talley glanced up I asked my usual question.

"It fishes real well in the spring," he said, tipping back his cap. "You can catch largemouth bass and white perch. And sunfish, of course." He'd grown up nearby and used to swim in the Choptank as a boy.

"What's that gadget you've got?"

"A metal detector. It's my new hobby."

"Are you finding anything?"

He opened the palm of a hand—three pennies and a slew of pop-tops. "We did better at the ballpark. Over there we made seventy-five cents."

Joe found it easy to laugh at himself. He'd probably squeeze an ounce of mirth from almost any situation, even the blackest. Looking silly was the least of his worries. Paula had just been laid off by an electronics firm after twenty-three years, and the Talleys were in a pinch. They tried not to be bitter about it. Most of Caroline County was feeling the pain.

The downturn didn't surprise Joe. He'd seen it coming. Americans were too spoiled, he thought. They'd had it too easy for too long.

"Did you watch the debate last night, Joe?"

"Just the highlights. I'm tired of the whole political process. It goes on forever now."

"Joe refuses to vote," Paula needled her husband. "So he shouldn't be allowed to complain."

"What about the economy?"

"It sucks!" Joe bellowed, although this, too, seemed to amuse him. He appeared ready to meet any calamity head-on and grapple it to the mat.

Paula leaned toward the Democrats, but she was no wide-eyed believer in Barack Obama as a magical cure for the nation's ills. "Whoever becomes president won't be able to do much," she offered. "Not for a while, anyway."

DENTON, MARYLAND, HAS an explosive history. It rose from the ashes—literally—after a company of Union soldiers, celebrating the Fourth of July in 1863, set off some skyrockets and other fireworks and burned it down. It lies on a wider, deeper stretch of the Choptank, dredged to make it navigable.

Ships once departed for Baltimore from Joppa Wharf bearing a cargo of tomatoes and watermelons, and returned with fertilizer, bricks, and oyster shells for paving roads. The main market, rooted in the center of town, sold farm produce and slaves.

The recession had hit Denton hard. In most neighborhoods, I saw properties for sale or about to be foreclosed. The median price of a house had fallen by more than a hundred thousand dollars in the past year, while the rate of unemployment had reached almost 10 percent because jobs in construction, the leading source of income for men, had dried up. The prospects for the future weren't bright, either, since the number of residents who hadn't graduated from high school was almost double the average for Maryland.

In West Denton, I stopped at Joppa Wharf, peeked into the restored passenger terminal, and ate a sandwich while I leaned against the car and then consulted my atlas and noticed roads that tracked the Choptank along the Eastern Shore until it flowed into the bay at Cambridge. Here was an opportunity no vacilador could pass up, particularly one who loves rivers, so I put off the plan to go west on U.S. 50 and took Highway 317 to Oxford instead.

Located at the mouth of the Tred Avon River, another Choptank tributary, Oxford was one of Maryland's only two legal ports of entry during the colonial era—Annapolis was the other—and grew rich by shipping tobacco to England, but the Revolution quashed any further trade with the British. Though the farmers switched to wheat, Oxford languished until the railroad came in 1871 and sparked an oyster boom. The oysters could be packed or canned for transport now, but the beds were so heavily pillaged the boom petered out by the 1920s.

The fields of soybeans and stubbly corn around Oxford were a rich gold color, and the town was a delight, with almost every street delivering a view of the Tred Avon or the Choptank. Fewer than a thousand people live here year-round, and often still earn their keep by working the rivers and the bay.

A little ferry started crossing the Tred Avon to Bellevue in 1683. From April to November, it continues to operate. I made the trip myself that afternoon. It lasted about eight minutes each way, not even long enough to read the extracts section in my copy of Moby-Dick.

Eason's Produce sits in a field off Oxford Road. The cornucopic array of fruits and vegetables would have won a blue ribbon at any fair. This was the last of summer's bounty, and doubly seductive because of it— yellow wax and Blue Lake beans, tiny beets like rubies, orange zucchini flowers, fat white peaches, and melons, of course.

Bill Eason presided over the stand, assisted by his granddaughter Hannah—"with two h's"—a bubbly blonde high school student with a winning smile. Hannah first hired on as a seven-year-old, and made five dollars a day. Try as she might, she couldn't figure a way to spend it all. Proud to be from the Eastern Shore, she assured me there was no intelligent life west of the bay.

"It's an old joke," she added, not wanting to sound mean. "They say the same about us." Her grandfather looked on fondly.

Bill Eason acquired his land in 1959, and tore out an orchard to farm it. He used to grow his own sweet corn, but Talbot County has more people and less water these days. He doesn't want to fuss with irrigation and gets his corn over in Caroline, along with his cantaloupes. Once a week he travels to Pennsylvania to buy heirloom tomatoes and lima beans—"the best I've ever seen"—from some Amish farmers.

His asparagus is homegrown, as are his strawberries, but the deer can be brutal on crops, and Bill isn't as tolerant of nuisances as he was years ago, so he shops almost as much as he farms. When I knocked on a cantaloupe to test its ripeness, he gave me a big juicy one free.

"If you don't eat it right away, it won't go mushy on you or nothing," he guaranteed.

Meanwhile, I'd started fondling the heirloom tomatoes. I knew it was a sin, but I couldn't stop myself.

"Don't let those ugly stripes on 'em steer you wrong," Bill advised. "They won't affect the flavor."

The stripes resembled little wounds that had healed. The tomatoes might have burst at some point during the growth cycle, then formed a scar. They were very soft to the touch and smelled of the vine, much more fragrant than the odorless hothouse varieties. The heirlooms were not only red but also green, yellow, and a purplish hue almost as dark as an eggplant.

Some regular customers turned up, an older couple who owned a summer place. The town draws its summer folks from Baltimore and Washington, and they're usually well-to-do. Bill was too polite not to introduce me, but he described my trip in more grandiose terms than I'd have volunteered.

This didn't sit well with Phil, the new arrival. "Produce stands of America, eh?" he asked snidely. "State of the nation through its vegetables, am I right? Better deal with the financial crisis!"

That was the extent of our conversation. Phil's portfolio, I gathered, had recently been hammered. I didn't fare much better with his wife.

"Bill says you live in Ireland," she stated flatly, as if submitting evidence. "I travel a lot myself."

"Where do you like to go?"

"I've been to Canada and Alaska lately, but I am *always* glad to get back to the real United States."

When they left with a watermelon, I hoped they'd drop it. I paid for half a dozen heirlooms and fondled the corn. I was out of control, really, and wished I had a camp stove like John Steinbeck so I could boil up a couple of ears.

"Do you have a kitchen at your motel?" Bill had read my mind.

"Just a microwave."

"That'll work. No reason to drown your corn in too much water. I'll show you how."

He cut off both ends of an ear with a butcher knife, and peeled away half the husk because it had been treated with pesticides. The kernels were small and white, and the silk was dry rather than wet—very fresh corn. No worms had got at it, either.

"Pop it in the microwave for two and a half minutes," Bill went on. "A Chinese couple came by the other day, and I did up two ears for 'em like that. Sure enough, they asked for two more."

Next we talked about soybeans and ate some edamame. Talbot County seemed in good shape compared to Caroline, I thought, and Bill agreed that was probably true, although some farmers were struggling.

"We've been lucky," he said, recalling last year's floods in Texas and how Hurricane Gustav had trashed Louisiana this past August. "We haven't had any of those natural disasters."

That's how Bill Eason viewed the world, through the prism of nature. The Dow Jones and the NASDAQ barely impinged upon his mind. Such security as he had was tied to the earth and its seasons, and though that could be risky, it was still safer and saner than being a prisoner to the stock market.

Bill put my cantaloupe and four ears of corn in a paper bag, and gently laid the tomatoes on top, then wrote his address in my notebook so I could send him a book when I finally quit traveling and got around to writing it.

THOUGH I'VE BEEN fortunate enough to eat at a restaurant or two with a Michelin star, I doubt any chef could surpass the meal I fixed late that afternoon. As instructed by Bill Eason, I stripped an ear of corn, popped it into the microwave, set the timer, and stood back, certain the ear would blow up and send a shower of scorched kernels across the room. It came out piping hot and cooked to perfection instead, so I sliced an heirloom tomato on a paper plate and sprinkled it with the sea salt and pepper I'd bought in Oxford.

I'd also splurged on a good bottle of Chablis. After pouring a chilled glass, I sat at a desk—my "business center," in motel-speak—and dug in. The corn was sweet and tender, and the tomato juice ran down my chin. For dessert, I split the cantaloupe into quarters and ate it with my hands, right down to the rind. Motels always have too many mirrors, so I couldn't avoid seeing the dopey grin on my face.

IN THE EARLY evening, I followed the crooked course of the Choptank to Secretary, where it swings roughly west toward Cambridge and Todd Point above Cornersville to join the Chesapeake. A concrete bridge over the river, built during the Depression but now defunct, had come back to life as a fishing pier that's open around the clock all year. Anglers catch perch, hard heads, catfish, sea trout, and crabs.

In 1960, the year of Steinbeck's journey, Cambridge was fiercely redneck and racist to the core. African Americans, fully a third of the population, were confined to the rundown Second Ward ghetto. The schools were segregated, and blacks were casually deprived of their rights. With jobs at a premium—29 percent of the blacks were unemployed, as were 7 percent of the whites, quite high for Maryland then—Cambridge amounted to a disaster waiting to happen.

The showdown occurred in 1963. For the previous two years, local African-American activists and their supporters, branded as "outside agitators," had staged sit-ins and demonstrations to the chagrin of elected officials. That July eleven protesters attempted to enter Dizzyland, a café whose owner, Robert Fehsenfeld, was a rabid segregationist.

Fehsenfeld blocked the door and shouted curses. When the protesters knelt on the sidewalk to pray and sing, he kicked them, carried one woman away, and smashed an egg on the head of a white youth involved, while onlookers hooted in approval. The police, all white, refused to intervene.

The protesters returned to Dizzyland later that week. This time Fehsenfeld stood aside and let them pass.

"You're not wanted here!" he cried. "Understand, you come here at your own risk."

Then he locked the door behind them. Twelve white thugs were waiting inside, and they beat the protesters to a pulp.

Mobs from both camps ranged around town through the night, leaving seven white men wounded. For the second time that month, the governor called in the National Guard, whose soldiers shut down the bars in Cambridge and enforced a nine-o'clock curfew. The Guard would act as an occupying army for more than a year.

Four years later, Cambridge still hadn't healed. When H. Rap Brown of the Student Nonviolent Coordinating Committee urged an angry black crowd to "burn this town down if it don't turn around," an assailant wounded him with a shotgun. The town did begin to turn around at last, however slowly, and it's almost evenly divided between the races now and harmonious enough for them to gather together on occasion.

They were doing so at Sailwinds Park that evening, in fact, where Crabtoberfest was going on—a big civic party that combined an affection for the Chesapeake's blue crabs with the sudsy ardor of Munich in early autumn. It did no good to ask what had inspired the odd union. Nobody I talked with seemed to know or care because there was so much food and drink around.

You could hang out at a *biergarten* inside an auditorium and gorge on sauerbraten, sausages, braised pork ribs, dumplings, spaetzle, and Paulaner or Dogfish Head beer, but if your lederhosen already felt a little tight, you could skip the Bavarian feast and buy a bucket of steamed crabs and corn for ten dollars as I did, joining some other revelers at a paper-covered table under a canopy.

"You ready to crack 'em?" inquired an amiable guy who had a fair bit of crab on his shirt.

"I think so. We've got Dungeness crabs in California."

"No crab like the blue crab. Bring one outta the bucket." I brought out a hefty specimen, and he gave it a brief physical exam. "What we're looking at here is a jimmy. That's a boy crab. See the tips of those claws? All plain? On a lady crab, they's painted red."

"That's good to know."

"Go on and start." He handed back the crab. "Don't be afraid to make a mess."

I made an excellent mess. I broke off the crab's claws and legs, then turned it over and loosened the apron with a knife, scraping away the gills and mustard and forking in the meat. I snapped open the legs and busted the claws with a wooden mallet. The shell fragments flew, but no one objected. We were all very messy by now. I'd certainly had a memorable day in the eating department.

A school bus pulled up at the auditorium, causing a commotion. Down the steps came a troupe of African Americans between the ages of eight and eighteen or so. The girls and women wore satin dresses in rose and black, with red tassels around their ankles, while the young men were in red T-shirts and black slacks.

As precisely as a drill team, the troupe marched inside and took up a position in front of a stage, where two men shouldered harnesses fitted with four snare drums. At a signal from their leader, they proceeded to rock the joint, laying down a thundering backbeat.

The dancers moved in synchronized fashion and looked radiant and full of joy. They were athletes, really, and their routine called every muscle into play. They stomped their feet, raised their eyes toward the heavens, and smiled at what they saw there. Here was the gospel spirit in action. The troubles of the 1960s seemed very far away, and America not such a bad place after all.

In an elevated mood, I left Crabtoberfest and promptly got lost. My eventual rescuers stood outside a church, seven women and a silver-haired gent. They'd just left a discussion group, where the subject may well have been how to help unfortunates like me, and they were glad to do a good deed.

"You were lost," the gent laughed. "And now you're found."

When I recognized the road to Easton and Oxford, I celebrated with a nightcap at The Portside, a cozy restaurant on the water. I met a boat builder there, who also operated a charter service and had "loaded up" some clients with snappers, or small bluefish, that morning. He claimed to have an accent unique to the Eastern Shore derived from the English of Shakespeare, and he described it as Elizabethan.

On Smith Island in Chesapeake Bay, where colonists from Cornwall and Wales arrived in the 1600s, you can reportedly hear traces of a West County dialect, so I pursued the conversation, but the builder and a friend were now weighing the potential drawbacks of dating a recently divorced woman—dealing with the threats from her violent ex-husband, for example.

"I'd say go for it," the Elizabethan told his pal. "He's probably just a bullshitter."

"What if he isn't?"

"You'll be the first to know."

AMERICA LOST ITS luster the next morning. The price of my room included a free breakfast of rock-hard bagels, calorie-rich muffins, anachronistic slabs of Wonder Bread, and syrupy fruit salad from a can. As I surveyed the dreadful buffet, I cursed myself for being so greedy and devouring Bill Eason's whole damn cantaloupe instead of saving half for just such an emergency.

Another humid, drizzly morning. St. Michaels, west of Easton, was dozing that Sunday, its curio shops and boutiques still closed. Route 33 wrapped itself around McDaniel, Wittman, and Sherwood, and ran through large flat tracts studded with oaks and loblolly pines. A drawbridge over Knapps Narrows led to Tilghman Island. With a land mass of only 2.7 square miles, the island seemed about to be swallowed by the advances of the Choptank and the Chesapeake.

Here, too, the oyster trade once flourished. When Captain John Smith charted the area in 1608, the Powhatans could wade into the bay and pick them by hand, but the newcomers soon depleted those stocks and moved offshore in log canoes, where the watermen relied on long, heavy tongs to get at the beds. The work was brutal and the results unpredictable. Often each pass, or "lick," yielded just a few keepers.

All that changed with the introduction of the dredge—a wire basket, raised or lowered with a winch, that efficiently dislodged and scooped up the oysters. Dredging caused such severe damage that Maryland banned it from 1820 to 1864, only relenting after a strict new set of regulations was in place. A dredge could be operated only under sail now, thereby reducing the negative impact.

At the peak of the Chesapeake's oyster bounty in the 1890s, the sailing vessel of choice was the skipjack, light and fast, with a single mast and a v-shaped hull ideal for maneuvering in the shallows. It took no special skill to build one. Even an ordinary carpenter could do it. About two thousand skipjacks were on the bay at the turn of the century, but they were gradually abandoned, destroyed, or fell to disrepair as the oyster stocks dwindled.

Only about thirty or so skipjacks remain, and those still going after oysters—the last commercial sailing powered fleet in North America—are berthed at Dogtown Harbor. Two watermen were leaning against a pick-up there, nursing cans of Bud and trying to regain the momentum they'd lost at a tiki bar the night before.

At first they waved me away, too hungover to answer any questions from a stranger. Who could blame them? Their lives are tough even in a good year. Though a waterman may own a boat, he often needs a second job to pay the bills. Hand tonging is still the primary method of harvesting and no less taxing. The beds are no less depleted.

"So you want to know about skipjacks?" one of the men reconsidered, shouting to me as I roamed.

I walked back to the truck. "Any here now?"

"The *Kathryn*. Come on, I'll show you."

The *Kathyrn*, sleek as can be, dates from 1901. Fifty feet long, she carries a crew of six to handle the dredging, cull the oysters, and tend the sails. On Mondays and Tuesdays in season, the skipjacks can use a motorized yawl to push them around if there isn't sufficient wind. (Most skipjacks operate only on power days, in fact.) The limit on oysters is 150 bushels a day, but they rarely meet it.

Oysters are odd creatures—protrandric, in the language of zoologists. They spawn the first year as males, then grow bigger and more energetic and release eggs as a female after that. The largest and toughest are called "counts." Only the most ardent aficionado dares to swallow them raw. Counts are best in stews, while selects are smaller and second-best. Standards are the smallest and most valuable of all.

It's easy to get lost in the lore of the Eastern Shore, an unusual spot that strikes a delicate balance between satisfying the tourists and sustaining the locals. The watermen may be under pressure, but they won't just disappear. When a man loves what he does and thrives on being independent, he won't surrender the thing that gives him meaning without a fight. The maverick streak may be dying out in American life, although not at Dogtown Harbor.

From the harbor, I drove to Neavitt at the tip of a peninsula between Bellevue and Tilghman Island. The road ended at a marina, where all was incredibly still. Only the minute splashes of silvery baitfish broke the surface calm. The Choptank looked imperturbable, an aspect of the eternal. I watched it do nothing, as entranced as one of Melville's water gazers.

"Posted like silent sentinels all around town, stand thousands upon thousands of mortal men fixed in ocean reveries," the master wrote.

The *Northern Star* from Neavitt and the *Holy Mackerel* from Deale, both fishing boats, were docked at the marina. They'd been swabbed down, and were spit-clean and ready for their next voyage. A lanky youth touched up the paint on another boat, saluting me with his brush.

"It's been fair of late," he said, regarding the catch. "Anyway, we're surviving."

RED EYE'S DOCK BAR on Kent Island Narrows can be dangerous on a warm Sunday afternoon. In no hurry to cross the Chesapeake Bay Bridge, I dallied there on my way to Virginia. The urban sprawl of greater Washington, D.C., lay on the other side, depicted in my atlas as an agonized orange blob. Though I'd vowed like Steinbeck to avoid major cities, U.S. 50 bisected the capital, so I left the highway for Mears Point Marina to postpone the drive, not knowing what I'd find there.

What I found was Red Eye's. Forget about Maryland—I'd made a detour to Key West. Surfboards and trophy billfish decorated the open-air bar. You could practically reach out and touch the bay. The marina, with about five hundred slips, supplied a steady stream of thirsty boaters, but landlubbers also were welcome. Sports fans hunkered before the TVs, fixed on football and the Mets' last game of the season. They needed to beat the Marlins to win a wild-card slot and didn't, deflating the hopes I'd built up in Manhattan.

The all-American scent of red meat sizzling on a barbecue wafted from a food stand. On a little stage, some musicians fiddled with their guitars and amps, tuning up for a gig. The Fourth of July had been enshrined in perpetuity at Red Eye's, but there'd be no bikini contest today, the bartender apologized as he collected my empty beer bottle.

"They already held the championship," he moped.

"Who won?"

"The blonde."

"Some things never change."

"You want another?"

"I do, but I won't."

The Chesapeake looked stunning from the bridge. You'd never guess how polluted it is, a huge dumping ground for the nitrogen, phosphorus, sediment, and chemicals that wash into it from car emissions, fertilizer, manure, and treated wastewater, causing algae blooms that deprive the blue crabs and oysters of oxygen. In effect, they're suffocating.

The bay's stewards projected that the Chesapeake might hold as many as 200 million crabs of spawning age in 2008, but the tally came to just 120 million. Oysters are even more endangered, barely viable now. Pity the poor shellfish and the watermen. The country's biggest estuary is slowly being poisoned, but it's tough to point a finger from behind the wheel of a car.

Past Annapolis, I geared up for the challenge of Washington's tangled streets. I'd spent time there before, and felt educated when I departed. Every American should visit the district at least once, if only to demystify it. It's ennobling to tour such monuments as the Lincoln Memorial, as corny as it sounds. They instill a tremor of idealism, however momentary, and remind us how far we've drifted from the infant dreams of the Republic.

Soon Washington sucked me into its vortex. In rural areas, you can motor along and daydream, but an unfamiliar city kicks you in the shins and wakes you up. It's easy to get confused. My route through D.C. looked so clear on the map I never gave it a second thought. U.S. 50 turned into New York Avenue, then glided by the White House and over a bridge on the Potomac.

Nothing could be simpler. That's what we tell ourselves, full of false bravado, even when we know better. Nothing could be simpler—the sentence should be struck from the English language.

For the next hour or so, I became an accidental sightseer. Lost again, I saw such awe-inspiring wonders as the Bureau of Economic Analysis and the Passport Office before I crossed into Virginia on Interstate 66, not U.S. 50. The calm of Neavitt seemed very far away.

Of the many suburbs where I might spend the night, I chose Falls Church. The name was more idyllic than Tyler Park, and less cute than Sleepy Hollow. The church in question once stood on a main road to the Great Falls of the Potomac, where the river flows through a gorge and drops seventy-six feet in less than a mile.

Too tired to be picky, I checked into the first motel I passed on the Arlington Pike. A Vietnamese cultural society's annual luncheon had just concluded there, and the guests still lingered in the lobby. The men wore dark business suits, while the women were graciously attired, some in traditional dress, and the children were noticeably well mannered.

As opposed to the Bureau of Economic Analysis, this was a sight that cheered me up. Falls Church, an extraordinary melting pot, renewed my always tentative faith in the American experiment. The northern Virginia phone book listed thirty-one restaurants advertising pho as a specialty, for instance, and Eden Center Mall catered almost exclusively to the Vietnamese.

On my evening stroll, I passed a kebab parlor that split its space with a Salvadoran taqueria serving "delicious pupusas." El Tutumaso, a Bolivian café, competed from an adjacent strip mall. About forty thousand Bolivians live within a few miles of each other between Falls Church and Arlington, and they frequently own small businesses, including Italian restaurants.

Cecilia's sells pizzas by day, but it's a disco by night that sometimes features famous entertainers imported from La Paz. While you can order pasta at Tutto Bene, the *salteña* is an off-the-menu item—Bolivia's empanada stuffed with chicken or beef and a soupy sauce of raisins, peas, potatoes, olives, and eggs. Tutto Bene sells about three thousand every week.

PISTONE'S ITALIAN INN has been around too long for the Bolivians to be involved. It enshrines the spirit of the 1950s and sits on a little hill above the Arlington Pike, with an agreeable terrace for outdoor dining.

The Sunday Jam, with Art Beverage tinkling the ivories, hit its stride when I entered. A three-piece combo launched into a killer version of "They Call the Wind Maria," and you could feel the ghost of Old Blue Eyes snapping his fingers to the beat and asking for another double on the rocks.

Portraits in oil lined a wall in the intimate, horseshoe-shaped bar, perhaps dear departed Pistones, or maybe treasured regulars who'd run up a record tab. Most regulars that night had left their youth behind years ago, but they still conveyed its lively, robust energy.

Clifford Dewey qualified as the life of the party. He often drives over from Bethesda, Maryland, in the white Lincoln Town Car he calls the Tuna Boat. An outrageous flirt, Dewey was quick with a quip or a slap on the back. The gals doted on him. Sinatra would have approved.

"Having a good time?" he asked as I sat down, and before I could answer he bragged, "I've never had a bad time in my life."

The bartender poured me the biggest glass of Chardonnay I'd ever seen. I could have been drinking from a goldfish bowl. That was in keeping with the charm of Pistone's—flamboyant, letting it all hang out. After the combo played the last notes of "Maria," a demure woman released her inner self, bloomed into a chanteuse, grabbed the mike, and belted out an anthemic "Mack the Knife." Anybody can sing at the Sunday Jam, whether or not they can carry a tune.

"I'll be singing in the parking lot on the thirty-second of October," Clifford Dewey whispered, his eyes twinkling. "Get it?"

I did get it, and we began to talk. Dewey's business card read *C. D. Dewey & Associates, International Financing*, so I assumed he'd be an expert on the economy and our prospects for the future.

"They're frightening," he responded, but his tone wasn't pessimistic. Instead he took the long view. He meant frighteningly positive. The country had weathered such turmoil before, he pointed out—the Depression, of course, and also the big stock market dip in the 1990s. He believed that we'd recover in due time. As a self-made man, he trusted in the potential of human beings to better themselves if they're given half a chance.

Dewey reeled off his autobiography for me. His was a success story stamped with the imprimatur *Only in America.*

"I'm lucky," he said modestly. "The Good Lord gave me a shitload of brains and an elephant's memory. I had one of the top IQs at my high school in Massachusetts and the lowest grades. I didn't even graduate. I started pumping gas at sixteen."

He joined the navy to escape his fate as a pump jockey, then took a job as an auto mechanic on his return and ascended the company ladder, eventually signing up as a parts salesman. He rose to the rank of general manager at twenty-five, and when the firm cashed out as a franchise, so did Dewey. He received about a quarter of a million dollars in 1985 and built up a portfolio of investment properties. He still had a finger in many pies, including some real estate in Dubai.

Though he felt confident about a recovery, he did admit to transferring some of his assets to an FDIC-insured bank. It was the working people who were most at risk in the current climate, he thought. If you had only a paycheck and no savings to depend on, you were terribly vulnerable.

When a waiter set a slab of lasagna before Dewey, he urged me to try it, but I begged off. It was almost the size of home plate, too rich and heavy after a rough day of travel, so I cast my lot with the Bolivians instead—proof of how little I knew about Bolivia's cuisine.

Evo Morales wasn't at Tutumaso that evening, but his distant cousin might have been tucking into a plate of *pique lo macho* (steak, sausages, onions, tomatoes, and peppers served over french fries) or *silpancho* (breaded beef fried and mixed with potatoes and rice). Family groups, young and old, were convened at most tables. Kids dashed around the room and hid in corners, while the teenagers watched videos of Bolivian hip-hop. The atmosphere was warm, gentle, and loving.

As the only gringo in the room, I attracted some friendly glances. After studying the photos on the menu, I ordered *charque*, a dish that dwarfed Pistone's lasagna. It consisted of shredded dried beef, posole, boiled potatoes, and hard-boiled eggs, and came with *llajua*, a bright green hot sauce I should have used with more restraint instead of demonstrating my new fondness for all things Bolivian.

Here was an America I could believe in, Clifford Dewey's land of opportunity come to life. Someday a boy or girl at El Tutumaso, rescued from poverty's extremes, might have an identical success story to tell. Immigrants are essential to the nation, reinvigorating its most basic principles. Our edge in innovation would suffer without their input. Half the doctorates awarded in the United States would go to foreign students in 2010.

At the most basic level, of course, immigrants do the work Americans turn down, vividly demonstrated in Cambridge, where the crab-packing houses were short of hands. Ordinarily, they depend on H2B laborers from abroad, who hold special visas for temporary, seasonal, nonagricultural jobs.

Only sixty-six thousand such visas were granted in 2008, though, and the laborers had all been hired by the time the crabs were ready, so the packers held a job fair and hoped to find three hundred replacements. Even in a deep recession, just fifteen applicants showed up.

BREAKFAST AT Eden Center Mall, already buzzing at nine-thirty. A sleek-haired dandy, vaguely sinister, banged away at a pinball machine, while Saigon techno pop bounced off the walls at Café Dang. Elsewhere wizened men, close contemporaries of Tomoji Tanabe, brooded and stroked their chins over chess boards, ignoring the activity around them.

Two boys struggled to tote a twenty-pound sack of rice from a market to their mother's car. A hesitant woman peered at the gowns in the window at Ha Van Bridal, a look of intense concentration on her face, maybe pondering her future. To commit or not to commit? There were many jewelry stores for choosing wedding bands, and also hair salons, an herbalist, and a moneylender.

At a bakery, I ate a croissant and drank Vietnamese coffee, a strong, dark roast filtered and blended with sweetened condensed milk, and asked for a *banh mi* sandwich to go. The counter girl sliced a crusty baguette in half and layered it with barbecued pork, then added tomatoes, cucumbers, pickled carrots, shredded daikon, and sprigs of cilantro.

"Jalapeños?"

"Yes, please."

She wrapped it neatly and put it in a paper sack. I had to stay my hand from unwrapping it on the spot. Lunch, my eye. That sandwich probably wouldn't last until noon.

Leaving Eden Center, I found U.S. 50 again, a miracle of sorts. The highway rolled by Chantilly and away from that dense orange hazard zone in my atlas. I was traveling through Loudon County now, the fourth-fastest growing in America and also the wealthiest, with a median household income of about $107,000. The heavy hitters often worked for high-tech or Internet-related companies. The county's motto, "I Byde My Time," might still apply to the horse farms and vineyards around Leesburg and Bluemont, but the rest of Loudon had been dragged inside the commuter rim.

Loudon County does still have a few open tracts of land. Near Aldie, I blinked at what appeared to be a fortified compound for gnomes. Several small white houses—the size of outhouses, really—with red corrugated roofs and two square windows like eyes were perched on an almost treeless hillside. A wooden guard tower hovered in the rear, tall enough to grant the little person on duty a 360-degree view of the area.

This was Pev's Paintball Park, a forty-eight-acre parcel with fourteen playing fields. Its founder, Mike Peverill, owns the largest chain of "paintball only" stores in the country. On a busy weekend, the park accommodates up to 250 players intent on annihilating each other. Corporate groups sometimes reserve Pev's as a tool for letting their employees vent their frustrations and resolve their disputes.

The square-jawed jock in charge of Pev's shared this with me. He was a recent college grad, bored and biding his time until the next move revealed itself.

"It's slow during the week now," he said. "The kids are back in school."

"Do you get a lot of children?"

"Sure do. They use the park for birthday parties. We do bachelor parties, too. And bachelorettes."

Here was a new cultural twist. Apparently a groom-to-be required more than a surfeit of cocktails and a lap dance before he faced the altar. He needed to be shot with a ball of paint.

Although the nation's fascination with weaponry has never been mine, I'd be the last to criticize somebody else's idea of harmless fun. It's been estimated that five million Americans play paintball every year, after all, and the hobby isn't cheap. A round at Pev's costs fifty-four dollars if you rent the gear. When adults take up simulated warfare for pleasure, though, it does suggest their lives may lack adventure.

There's no small irony in Pev's location. It's just miles from Manassas, where nine hundred young soldiers, some still in their teens, died in 1861 during the First Battle of Bull Run. The battlefield is a national park at present, and though John Steinbeck confessed to being lax about visiting such places in *Travels* and even put Yellowstone in the same category as Disneyland, he might have felt differently here.

Nobody was in period costume when I entered the park. No Civil War reenactors were on the prowl, either, and the battlefield had been left largely untouched out of respect for hallowed ground. It's impossible to walk over that ground without feeling haunted. The ghosts of Bull Run inform every step.

At Manassas, the tide was supposed to turn in the Union Army's favor and hasten the war's end. The troops numbered about thirty-five thousand, mostly ninety-day volunteers who'd heeded Lincoln's call to action. They'd never been trained for combat, rejoiced in their new uniforms, and idled to pick blackberries as they marched on a crucial railroad junction. If captured, the junction would give General Irvin McDowell the best overland approach to Richmond, the Confederacy's capital.

Gangs of civilians tagged after the army, keen to witness the spectacle. They carried picnic baskets, certain they'd be celebrating a quick surrender or a rout. Yet Confederate general P. G. T. Beauregard lay in wait at Bull Run with twenty-two thousand men, soon to be joined by ten thousand more men from the Shenandoah Valley.

On July 21, at daybreak, Union soldiers fired on an enemy stronghold. The Confederates retreated, consolidating their forces on Henry House Hill. McDowell tried to press his advantage, but his green volunteers lacked the will and experience, and they withdrew in the late afternoon. Weary and disheartened, they were enveloped in a melee on the road back to Washington. The civilian observers also were racing from the scene in their carriages. Caught up in the chaos, the soldiers lost any hint of discipline and fled in a panic.

The armies met at Manassas again in August 1862, although they were composed of hardened veterans by then. Second Bull Run lasted for three days, elevated the Confederacy to the pinnacle of its power, and left another thirty-three hundred men dead.

INDIAN SUMMER. It came out of nowhere with a blast of heat and light that banished the clouds. On Route 211 past Warrenton, I drove up and down, up and down through the foothills of the Blue Ridge Mountains, hooked on the pastoral sublime.

There were lush green meadows board-fenced for horses or cattle, dry stone walls, farm ponds stocked with bass and catfish, and dragonflies on the wing. The Rappahannock River sparkled in the sun. After a tour of Manassas, I felt grateful for the gift of such a splendid afternoon. This was Barack Obama territory if you trusted the signs, twice as many as McCain's. Though George W. Bush won Virginia in 2004, most pollsters judged it a toss-up in 2008.

APPLES AND COLD CIDER read another sign, this one for Williams Orchard in Flint Hill off the two-lane road to Front Royal, once known as Helltown because of the rowdies who tore it up while chasing after whores and whiskey.

The road, all tight curves, afforded fine views over a valley after each switchback. The orchard was at the base of a steep incline. Apple trees heavy with fruit stretched in every direction. The scent of ripeness, brought on by the warmth, was almost dizzying.

Two women were hoisting bushels of apples into their truck. They looked like members of a commune, muscular and not fussy about their clothes, ready to dig post holes or string up barbed wire, servants of the functional. Maybe they'd be baking pies for the followers of a little-known swami later on. Flint Hill, this part of Rappahannock County—my California antennae twitched. I sensed the presence of seekers.

In a weathered barn, there were more apples in baskets—Yorks, Romes, McIntoshes, and Jonathans—along with cool cider in bottles and jugs. Farm machinery was stored in the dark interior, where spiderwebs hung from the beams. When a pup rushed up to sniff my leg, a woman shouted, "Andy!" and the pup dashed away to sniff at something or somebody else.

The woman's name was Liz. She ran the stand for the Williams family and wondered how she could help me.

"Well, I'd like some apples," I said, stating the obvious.

"We've got all kinds. What's your pleasure?"

"Something I haven't tasted before."

She selected a bright yellow apple with a pink blush. Using a pocket knife, she cut a wedge and held it out on the blade.

"Try that. It's a Virginia Gold. They're a cross between an Albermarle Pippin and a Golden Delicious."

The apple, very crisp, managed to be both tart and sweet. I bought half a peck for a mere five bucks and felt as if I'd just picked the Williams's pocket. They'd been farming the orchard for more than seventy-five years, and also sold vegetables and natural beef.

Liz bagged my Virginia Golds. "They'll last straight through the winter. They won't go bad until spring."

"I'll be happy if they last until Kansas."

"What'll you do in Kansas?"

I told her about Steinbeck and my trip.

"I'm envious," she laughed. "I'm a terrible traveler. Not like my daughter. She's got the travel bug. She insisted on going to college clear across the country in California at Humboldt State."

Humboldt State is in the redwood country of the northern coast, where marijuana, not apples, is the cash crop. Liz flew to San Francisco once and rented a car to visit the college, but she was too chicken to take Highway 1 along the coast, even though she wanted to see the Pacific. She feared she'd be so mesmerized she'd drive right off a cliff.

"Where does your daughter go when she travels?"

"All over. She'll go anywhere. I like to follow her in my atlas."

A Mexican rode by on a tractor and waved. I walked into the orchard to inspect the trees. They were old and gnarled, and some branches trailed almost to the ground, drawn down by so many apples ripe for the picking.

I hadn't been wrong about the Flint Hill area. It represented an offshoot of the New World born in California in the 1960s. The locals bred goats for milk and cheese, and grew lavender and medicinal herbs.

Their veggies were strictly organic. They raised purebred Clun Forest sheep and Scottish Highland cattle. Their Yorkshire pigs ate fescue grass, and were fed no hormones or antibiotics.

Teachers advertised classes in weaving, ceramics, and yoga. Massages and acupuncture treatments were widely available. No doubt a cultivar of Humboldt's potent skunk had also found a purchase in the Blue Ridge foothills.

A man could live here, I thought. For an evening out, you'd drive to nearby Washington, a five-block-by-two-block grid laid out in 1749. The surveyor was George Washington, age seventeen. The town was the first of the country's twenty-eight Washingtons, a plaque certified.

Dinner at the Inn at Little Washington? Well, maybe not. The fixed price on Saturday night was $178 before you chose some wine from the 2,400-bottle cellar. For a surcharge of $450, you could sit at a table in the kitchen and watch the chef prepare carpaccio of herb-crusted baby lamb with Caesar salad ice cream. Even falling into bed could be painful when a room with a full bath cost $505. The inn catered to silver-haired patricians and fat-cat lobbyists on a weekend escape from D.C., I suspected.

Sperryville was more humble. An artsy-craftsy town on the Thornton River, it acted as a gateway to Shenandoah National Park. The summer high season had just ended, and the leaf peepers of autumn had yet to show, so the streets were quiet and the river barely a rill.

The Sperryville Country Store, an ordinary grocery by its exterior, fooled me. Inside I found Manchego cheese from Spain, imported Belgian ale, multigrain bread from a resident bakery, and thick strip steaks properly aged. I'd stumbled on a backwoods version of Dean & DeLuca.

The man at the cash register, in Bermudas and an apron, appeared to be the owner, so I complimented him on his stock and mentioned all the Obama signs I'd seen since Warrenton.

"Is that a fact?" he asked archly, turning his back.

"I gather you're not the one who put them up."

"No, I'm just an old southern boy at heart."

"That says it all."

"I guess it does."

...

THE DAY SLIPPED away from me in the lovely confines of Flint Hill and Sperryville. It was too late for even a short hike at Shenandoah National Park before dark, so I went southeast to Culpeper instead, realizing that I hadn't yet seen a single roadside attraction, not one papier-mâché dinosaur or petting zoo. Hitchhikers also were missing from the traditional equation, all those hobos, bindlestiffs, and minstrel vagabonds of legend.

Culpeper is the seat of Culpeper County. Its slogan, "Still Making History," caused me to scratch my head. The sturdy brick buildings downtown—historic, naturally, and newly revitalized—were scrubbed clean and painted inviting shades of red or pale blue. The old train depot, also recently restored, was a trophy during the Civil War, coveted by both sides for its telegraph line and easy access to the railroad.

Once Culpeper was a hub for dairying and beef cattle, but most farmers quit after a government buyout in the 1980s. That freed up acres of land for developers. A housing spree began a decade ago, with subdivisions built at warp speed and crews of Mexicans arriving to do the labor. The spree had ended, of course, but the Mexicans hadn't left, a sore point in certain quarters.

Now Culpeper banked on its tranquil atmosphere to attract harried Washingtonians ready to swap the urban frenzy for a simpler lifestyle, if such a thing exists. Tourism figured in the plan as well, with horseback riding, golf, biplane flights, and an array of B and Bs. You could visit the boyhood home of Eppa Rixey, inducted into baseball's Hall of Fame in 1963, and Belmont Farms Distillery, the only legal purveyor of "moonshine" in Virginia.

That evening, I fell into a trap that loneliness sets for travelers. Though I knew better, I conned myself into believing that an hour or so at the motel bar might relieve the symptoms, blissfully ignoring the fact that such bars are the venue of choice for veteran cranks and other self-regarding bores every bit as lonely as I was.

The only other customer on this dreary Monday was a veteran crank attired for golf in an Izod shirt and jackass slacks. He stared blankly at Fox News, while the bartender sliced lemons and limes, attacking the fruit more violently as the negatives escalated in a dismal financial report.

"I hate the news!" she cried, stabbing a lemon. "It's so upsetting!"

"Scare tactics," her ally muttered. "You can't trust the damn govern-ment anymore."

"I feel it's all beyond my control," the bartender shuddered. "Thank God, I'm blessed." Her blessing, it seems, was a lower mortgage payment renegotiated prior to the collapse. "I'll never be foreclosed. I'll come out of this just fine."

"They should never have allowed it to happen," said the guy in slacks. "They weren't paying attention!"

"Who do you mean by 'they'?" In a split second, I wished I'd never opened my mouth.

For the next ten minutes, I listened to a highly polished, well-rehearsed harangue. In broad strokes, old jackass slacks blamed the government for failing to protect its citizens from making such stupid decisions as buying real estate and material toys they couldn't afford. Absent from his argument was any notion that an individual bears some responsibil-ity for his or her actions.

"I'll say it again," the bartender piped, her voice overflowing with emotion. "I am truly blessed!"

She was not alone in her sympathies. Organized religion is a power-ful force in Culpeper County. There are more than a dozen Baptist churches, some dating from the 1800s and Crooked Run Baptist from 1772. The Presbyterians, Episcopalians, Methodists, Lutherans, and var-ious evangelical sects have congregations, too, although the county lacks a synagogue and has only one Catholic church.

Had I been younger and even more foolish, I'd have countered the man's argument with FDR's admonitions—no plague of locusts had de-scended on us and so on. Instead I crawled into bed, ate a Virginia Gold apple, and read some Emerson.

"God will not have his work made manifest by cowards," he wrote in *Self-Reliance*.

EAST STREET IS Culpeper's Park Avenue, famed for its lavish Greek and Colonial Revival–style houses. With a tourist brochure in hand, I started for it the next morning and almost got run over by a maniac in a careering van. Ed Perryman shared my fate. We jumped back on the sidewalk in synchronized fashion, as if we'd been practicing the trick. As survivors of a near fatality will do, we introduced ourselves and expressed our disbelief at what the world was coming to.

Anyone would put their trust in Ed Perryman. There was no guile in his face, just a sunny quality of acceptance. He was neat, too. You could see that in his crisply ironed short-sleeved shirt and his new khakis. A ballcap rested on his head. What would Americans do without ballcaps?

"I'm going to be eighty pretty soon, in November," Ed began our conversation, without much prompting. "I've been retired since '91, used to be with a paper company. I keep busy making furniture for those who ask. I did farm work as a boy for a dime a day—'course, you could buy two pounds of beans for a quarter back then. It's not like that anymore. The future looks pretty bad to me."

"Why is that?" I wondered if a bleak outlook necessarily accompanies the aging process. Steinbeck, though in denial, showed evidence of it. Often the future looked pretty bad to me, as well, but I wasn't an eighteen-year-old computer whiz versed in the potential applications of nanotechnology.

"There's too much modern stuff," Ed declared cheerfully. "Too many white collars and not enough blue. Machines do the jobs on farms that eight or sixteen men used to! 'Course, the young fellas in Culpeper don't want those jobs, not really."

"You sure about that?"

"I am sure. They're too spoiled for hard work," Ed said with absolute certainty. "That's where the Mexicans come in. They're good people, hard workers. They're good to me, and I'm good to them. You know what really bothers me?"

I braced myself for a major revelation.

"I can't stand all this red tape. If I want to build a pigpen, I've got to get a permit now. Why is that? I know what I'm doing." There it was, Emerson's self-reliance in spades. "I'm a Baptist and never been in trouble in my life. Never been in a jailhouse, either. I've had a couple of speeding tickets, all right, but everybody gets a few of those."

The granting of permits was front-page news in Culpeper, in fact,

especially regarding the use of firearms. If a varmint ravaged your vege-
table patch in the old days, for instance, and deserved to meet its Maker,
the sheriff simply issued one. He still would, but only if you had at least
an acre of land. In a crowded subdivision, a bullet could go astray and
wound an innocent bystander, he asserted.

The sheriff's stance had infuriated the Virginia Citizens Defense
League, based in Newington and described as "gun fanatics" and "loonies"
by their foes. Some members of the league attended a town meeting
with pistols on their hips, harping on about the right to bear arms even
though they lived elsewhere. The matter was referred to committee.

Ed Perryman scanned Main Street for further threats to his well-
being, but the coast was clear. "Good luck to you, then," he said, gingerly stepping off the curb. "Looks like I may get to celebrate my birthday
after all."

I continued on to East Street, a hotbed of McCain supporters. Virtually every household advertised its preference for the senator. The homes
were as grand as I'd imagined, beautifully groomed and defying the in-
roads of time, set apart from the hurly-burly in an enclave of wealth and
privilege.

East Street might back McCain, but Barack Obama's foot soldiers
had taken command of Main Street. The Campaign for Change operated from an upstairs suite of offices cluttered with fliers and bumper
stickers, puff pieces and photos of the candidate. In its cramped alcoves,
volunteers busily addressed envelopes and worked the phones under the
watchful eye of Nish Suvarnakar.

Suvarnakar radiated an utter devotion to Obama. As the regional field
organizer for Culpeper and Rappahannock counties, he cared about little
else except getting his man elected. He had no time for small talk, and
no interest in the fineries. When I blundered into the suite, haphazardly
as usual, he grilled me long and hard about my purpose before he answered a single question.

Tall and imposing, with a controlled fierceness about him, Suvarnakar had earned a degree in comparative literature from the University of
Pittsburgh in 2001. He'd dabbled in acting there, and you could see
traces of it in his manner. He fixed his audience—me, that is—with

his gaze and never wavered from his message. As an organizer, he was especially effective with African Americans and the young.

Obama's troops had stolen a march on McCain's, he explained. The campaign had opened their office two months before the Republicans caught on and responded in kind. Probably they'd been resting on their laurels, I thought, since Bush had romped through Culpeper County in 2004 with 64 percent of the vote.

Though Suvarnakar worried about the chances of a perceived "black man" in the South, he sensed a restlessness in town. Independents and some GOP stalwarts seemed ready to distance themselves from the Bush administration and its policies. They felt terribly let down, he believed, and disinclined to waste another chance. There was a bit of play in the system, a glimmer of hope for those who shared Suvarnakar's convictions.

In the interest of fairness, I knocked on the Republicans' door, too, but it was still locked at noon, so I walked over to North East Street to see Eppa Rixey's stately white house, now divided into apartments. A curbside display pictured his Big League Chewing Gum card and his "Life Time Free Pass to National League Games," an honor bestowed by Commissioner Ford Frick.

Unlike most ballplayers of his era, Rixey was a blue blood with a master's degree from the University of Virginia. He began his career with the Phillies fresh from college and later moved to the Reds, racking up 266 career wins—a record for southpaws until Warren Spahn broke it in 1959. Respected for his dry wit and gentlemanly qualities, Rixey greeted his election to the Hall with typical modesty.

"I guess they must be scraping the bottom of the barrel," he quipped, perhaps thinking about the 251 games he'd lost, and passed quietly away that same year.

BELMONT FARM DISTILLERY lay behind a cornfield off Cedar Run Road on the outskirts of Culpeper. Chuck Miller and a hired hand were toasting chunks of apple wood over an open fire when I pulled up, while sparks and ashes sailed around them and Willie Nelson sang "Bubbles in My Beer" on the radio.

Miller's straw cowboy hat, punched through with holes, looked as if the dog had made a meal of it. He didn't seem to mind, though. The hat might even have been a favorite of his, rescued from oblivion the way some men hang on to a faded flannel shirt or ravelly sweater for the comfort it gives. He cultivated an air of eccentricity.

A lanky former airline pilot, Miller played the country boy to the hilt. He liked to tell how his bootlegger granddad never once got caught by the law, only by the IRS. The revenuers forced him to sell eleven of his houses—that's right, eleven—to pay his bill for back taxes. Good old granddad had whispered his secret recipe for moonshine in his grandson's ear, Miller swore, and one almost believed him.

He and his wife, Jeanette, bought their 189-acre farm in 1975. It had always been a grain and livestock operation, and they dealt in grain, hay, horses, and cattle at first, too. Now corn is their major crop, enough to make 150 cases of liquor per acre.

Deep in concentration, Miller looked up at my approach. He has jolly eyes, bright blue, and a practiced smile.

"We're toasting some apple wood," he said, fiddling with his hat brim.

"What will you do with it?"

"Put it into a mesh bag, then sink it into a vat of whiskey. It adds some flavor."

Miller makes two whiskeys, Kopper Kettle and Virginia Lightning. Kopper Kettle is a triple-grain product—wheat, corn, and barley—mashed and fermented in copper tanks, then double-distilled in a pot-still before aging for two years in a barrel. Virginia Lightning is pure corn whiskey. It's not as raw as real moonshine, but it weighs in at a solid 100 proof and can knock your socks off. Kopper Kettle's a smoother, milder 86 proof.

True moonshiners haven't entirely disappeared from the Virginia hills, in fact. In Franklin County, the state's moonshine capital, folks horde more sugar, a primary ingredient, than they could possibly consume. A Mason jar remains the favored container for white lightning—also called popskull, skull cracker, ruckus juice, happy Sally, and plain old rotgut—occasionally with a peach at the bottom for color.

NASCAR might yet be a speed demon's fantasy if it weren't for moonshine. Some of its early heroes honed their tactical skills by out-running the authorities on their delivery routes. Junior Johnson got his start at fourteen, for example. As for the word "bootleg," it derives from the colonial period when the rascals who sold whiskey to Native Americans, often to the disgust of their compatriots, tucked a bottle into a boot and covered it with a pant leg.

Chuck left the apple wood to his helper and guided me around. Once he wanted to open a winery, but the vineyard he planted kept flooding, so he hit on the moonshine scheme instead, renovating an old work-shop for the distillery and incorporating materials from a defunct church, including two pews. He has a pack rat's affection for his two-thousand-gallon potstill, solid copper and built at the end of Prohibition, and also owns an antique Filabelmatic rotary gravity pressure filler for his bottles, a relic from 1945.

"You're a good scavenger," I complimented him.

He took it in stride. "Gotta be if you're going to make it in this old world."

"What can you tell me about your secret recipe?"

Miller looked askance. "Nothing. It's a secret."

At the distillery's gift shop, Chuck introduced me to Jeanette. The shop stocks an assortment of geegaws, apple wood chips among them, and there's an Informational Room where you can watch a History Channel video about Belmont Farm, or read about it in *National Geographic*. Miller doesn't miss an angle when it comes to promotion.

After breathing the vapors from so many vats and barrels, I felt ready for a free sample, but the law forbids Chuck from pouring any, so I bought a fifth of Kopper Kettle on faith, and my faith was later rewarded. With nothing more to be said of distilling, the talk turned to the presidential candidates. Miller saw lots of similarities and enumerated them.

"One, they both want out of I-raq," he contended. "Two, they both want progress in Afghanistan. But McCain supports free enterprise, and that's better for businesses like us. Obama will raise taxes. He's a social-ist. I'm not in favor of killing little babies, either."

Jeanette cringed. "It's just so emotional this year. Chuck and his brothers fight about it all the time."

I remembered John Steinbeck's return to Monterey in *Travels*, and how he battled nightly with his Republican sisters. "We ended each session spent with rage," he wrote. "On no point was there any compromise. No quarter was asked or given." There wasn't much compromise in Chuck Miller, either, nor did it seem likely he'd be swayed by the Campaign for Change.

SHENANDOAH NATIONAL PARK would have provoked John Steinbeck's dismay. An industrial-strength giant, the park encompasses two hundred thousand acres in the Blue Ridge Mountains, and generates millions in tourist dollars every year. A great many visitors never leave their cars except to use a restroom, admire a view, or purchase a souvenir, and the main roads can be as choked as the New Jersey Turnpike.

With more time and better gear, I'd have escaped for a night into the eighty thousand acres designated as wilderness, but I only had my sleeping bag and a cheap tent I'd grabbed on the fly in Culpeper, too flimsy for any challenging camping.

Lewis Mountain, set aside for African Americans when Shenandoah was still segregated—a system of apartheid that lasted, rather incredibly, until 1950—is the most rustic of the four developed campgrounds. I reserved a site there and joined the motorcade on Skyline Drive, a road that runs for 105 miles along the crest of the Blue Ridge between the Shenandoah River Valley and the green hills of the Piedmont.

The motorcade moved at a funereal pace. At every turnout, somebody had braked to photograph a scenic vista that seemed about to wilt from overexposure. "One goes, not so much to see but to tell afterward," Steinbeck rightly commented. Here stood nature, reduced to a postcard image, and I cursed the traffic and thought, as I often did on the trip, that Americans had become a docile, sheeplike breed.

Unable to contain my displeasure, I ditched Skyline Drive for Hawksbill Mountain, another top draw, and hiked up a rocky, moderately steep trail to the summit at forty-one hundred feet, the park's highest point.

Below lay the turbid Shenandoah River, where redbreast sunfish and black bass were dying from pollution just like the oysters and crabs of the Chesapeake, although not as rapidly.

There'd be no singing of "Oh, Shenandoah" that afternoon. My Pete Seeger moment had come and gone. Instead I chatted with a man prowling the summit, who held a gadget new to me.

"It's a GPS Ranger," he told me. "It shows you what you're looking at."

"You're looking at the mountains and the valley."

He grinned. "You're kidding, right?"

"Right."

"It's more the background stuff. How Hawksbill came into being. The geology of it." He handed it over for inspection. "There's videos and music."

"Is it expensive?"

"It must be, store-bought. But I rented mine for ten dollars at the Byrd Center, Mile 51."

"Ever heard of Thoreau?" I asked, recalling my recent reading of Emerson.

"Sure have. He wrote *Walden*."

"Thoreau could study a tree and judge how tall it was without any instrument except his eyes. Same with a mountain."

He seemed skeptical. "No lie?"

"Nope, I'm being serious."

Americans used to travel to beautiful spots to get away from it all, but they bring it all with them now. The campers at Lewis Mountain had transformed it into a suburb complete with patio furniture, Weber grills, stereos, and battery-powered DVD players. One old boy had even dragged up his recliner and sat in the shade of an RV awning, regally dispensing peanuts to gray squirrels.

I decided against putting up my tent, too intimidated to wrestle with it in front of the spectators. Some had already popped open their first beer of the day, and they'd be delighted to watch a floor show starring a greenhorn from New York acting like a Webelo desperate for a merit badge. Instead I retreated to Lewis Mountain Cabins, where fortunately they had a vacancy.

The cabin was okay. It was just fine, in fact, secluded from Skyline Drive and enclosed by the woods, with shake shingles outside and knotty pine paneling within. One could protest the absence of paperback thrillers, a cribbage board, and some cooking utentsils, but beggars can't be choosers.

On the deck, in a sweet wash of twilight, I returned to Emerson's jottings about Thoreau. When asked at a dinner party which dish he preferred, Henry David would reply, "The nearest." He despised such gatherings and said with a sneer, "They make their pride in making their dinner cost much; I make my pride in making my dinner cost little."

I hadn't lied about Thoreau's gift. As Emerson attested, he could ascertain "the measures and distances of objects which interested him, the size of trees, the depth and extent of ponds and rivers, the height of mountains and the air-line distance of his favorite summit . . ." Thoreau's GPS Ranger came built-in.

My own dinner cost little except for the pricey Manchego I bought at the market in Sperryville. Otherwise I ate bread and tomatoes, feeding the crumbs to a hungry jay.

Shortly after dawn, I woke refreshed and set off on a long walk before packing up. The park is almost wholly forest away from the developed areas, with more than a hundred species of trees. Once you've gone half a mile or so, you're alone and wonder if you'll be lucky and see a white-tailed deer, or unlucky and meet a black bear.

The bears were still roaming and foraging in late September. They'd continue until a cold snap sent them into their dens, normally in October or November. Given that information, I convinced myself that a bear, if not Bigfoot himself, was stalking me when I heard a racket in the underbrush.

The racket grew louder. I cocked an ear—two bears at least, I figured, but the commotion died down and resolved itself into a flapping of wings. Spared a hideous mauling, I crept forward until I stood about twenty yards from a flock of wild turkeys feasting on acorns, berries, grasses, or some combination thereof.

The turkeys were giants. The biggest males must have tipped the scales at thirty pounds or more, powerful enough for me to keep my distance.

They didn't spook and disappear at the sound of my footsteps, either, too preoccupied with their rooting around or perhaps slightly domesticated, since hunting is banned in the park, although poachers do sneak in.

Benjamin Franklin promoted the wild turkey as a better symbol of the Republic than the bald eagle, "a bird of bad moral character"—a carrion eater, not a raptor—"that does not get his living honestly." Wild turkeys, albeit vain and silly, were native to America, Franklin argued, and so courageous they'd assault a grenadier of the British Guards should one invade their farmyard with a red coat on.

VIRGINIA IS A very comely state, I concluded as I crossed the park to Luray. I'd only covered a small section of it, but if I failed to wind up in a cabin on a California river, I'd settle for a bungalow around Flint Hill with a white-faced jockey on the front lawn holding a lantern, or else a ring for hitching up a horse.

Those lawn jockeys cropped up all over Virginia. In my errant days as a frat boy long ago, I helped to liberate one during a sodden run to Skidmore College in Saratoga Springs on a hapless, last-minute search for a date. My pals named the jockey Johnny, and he began to accompany us on such expeditions until he fell to his untimely death from a second-floor window—strictly an accident, everyone claimed.

This story, though extraordinarily brainless, still amuses me. What's youth for if not to supply the evidence that you really have matured despite what others might think? People are remarkably various when it comes to what produces a smile. In Virginia, for example, a ride-around mower is a surefire way to generate a grin for their operators.

Actually, I first noticed the phenomenon in Maryland. The men and women riders always looked supremely content. I never saw anyone frowning or furrowing a brow. The mowers are more potent mood elevators than Prozac, maybe because they lend a sense of industry in those idle moments when a lack of purpose seems to be our destiny on earth. Anyway, I wanted one for my fantasy spread in the foothills.

Luray lies between the Blue Ridge and Massanutten mountains in Page County. It's another peaceful rural town of about five thousand—long-term residents, retirees, some commuters, and a smattering of vegans, therapists, and holistic practitioners. The valley farmers raise beef cattle, hay, and a little corn.

Tourists frequent the famous caverns, where they can wander through a garden maze and listen to the world's only Stalacpipe organ, where electronically activated rubber mallets strike the stalactites to produce tones. (It's questionable whether the world needs more than one, really.) They rent canoes, kayaks, rafts, and inner tubes to drift down the South Fork of the Shenandoah River, and fish and swim in Arrowhead Lake.

At a bank where I used the cash machine, I waited behind two elderly women who were loudly conversing. Volume control is a problem for some Americans. The loud talkers don't seem to care that anybody in a twenty-yard radius can hear every word they speak. Maybe they're unconsciously bothered by the vastness of the United States, and feel they must combat it with noise.

"I can't read in bed no more," the first woman bellowed.

"I can't, either," shouted the second.

"I like to read settin' up. I won't go near my lounger now."

"Me, neither! I take a straight-back chair."

"Good Lord! Give me a straight-back chair every time."

"It's better on my spine!"

"Mine, too!"

Luray's Main Street, lined with cute shops, went up a hill and then down it. The amenities were excellent—an arts center, a theater showing five first-run movies, a gourmet grocery. Along Hawksbill Creek, the bird life was abundant. The blue streak of a kingfisher flashed by, while a heron dredged for fingerlings. Trout season opened soon and would last until next June.

The joggers on a path by the creek all greeted me with a nod or a gesture. I almost tired of saying hello. Not every small town is so friendly, but Luray seemed determined to be welcoming. More than half the residents both live and work there, and they're attached to the community.

As in Culpeper, they're active in their churches—about thirty or so, nearly all Protestant—and belong to the VFW, the American Legion, the Masons, and the Rotary Club. They're also conservative and Republican. A team of Luray girls had recently played teeball on the White

House lawn, in fact. George Bush won 65 percent of the vote in Page County in 2004.

The folks in such rural areas had the fewest bones to pick with Washington, it appeared. The more distant they were from a big city, the more they approved of the state of the nation. Perhaps, too, the locals were only concerned with local issues, not with what happened beyond their neck of the woods.

Whatever the case, I knew one thing for certain: I needed a real dinner after my steady diet of cheese, bread, and tomatoes. The Mimslyn Inn came recommended. Its Circa '31 restaurant, so called because the inn opened in 1931, reportedly served the best food and finest Virginia wines in town.

The Mimslyn is Luray's most majestic building. It looks like an antebellum mansion and functions like the stuffiest of country clubs. An antique dress code at Circa '31 "suggested" a jacket and tie—I'd already broken that rule—and encouraged women to forgo slacks in favor of skirts or dresses. The restaurant's patrons were dining with a listless solemnity that would rob a good T-bone of its juice.

As I pretended to browse a menu and racked my brain for an exit strategy, the hostess assisted me.

"Our Speakeasy Bar does casual fare," she sniffed. "Might you be more comfortable there?" Never had I been so happy to be dismissed.

The Speakeasy was a misnomer. There wasn't any sense of illegality or trespass, only a football game on the tube and a pair of tipsy guys attending to it. I asked for a glass of Virginia Chardonnay, thinking it might salvage the evening, but it tasted thin compared to the robust Chardonnays of California, although maybe I'd chosen badly. Luck had deserted me that evening. About to cut my losses, I rose from a barstool just as a waiter dropped a plate from his tray at my feet, where it shattered.

"Sorry," Jon Mayes apologized.

This was Jon's last day on the job, so wouldn't you know an accident would happen? He'd signed up to join an archaeological dig that started the next morning—not abroad but in Virginia, he explained as he cleaned up the mess.

The Speakeasy was so quiet we had an opportunity to talk. At twenty-six, Jon admitted to being confused about life. Almost every young person in Luray, Stanley, or Alma was confused, he thought, torn between the demands of tradition and the desire to follow their own destiny.

As a child, Jon had been taught to respect America and the flag, and to revere the bravery of our armed forces during World War II, a heroic period still honored and celebrated in Luray. The town embraced its military heritage and would not soon forget the sacrifices its soldiers had made.

For those of Jon's age, though, the world had rushed in and filled them with new ideas and choices. Their dreams and wishes were often at odds with the older generation, and they felt guilty about it, as if they'd betrayed their families. Jon did not support the war in Iraq, for instance, yet he'd only confess it to close friends.

Luray resisted change because of its reverence for tradition, he believed. People are mostly satisfied with their lot and won't risk endangering it. They're only dimly aware of international affairs and not much interested in foreign countries. You can't say a negative word, however, or the older folks take offense. They don't understand how confining Luray can be if you're twenty-six and intellectually curious.

"I hope your dig goes well," I said in parting.

"Well, it's an improvement," Jon replied. "It's something. No more plates to drop, anyhow."

THE SHENANDOAH VALLEY outdid itself on the first of October, my sixth day on the road, all sunshine and blue sky. A fleet of cumulus clouds drifted by, and the mountains turned a dusky shade of purple even at noon. Green fields fanned out toward the horizon with cattle here and corn stubble there.

Trees grew in copses by barns and along creeks and streams. The temperature hovered in the mid-seventies, T-shirt weather again. Instead of the patchwork look of Iowa or Kansas, the farmland was gently contoured and more visually arresting. I took some photos, but the valley demanded a Constable or a Corot to do it justice.

In Stanley, I sat in the shade to drink in the scenery. I'd gotten off to a better start than John Steinbeck, I reckoned. He traveled to New England first, and the weather, already wintry, contributed to his depression. Maine went on forever, he complained, and its legendary taciturnity added to the chill, while I'd been warmed by much of what I'd seen in Virginia and on the Eastern Shore.

In New Hampshire, Steinbeck tried to coax a political opinion from a Yankee farmer without success. "And that's what I found all over the country—no arguments, no discussions," he griped, but the fault was his own, I guessed, for failing to engage. My experience couldn't have been more different. From Greensboro to Culpeper, I'd been treated to an earful. The voters were energized and polarized, ornery and contentious.

If you had told Steinbeck in 1960 that a man of African-American ancestry would run for president someday, he might have laughed. The Supreme Court had only just ordered public schools to desegregate, after all, and the civil rights movement had not yet reached its peak. Race relations were hardly ideal in 2008, but the kind of healing I'd witnessed in Cambridge had gone on elsewhere, too, and spoke well of the nation.

Americans still had it easy when Steinbeck set out. The rate of both unemployment and inflation was quite low. A stamp cost four cents and a gallon of regular thirty-four cents. As he wrote to Pascal Covici, he met with no "terrifying poverty," and I hadn't, either, although almost everyone felt slightly uneasy about their finances and the future.

From the moment Steinbeck left Sag Harbor, he felt homesick despite Charley's company. He sent his wife a letter almost daily, while I had the luxury of keeping in close touch with Imelda by e-mail and inexpensive calls to Ireland. Whenever she asked how things were going, I answered, "Just fine," and that was true. If some aspects of the country angered or upset me, they hadn't yet soured me on the trip.

ILLUMINATING FACTS EMERGE out of nowhere on the road. If I hadn't stopped in New Market along Route 259 on the way to West Virginia, I'd never have learned about the Rockingham County Baseball League, founded in 1924 and the second-oldest organization in continuous operation after the majors.

The Shockers, New Market's home team of amateurs, tackle the likes of the Shenandoah Indians and the Clover Hill Bucks at Rebel Field every summer. In their five years as a franchise, they've yet to post a winning record, though. Smokey Veney, the club's manager, had a big-league excuse for the press. He blamed the lack of pitching, but he hoped to correct it next season.

New Market looked spruced up, as if it anticipated a visit from the cousins over in Timberville. Flags billowed on Congress Street, where the oldest houses, elegantly restored, date from the colonial and federal eras. This was a Stars and Stripes sort of place, with a Norman Rockwell veneer.

For ten bucks you could go on a walking tour of "An All-American Town," or opt for "Boys, Bugles, and Skirts," a survey of the Civil War years. The docent affected the garb of the 1860s. Another tour focused on the exploits of the Scottish immigrant Jessie Rupert. As an outspoken abolitionist, she had earned the enmity of her Confederate neighbors. It might still be a little risky to praise the Union Army in New Market.

Rockingham County produces nearly one fifth of Virginia's entire agricultural output. Chickens, turkeys, dairy cows, and beef cattle are the primary sources of income. The poultry plants and farms hire many Hispanics, so New Market has taquerias now, it has chimichangas and shops selling jalapeños and votive candles. Even more isolated than Page County, it's more conservative, too, with Bush carrying 75 percent of the vote in the 2004 election.

On I went to Timberville, incorporated in 1884. At the Plains District Memorial Museum, there was plenty of history on show. History's become a commodity in these far-flung towns, almost a living, breathing entity that threatens to erase the present and deprive it of any meaning.

The first drugstore, the first tannery, the first saddle and harness shop, it's life as a quaint daguerreotype. Why can't life be so simple and orderly in 2008? As for the future, don't even go there.

To the west of Timberville I saw the ridged Appalachians, a panoramic view. At Fulks Run Grocery, I could smell the forest outside the store, but inside, a mouth-watering aroma of ham prevailed. The grocery doubled as Turner's Ham House, largely a mail-order business. Shopping carts were piled with hams in nylon nets, each sugar-cured with a secret recipe.

These secret recipes, like history, seemed to be everywhere. It tortured me to see the packets of boneless ham and realize I could be frying up a slice with some eggs and hash browns if only I possessed a skillet and a flame.

Then I crossed over into West Virginia, a state I associated with an old friend who fetched up in San Francisco during the hippie heyday and captivated everyone with his stories. He came from a poor coal-mining region of the Appalachians—only Arkansas and Mississippi are poorer per capita than West Virginia—and told folk tales with a twang probably never before heard in the rarefied precincts of Berkeley's English Department.

He stretched out every syllable of every word, so that time itself slowed down and expanded, and he played a hammered dulcimer, too, and made us all want to board a psychedelic bus and explore his home ground. And now I'd gone and done it, although in a Ford Focus.

The boundaries between states are artificial, of course, but West Virginia looked different from Virginia, more frayed at the edges, with a greater distance between the towns on Route 59. A billboard for the World Famous Smoke Hole Caverns in Petersburg, faded and peeling, could have been a Walker Evans photo from the 1930s. One might assume the caverns had crumbled to dust by now, but they're still open to the public.

Mathias is so dinky it would be the last spot on earth where you'd expect to find a strip club, but there it was—Paradise City on Crab Run Road, its doors shut tight against the daylight while the gals indulged in their beauty sleep.

Out of curiosity, I checked my laptop and discovered an online guide that rates the strip clubs of West Virginia. To win five stars, a club must meet all five of Jack Corbett's exacting criteria—employ fifteen or more dancers per shift; host a Web site (a no-brainer, Jack says); present featured entertainers; price the drinks at six dollars or less; and serve some food.

Jack's verdict on Paradise City? A half star.

I KEPT CLIMBING into the foothills. At an elevation of about fifteen hundred feet, the landscape became less scrappy and more densely forested. To the east, trees ascended a flank of the Appalachians and again made the air smell fresh and clean.

The road passed through Lost City, once known as Cover, on the Lost River and then through the actual town of Lost River, where I asked about the stream's mysterious name at the post office. Though the woman on duty could not be described as busy, much less overburdened, I must have interrupted her reading of Dan Brown or otherwise identified myself as a pain in the butt because she responded curtly.

"It disappears," she snapped.

"Just goes away, does it?"

"No, it comes back again."

"Whereabouts?"

"Somewhere. I can't precisely say."

I found the river on my own—more of a babbling brook in October—not far from the post office. It does disappear for a couple of miles, then resurfaces as the Cacapon River. It's a sweet little stream ideal for a picnic on the grass, or lying on your side in a pose of Keatsian languor while you draft a sonnet.

Nearby stood a lovingly renovated barn, with two wagon wheels propped against it and a vintage tractor out front. The barn, more than 150 years old, houses the Lost River Artisans Cooperative, a collective whose members practice such traditional crafts as caning, basketry, weaving, quilting, and woodworking, although painters, potters, and artists in stained glass and other media also belong to it.

The barn's divided in two. On the lower level there's a museum, naturally, while a shop upstairs sells a wide variety of goods, some produced by the co-op but all indigenous to West Virginia—cookbooks, Mason jars of locally preserved jams and jellies, ceramics, jewelry, and wine.

From a bin of CDs I plucked *Old Songs*, a compilation that ranged back to the Civil War. Ralph Hill and Wayne Strawderman, who performed the songs, looked as though they'd mastered their chops when they were boys at the knee of a musically inclined uncle. They both wore tractor caps, and Wayne relied on a pair of suspenders to hold up his blue jeans. He played mandolin and fiddle, while Ralph played guitar. They'd be no strangers to the high lonesome sound.

At the shop's counter, I met Brooke Baumann. Bright and articulate, she'd been a co-op member for a long time. In her flannel shirt and denims, she might have been a relative of Wayne's, but she grew up in Bucks County, Pennsylvania, and reached Lost River by way of Tacoma Park, Maryland, searching for a more supportive environment for creating her art.

Brooke designs floorcloths, or mats, and paints them in colorful acrylics under the name Goat On Roof. The mats often feature woodland critters—crows, pileated woodpeckers, barn swallows, lizards, and tree frogs. What attracted her to Lost River, aside from the area's beauty, was the cost of living, downright economical in contrast to Tacoma Park. She owns a house with enough land for her animals—Jupiter the goat and Ginger the dog—and pays only six hundred dollars a year in property taxes.

At first, Brooke wondered if West Virginia would suit her. It suffers unfairly from a hillbilly image, she thinks, in part because of *Deliverance*, even though the movie was shot elsewhere and James Dickey's novel isn't set in the state, but she gets along fine with her neighbors.

"They're interested in who you are, not what you are," she declared.

If she has a problem, she can count on some help—fixing her car, say, or shoveling snow from her road. Four guys felled a tree on her property not long ago in exchange for a hundred bucks and four beers. One neighbor brings her brook trout fresh from a lake and ready for the pan.

Lost River has become a popular retreat for people from Washington, only two-plus hours away. They buy or build second homes, and use them on the weekend or for a summer vacation—lobbyists, government workers planning to retire in the foothills, CIA operatives. Nine out of ten houses around Brooke's are vacant during the week.

"Must be pretty unsettling having the CIA next door."

"Not as scary as the bears," Brooke countered.

"You get a lot of them?"

"We do. Virginia dumps the troubled ones in our forest."

"Troubled? As in psychologically?"

"That's right. Bears who've attacked campers, or are proficient at raiding campgrounds." For a brief few seconds, my walk in Shenandoah National Park returned to haunt me.

Another reason for Lost River's popularity with Washingtonians, I discovered, is The Guest House, a sixteen-room inn that's friendly to gays and lesbians. The inn has a pool, a Jacuzzi, and a strikingly tranquil setting, and the chef acquires his ingredients from local sources. The words "organic" and "free-range" are frequently invoked on the menu. Except for the location, you could be in any sophisticated district of the capital—or America, for that matter. Lost River is a unique sliver of West Virginia, an island apart where the urban meets the rural in apparent harmony.

BEYOND LOST RIVER and Baker, the forest began to thin, and there were broad views of the mountains. I fiddled with the radio, looking for some country music, and hit on a station that mixed Faron Young, Hank Williams, Patsy Cline, and other classics with public service announcements. One advertised a church group's all-you-can-eat breakfast—tubs of grits and vats of red-eye gravy. The doors opened at five-thirty A.M.

The Baptists rule in West Virginia, where the population is almost entirely white. They claim about one third of all churchgoers, while other Protestant sects account for most of the rest.

In spite of the conservative thrust in religion, West Virginians have been politically liberal until recently, preferring Jimmy Carter to Ronald Reagan in 1980. They even chose the ill-fated Michael Dukakis in 1988, and Bill Clinton won twice, but the Republicans reversed the trend in 2000, and again in 2004, by a wider margin. Some attribute the switch to the waning power of labor unions.

Arkansas, Rio, Delray, and High View amounted to a string of tiny, unincorporated places, each with fewer than two hundred residents and no special attractions. Capon Springs does draw visitors to Hampshire County with its medicinal waters, though, first discovered around 1765. When West Virginia seceded from Virginia to side with the Union in 1863, it stole the hot springs, but they were deemed so valuable the state was forced to make restitution during the era of Reconstruction.

At Augusta, I swung west to join U.S. 50 again, crossing the Potomac in Romney in the Eastern Panhandle. I planned to stay the night in Keyser, the only city of any size for miles around. It had stoplights, paved sidewalks, and drinking fountains, a regular paragon of civilization, but I couldn't find a motel.

Keyser bills itself as The Friendliest City in the U.S.A—an outlandish boast, perhaps, but West Virginians do seem friendlier than normal. The shoppers at a central mall were very solicitous when I started asking questions, first of a young cashier in a bulletproof gas station kiosk who couldn't direct me to a motel and acted embarrassed about it. She urged me not to interpret her response as definitive.

"Don't worry, somebody else will set you straight!" she shouted through her squawk box. I thought she might cock a finger and add, "Just follow the Yellow Brick Road!"

Another friendly woman offered to let me use her cell phone. Only then did I remember my own cell, so I checked for motel listings in Keyser and came up snake eyes. The quest now refined itself. Where *would* I sleep tonight? My ultimate benefactor, a rail-thin, stiff-backed gent, solved the riddle. He must have been in his sixties, but he appeared to be much, much older. A lifetime of hard work had worn him down to the bone.

"I'm looking for a motel," I said with an invisible hat in hand.

"Motels are over yonder." The sentence took a lot longer to be uttered than you might suspect. He spoke as slowly and teasingly as my old pal in California, stretching out the syllables like taffy. "In Cumberland." Pause. "Off the interstate."

"In Maryland?" I'd already been to Maryland and wanted no part of an interstate.

"It's not too bad of a drive." Pause. "Where you from?"

"New York." That seemed the simplest reply.

"Fixing to stay long?"

"Just overnight."

"You ought to go see the ball eagles." Pause. " 'Fore you leave."

"The ball eagles?

"Out at the Trough." He clarified this painstakingly over the next few minutes. The Trough is a gorge on the Potomac where bald eagles nest. "Train from Romney'll get you there." Pause. "It's a sightseeing train." Pause. "You could go in the morning." Pause. "Be a shame to miss it."

He pointed me toward Cumberland. It wasn't too bad of a drive. The pastures in Fort Ashby and Short Gap were wonderfully sweet-smelling. I'd never smelled grass as sweet as West Virginia's.

Early in *Travels* Steinbeck bunks at an auto court in Maine and rages against the sterility of it. "Everything was done in plastics—the floors, the curtain, tabletops of stainless burnless plastic, lamp shades of plastic," he protested. He hated the water glasses wrapped in cellophane and the seal over the toilet seat, so he kicked it in and tried to soothe himself with some vodka and a hot bath.

We're too inured to mediocrity to object to it now, but the motel in Cumberland still demoralized me. I borrowed a page from Steinbeck, poured a healthy shot of Kopper Kettle, and popped *Old Songs* into my laptop. Almost immediately, I felt better and less alone. The room, deliberately antiseptic, filled with a warm, human glow. A fiddler and a slug of whiskey might be the prescribed cure for anybody's blues.

The songs were unfamiliar to me, but they wouldn't be to most West

Virginians. If you heard "The Wreck of Old 97" just once, it would stick in your mind forever. The rousing tempo matched the lyrics about an out-of-control mail train determined to reach Spencer, Virginia, on schedule.

Though the stoker threw on more coal, the engineer lost his air brakes at the seventy-five-foot-high Stillhouse Trestle near Danville, and Old 97 plummeted to earth and killed nine people—a true story. The engineer was found in the wreckage with his hand on the throttle. He'd been scalded to death by steam.

That number got my blood pumping. I poured another shot, bit into a Virginia Gold apple—still as crisp as ever—and listened to "Faded Love," a Bob Wills song. The lyrics weren't a patch on Old 97—"I miss you darlin' more and more every day/As heaven would miss the stars above"—but if you blocked them out, the melody was catchy.

My favorite was "The Legend of the Rebel Soldier," an anthem for those who'd like to fight the Civil War again. In a dreary Yankee prison, the rebel confronts his mortal fate before a parson. He asks but one question, "Preacher, will my soul pass through the Southland?," after which he lauds Georgia, Alabama, and the rest of Dixie.

The sympathetic parson will reassure him, we think, but that's not what happens. The last line goes, "Then the rebel soldier dies." He never gets his answer. Life is unfair, it seems, even for a Confederate with a cause.

A FRESH START, that's another American anthem. In a rush to return to West Virginia the next morning, I slapped *Old Songs* into the car's CD player for some extra energy. Wayne and Ralph were more bracing than caffeine. In my atlas, U.S. 50 ran almost straight from Burlington Junction to Parkersburg on the Ohio border—a piece of cake, I thought, but that was another oversight in planning.

They don't call West Virginia the Mountain State for nothing. The highway imitated a roller coaster. It dipped and climbed at abrupt intervals, and swerved and twisted at will. On most roads, you can safely ignore the posted speed limit, but on this stretch of U.S. 50 you'd go the way of Old 97 if you did. I crept along like a grizzled codger to the consternation of the natives, who couldn't pass me and vented their spleen by tailgating and gesturing obscenely.

The woods were also responsible for my dawdling. The leaves had changed color overnight, and the effect was hypnotic and entrancing. Oaks were the dominant species and contributed a palette of reds— scarlet, crimson, and rust—and most of the browns, while more than twenty different trees accounted for the shades of dull, pale, and bright yellow. Hornbeams and sugar maples threw splashes of orange into the mix. West Virginia's autumn carnival surpassed New England's, at least to my eye.

The highway was desolate, except for the color—no businesses or industries, and only an occasional farm on a cleared plateau. Instead of proper towns, there were unincorporated clusters that all looked the same. Some properties were in good shape and already decorated for Halloween, but others were run down, ringed with junk, and barely habitable.

Arsonists had been busy, too. A few torched and abandoned cars littered the woods, and some houses had been burned out. One failed motel rented its rooms to tenants now, while a wildly optimistic Realtor had posted his "For Sale" sign on a failed café tangled in ivy and covered with moss.

The settlements seemed frighteningly cut off and vulnerable. Where did you buy food or clothes, and how did you support yourself? You'd have no services to speak of in case of an emergency. Clarksburg was a good two hours away over that torturous road. Maybe the extreme isolation accounted for the surfeit of churches, one per cluster. The wish to connect with a higher power might well be enhanced.

The living was dirt cheap, though. Pensioners took advantage of it, and so did those who liked to hunt, fish, and avoid the government. Others sought the liberty to do whatever they wanted to do regardless of the law—dodge an arrest warrant or an alimony payment, say, or cook meth or grow some pot under heat lamps. The backwoods have always belonged to the lords of misrule.

Aurora stood out from the crowd, orderly and relatively prosperous, with a library and a small factory that manufactured wood products.

The town felt anchored rather than hastily assembled, permanent rather than fleeting.

At the Aurora General Store and Genealogy Archives, Dee Douglas sat in a rocker with a book on her lap, talking on the phone. The store was another museum of sorts. Instead of packaged history of dubious value, it told a tale of the town over the past century or so through the materials people had donated, creating an affectionate tapestry of everyday life.

The exhibits included antique tools and worn-out boots; dolls, model cars, and board games; a leathery old mitt Ty Cobb might have used; football jerseys and Cub Scout uniforms; and such vanished products as Rinso, King Syrup, and Aurora Mills Buckwheat Flour.

"I'm sorry about that," Dee apologized, hanging up. She's a former nurse, recently retired, with bobbed hair and a vibrant manner, who volunteers at the store.

"That's all right. I enjoyed the exhibits."

"I'm arranging a sixtieth-birthday party for Mary Stemple," Dee explained. "The Stemples are a big clan around here. Just about everybody in Aurora's related. Half the time you're talking to your cousin."

"No secrets, then."

"None at all."

"What are you reading?"

Dee lifted her book to show the cover. "A novel by Nicholas Sparks. I love to read."

That was music to a writer's ears. "Isn't it difficult to get books around here?"

"No, there's the library, and I swap with friends or order from Amazon. I'll go all the way to Clarksburg if I really want a book."

"Who are your favorite writers?"

Dee considered. "Danielle Steel would be one. Did you know that's a made-up name?"

"I did. I've lived in San Francisco, where she's from."

"Danielle's disappointed me lately. She puts words in those books we don't need!" Dee laughed at herself. "I sent her an e-mail about it, but she never answered."

"So Danielle's in the doghouse."

"For the time being. I bought her new one, *H.R.H.*, to give her one more chance."

Dee grew up in Aurora and attended the same school from first to twelfth grade. Her husband, Keith, is from nearby Temple Ridge, and they might never have left the mountains except that West Virginia was even more impoverished when they married. They moved to a Cleveland suburb, where Keith put in thirty-six years at a Ford plant.

He never felt comfortable in the suburbs, though. When his retirement loomed, he told Dee, "We're going home." Sure enough, he picked up his final check on the first of January, and they were back in Aurora on the second. Keith worked a hobby farm now, and drove the town's ambulance.

"And we love it here!" Dee exclaimed. "Oh, yes, we really love it!"

"Doesn't it bother you being so isolated?"

"We don't feel isolated," she said. "I don't want for anything. There's a good supermarket in Ohio only fifteen miles away. And we love to travel. We just returned from the Canadian Rockies and Jasper National Park. Oh, that was beautiful!" she sighed. "We've visited all fifty states."

"What about people who aren't retired? How do they manage?"

"It can be tough on them," Dee allowed. "Some commute to Clarksburg and hire on at Wal-Mart or Lowe's Hardware."

She related how shocked she'd been when Aurora's last foreign exchange student, a Nicaraguan, mentioned that his father was employed by a shoe company once based in Elkins, West Virginia. She hated to see America exporting its jobs overseas.

"Are people in Aurora interested in the election?" I asked.

"They are, and they aren't," Dee said. "They're more concerned with local issues." She and her husband had voted in the primaries, Dee for Obama and Keith for McCain.

"Will you stick with that?"

"I haven't made up my mind. Obama seems intelligent, but he's against guns, and Keith's a hunter. Black's not a problem—not in the least. I took care of lots of blacks as a nurse, and they were often nicer than the whites." She thought for a minute. "I don't know, maybe Obama can do something for us. We sure need it. Our country's a mess."

ON DEE DOUGLAS's advice, I paid a brief visit to nearby Cathedral State Park to see a 133-acre tract of virgin hemlocks. An overly enthusiastic ranger once compared their lush canopy to the Sistine Chapel.

On the trails, amid the ferns and rhododendrons, I gaped at ancient specimens eighty feet tall and twenty-five feet around, feeling the same awe John Steinbeck did regarding the redwoods, "ambassadors from another time." Black-capped chickadees flitted from branch to branch, while tufted titmice cried *peter, peter* without surcease.

The hemlock is opportunistic, handles poor soil, requires little sunlight, and can live for more than six hundred years, yet it still took a miracle in the person of Branson Haas for the trees to be saved. Such virgin forests were common when some Lutherans from Maryland first settled here in 1787, but as other pilgrims joined them—the Methodists, Brethren, and Amish—logging began in earnest.

The allure of Aurora, its clean air and pretty vistas, later captivated a judge from Harpers Ferry, who built a resort there in 1888 and sold it to Lee McBride, a Cleveland entrepreneur, in 1902. McBride transformed Brookside Hotel and Cottages into a first-rate spa "dedicated exclusively to health, rest, and pleasure," and spared no expense in pampering his guests.

The cottages, furnished to a high standard, were fitted with Oriental rugs and had porches that faced the Appalachians. Brookside operated its own power plant, and a farm for meat, eggs, vegetables, and milk. You could swim, ride horses, play pool or billiards, bowl, gamble at a casino, and attend concerts and dances—everything, in short, except drink. Alcohol was banned within a ten-mile radius.

The resort flourished until the early 1920s, when McBride's luck ran out. Beset with financial difficulties, he sold off his land, frequently to timber companies. One parcel of virgin hemlocks went to an unlikely buyer—Branson Haas, the farm's manager, who intended to conserve the trees rather than plunder them.

West Virginia had been consumed in a logging frenzy since the introduction of the band saw in the 1880s. By 1912, twenty billion board feet of timber had been harvested, while 8.5 million acres of virgin forest were decimated by 1920.

Haas started at Brookside as a menial laborer, putting aside enough money over the years to fend off the "galdarned timberman." His hemlocks, about seven million board feet, were worth a fortune, but he sold the parcel to the state for ten dollars in 1942, with a proviso that the trees would never be cut. He stayed on as their caretaker until his death in 1955.

Not much is known about Branson Haas, but that may well have been his choice. He was a modest man, I'd guess, and maybe shy in the bargain. One can easily imagine the inner glow he experienced whenever he rejected an offer for his hemlocks, and the kick he got whenever someone called him a crotchety old man who stood in the way of progress.

ABOUT MY STAY in Clarksburg I will be brief. For starters, it has the biggest mall in West Virginia. Two major highways, U.S. 50 and Interstate 79, converge there with predictable results. The FBI's Criminal Justice Information Services Division, a warehouse for fingerprints, is in Clarksburg, as is the National Instant Criminal Background Check System, which lets gun dealers weed out undesirables.

The historic district—the city when it *was* still a city—has some fine examples of Renaissance Revival and neo-Romanesque architecture, but nobody goes downtown in the evening anymore. I did, not knowing any better, and communed with the ghosts of commerce past. The buildings were as sturdy and stocky as fullbacks, but they'd been benched, at least for the time being.

For dinner, I tried a Mexican place. A busboy brought chips and salsa and asked, "Drink?" His English was severely constricted, a newbie from Michoacán or Cuernavaca. The right answer was "margarita," of course, but the margaritas in such restaurants are always weak, watery substitutes for the real item, although people still swallow them by the pitcher for the sheer ethnic frivolity.

"White wine," I said.

The busboy stared at me. "Whine?" He was puzzled, taxed beyond endurance. "Whine?" he repeated, then scurried away.

A grinning waiter soon appeared with a water glass filled to the top with a dark, yellowish liquid.

"What's that?"

"Your whine, señor."

To be fair, the chicken tacos weren't bad, but I dared not sip the whine. At my motel, I watched a stupid movie about an invasion from outer space, suffered a miserable spasm of loneliness, couldn't believe I wouldn't see Imelda for another month, cursed John Steinbeck and his dog, and fell asleep.

ON MY WAY to Parkersburg, I took a leisurely detour to Harrisville, the largest town in Ritchie County. Auburn, Pullman, and Cairo—pronounced Care-o—all have fewer than four hundred residents, but Harrisville has nearly a thousand, enough to support Berdine's Five & Dime, the oldest dime store in West Virginia, for the past one hundred years.

If you were scouting locations for an Andy Hardy remake, you'd be ecstatic about Berdine's. The store still sells penny candy, even horehound and sassafras, from an old oak display case. They empty the case during the summer, though, because the store isn't air-conditioned and the candy would melt. The ceiling's made of pressed tin, and the wood floors are aged and worn.

In the market for a foot-long pencil? They're just down the aisle to your left, not far from the ant farms and the magnetic King Tuts. Berdine's sets aside a corner for ornery boys, too, where they can stock up on itching powder and phony soap that turns your hands black.

HAS CAIRO LOST ITS MARBLES? a roadside sign inquired. Cairo's marble factory shut down in 1986.

Parkersburg was a railroad and river town from the Kerouac bible, all redbrick, train tracks, and back alleys perfect for polishing off a poorboy of muscatel in peace. Tattooed short-order cooks presided over funky little cafés, where Sal Paradise could bust his gut on ice cream and homemade apple pie, the only meal he ate as he hitched across the country.

Long ago, Parkersburg's waterfront bars and whorehouses earned it a rough-and-tumble reputation—the Sodom of the Ohio, Robert Mitchum called it after a quick spin there while filming *The Night of the Hunter.*

Parkersburg seemed particularly American, and not only because of the zillions of flags. The solitary diners at a lunch counter, glimpsed through a plate-glass window, were stolen from an Edward Hopper. Huck Finn might have drifted down the murky Ohio on his raft. George F. Babbitt, late of Zenith, would covet a house in the Julia-Ann Square Historic District—yes, another!—exhilarated to see his name inscribed on an arch next to the other movers and shakers.

The city's early moguls had made their money on oil and natural gas before and after the Civil War. The Rathbone brothers, former salt miners—salt lies in fifty-foot-thick deposits in the subsoil of West Virginia, often in proximity to oil—drilled a well in 1859 and hit pay dirt at a mere 140 feet. With oil selling for thirty dollars a barrel, the rough equivalent of two thousand dollars today, speculators were quick to follow. Burning Springs, Petroleum, and California were hot spots, while so much oil dribbled from the banks of the Kanawha River into the water the boatmen named it Old Greasy.

Parkersburg quickly evolved into a transport hub. Crossing the Appalachians by wagon was laborious and expensive, so the oil and gas traveled on flatboats and barges to the Mississippi and New Orleans instead, where oceangoing ships carried them to Philadelphia, New York, and Boston, and gave birth to a class of instant millionaires.

The moguls chose the nexus of Julia and Ann streets for their colossal abodes, each constructed on a monstrous scale that would require a man to father a dozen children, at least, if he hoped to populate the bedrooms. The wealthy merchants of the city, often German Jews, resided here as well—W. A. Hersch of Union Woolen Mills, and M. Oppenheimer, a dealer in clothes and furnishings.

Around Julia-Ann Square, there are currently 126 stately houses, many restored to their original majesty. One of them was once home to Captain William Butterworth Caswell, a lumber baron and founding member of West Virginia's Republican Party, and has thirty-four rooms over three stories. In Caswell's day, the extra rooms might have been used as servants' quarters, but what did the present occupant do with all that space?

The district's air of privilege grated on me. It made too much of itself, rejoiced too noisily in its own good fortune. The patriotic impulse had run amok in the square, decorated as if for a Fourth of July parade. Flags, bunting, eagles, and even a couple of Uncle Sam posters graced the windows and porches of mansions. On one front lawn stood a replica of the Statue of Liberty nearly eight feet tall.

How odd that in a humbling era for America these citizens should seize on its symbols so zealously. We're still proud to be Americans, they appeared to be saying, no matter how badly our country has behaved. There was a mild hysteria afoot, a need to invest those tarnished symbols with a meaning they'd temporarily lost.

Babbitt would have joined right in. He was a joiner par excellence, and belonged to the Boosters' Club and the Zenith Athletic Club. Parkersburg would afford him a spate of fraternal organizations to choose from—the Moose, the Elks, and even the Improved Order of Red Men, once a power to be reckoned with although now in decline.

The Red Men dress as Native Americans, and gather in tribes and councils under the leadership of the Great Incohonee. Their treasurer is the Keeper of Wampum, while the women's auxiliary is known as the Daughters of Pocahontas. The Improved Order of Red Men Museum in Waco, Texas, displays such artifacts as Aaron Burr's writing desk, a bugle recovered from the battlefield at Gettysburg, and a ring of Rudolph Valentino's.

The Shriners have the highest profile in Parkersburg. An impressive mural covers an outside wall of the Nemesis Shrine Temple, Ancient Arabic Order of the Nobles of the Mystic Shrine. To be a Shriner, you must first be a Mason, as were five U.S. presidents—Kennedy, FDR, Ford, Truman, and Harding. And to be a Mason—or an Elk, a Moose, or a Red Man—you must profess a belief in either a Supreme Being or, more to the point, God.

For most Americans, that wouldn't pose a problem. A recent Pew Forum on Religion I'd read found that 92 percent of the respondents believed in God or a "universal spirit." About one third had witnessed the divine healing of an illness or injury, and fully 9 percent of the Christians polled confessed to speaking in tongues on a weekly basis.

EARLY SATURDAY MORNING, I walked through the city's redbrick slumber to the Ohio, still a major artery for coal and grain. The river used to be quite shallow, but dams and dredging increased its depth to facilitate the flow of cargo ships. The Ohio's fish are mostly bottom feeders— catfish, longnose gar, and silver carp. Sportsmen go after big paddlefish with snag hooks and bows and arrows.

Of the river's 981 miles, 475 are sometimes unfit for swimming after any heavy rain because of the high count of fecal matter. Tanning, pulp, and paper factories contribute to the pollution—"chemical wastes in the river," said John Steinbeck, "metal wastes everywhere, and atomic wastes buried deep in the earth or sunk in the sea."

In the clear light of day, Parkersburg looked even shabbier downtown. There were many vacant storefronts and derelict buildings. Opposite a weedy lot stood C&D Pawn with the following painted on one wall:

GUNS   GOLD   MUSIC
LOWEST RATES

I wondered how a pawn shop might be faring in difficult times, but I hesitated to enter C&D, assuming I'd be accosted by a stereotypical broker—burly, balding, short-tempered, and devoted to screwing his customers. Yet the only person inside was Norma Jean Nedoff, who presented an entirely different image. Articulate and well mannered, dressed neatly enough for church, she'd been involved in the family trade for about forty years.

The "C" in C&D represented Charles, her late husband. "He died recently of congestive heart failure," Norma Jean confided as the tears welled up. "It was a long, slow decline."

"I'm sorry to hear it."

"He drifted off to sleep the way he wanted to go." She dabbed at her eyes with a tissue, and I felt awkward and ready to leave until she stopped me. "No, no, it's all right. I'm just not used to it yet."

We made some small talk until she regained her composure, and then I asked, "Has the economy affected your business?"

"We're really struggling." Norma Jean offered a halfhearted smile. "Lots of pawning, but not much buying."

C&D had once provided a good living for the Nedoffs and their partner, but not lately. Norma Jean coped by monitoring the price of gold and selling any she had on hand if she noticed an uptick. She'd stripped her inventory of every wedding ring, all melted down now. The divorces weren't happening fast enough to compensate.

A pawnshop can be a sad place, obviously. The extent of Parkersburg's travail could be measured in the junk people had consigned in exchange for no more than the cash to buy a case of beer—old drills and chainsaws, a busted weed whacker, eight-track cassette tapes, a ragged golf bag with one iron, car batteries, rusty jumper cables. Norma Jean must sometimes fork over a few dollars just for the sake of kindness, I thought.

"It'll probably pick up here come hunting season," she predicted. Rifles, fifty or more, lined a wall rack. "The boys have got to have their guns."

In spite of her problems, Norma Jean had no intention of quitting or moving. Her son and her daughter, one an orthopedic surgeon and the other an executive with Motorola, had both invited her to live with them, but she'd declined.

"I wouldn't do it for nothin'," she insisted. "This is my home." She became nostalgic then, dreamily revisiting the past. "Parkersburg was so beautiful before they let those old buildings go! I decorated my house with antique prints and photos of the city."

Norma Jean's stocks and shares had taken a dive, but she could still afford a comfortable old age. That wasn't true of her partner, who had six kids and nothing squirreled away for the future.

Inevitably, we got around to the election. "Did you watch the first debate between Biden and Palin the other night?" I asked.

"I watch every minute of every debate." She spoke firmly, as if she believed it was her duty as a citizen to watch. "During the debate between McCain and Obama, I was visiting my daughter, and her boyfriend—he's big on McCain—made so many snide comments, I pretended I wasn't interested and snuck upstairs to see it on another set."

"Any opinions on Palin?"

"I don't like her. She's so phony. She has a lot of personality, though. I'll give her that."

"So you're for Obama?"

"I am. My husband was a hunter, and he voted for Bush twice."

"Can Obama win here?"

Norma Jean shook her head ruefully. "West Virginia isn't ready for a black man, I've heard the rednecks say as much, only they don't put it so politely."

From C&D, I returned to the river through a Parkersburg that still slumbered even as noon approached. The streets were like palimpsests, a faded sketch of an earlier and more vital form. A sense of loss seemed to haunt much of the country, although its precise nature wasn't easy to define. It manifested itself as a vague anxiety rooted, perhaps, in the discrepancy between the idealized America of schoolbooks and the present reality.

On October 4, the hazy heat of Indian summer still held. The gridiron warriors—"suicidally beautiful," as the poet James Wright from neighboring Ohio put it—would sweat buckets under their pads that afternoon. In West Virginia, the clashes would be titanic. Football mattered here.

My farewell to the state was fond, if not misty-eyed. It gave one faith to see the good works being performed unheralded in such towns as Aurora and Lost River—and surely elsewhere, too—and the stunning Appalachian landscape was a justifiable source of pride. As for the drive from Burlington Junction to Clarksburg, I could make it every autumn for the rest of my life and still feel a sense of wonder.

In the Hocking River Valley of Ohio, just across the Parkersburg-Belpre Bridge, the woods flared with a first burst of fall color. Blackbirds fluttered around an old barn bearing an ad for the Red Man chewing tobacco once endorsed by Napoleon Lajoie, who owned a .338 lifetime batting average. "Lajoie chews Red Man," the slogan went. "Ask him if he don't."

The Hocking isn't a glamorous stream. It's as dull as a mud puddle and limps along even more slowly than its big brother, the Ohio, but the banks in Hockingport were still elbow-to-elbow with campgrounds, RVs, and pickups hauling trailers, a regular working man's paradise. The barbecues were lit and smoking, and the kids who hadn't listened to their moms and refused to put on any sunblock were already badly burned.

I knew this scene well. I'd lived it every summer of my childhood, dragged by my parents from Long Island to the Midwest for our annual two-week fishing vacation. Though my father loved his job in New York, he came from the Upper Peninsula of Michigan—my mother was from Minnesota—and missed the outdoors, so he insisted on renting a cabin at a lake near his roots to recharge his batteries.

On these trips, I learned the esoteric pursuits of the heartland from my uncles, aunts, and cousins. I played canasta, pinochle, and cribbage; ate pasties stuffed with such weird vegetables as turnips and rutabagas; and mastered the art of casting a Jitterbug without hanging up in the lily pads. Occasionally I caught a bass or a crappie. The Norwegian relatives on my mother's side spoke like the cast of *Fargo*. "Oh, ja," they said. "You betcha."

Riverside Bait in Hockingport further stirred my memories. It sat right on the water, and its irresistible greeting—"Cold Beer, Welcome"—made me realize I *would* welcome a cold beer. The dark interior was a refreshing sanctuary, where night crawlers and red worms slithered around in their mossy bins. Minnows bobbed in a tank, while doomed crickets chirped their final chirps. I recognized some of the lures for sale, among them the deadly Rapala from Finland, a favorite of my Uncle Ned.

The shop's rear door opened onto the river. Little dimples rose all along its surface, and I saw the boil of a feeding fish now and then. Anglers cast to them from their boats and the shore, oblivious of the splashing swimmers and the antics of a madcap speeder on a Jet Ski.

John Davis, Riverside Bait's owner, emerged from an alcove. Tall and fit, with white hair and a matching mustache, he looked a hardy type who relishes a physical challenge. He'd been in the military, had worked as a trucker, and liked to ride motorcycles, but his true passion was fishing. Even in January, he could be found wetting a line somewhere, with a fire going to keep the guides of his rod free of ice.

Gizzard shad caused the dimples, Davis told me. "They're baitfish, and they're running now. The white bass go on the bite."

"What else can you catch here?"

"There's big crappies down deep. Catfish, smallmouths."

"Any pike?"

"Sauger. It's kinda like a walleye. The Hocking's loaded with fish."

As if on cue, a pretty woman appeared in the doorway, holding a fat white bass on a stringer. She beamed as people do when they cash a lottery ticket or bet on the right horse.

"That's a beauty, hon," Davis said approvingly. The woman clapped in delight, then vanished.

"Nice fish."

"She's my wife."

Davis had a setup one could envy—the easy life, or so it seemed. He described himself as semiretired, and lived above the shop in spacious quarters with a deck on the river. In a township that had once been dry, he'd built his business from scratch, circulating petitions and collecting signatures to obtain the necessary support. He'd found the right hole to fill, because the beer was flying out the door.

"How're you doing, Slick?" Davis addressed a ponytailed customer still battle-scarred from Friday night.

"I been better."

"Stay out too late, did you?"

"Way too late."

Davis gave Slick's twelve-pack of Bud a friendly pat. "That'll fix you up."

I passed up the Bud and bought a six-pack of imports, marking me as a city slicker. If John Davis seemed to have an easy life—even though no life is entirely easy—I thought he might feel good about the country, but I'd read him wrong.

"I'm terribly disappointed in Bush," he said, shaking his head in disgust. "I'd say he's counting the days till he'll be out of there."

"Did you vote for him?"

"Yes, I did."

"Will you vote for McCain this time around?"

"Probably. I'm an American, not a Democrat or Republican. I just vote for who I like."

"What do you like about McCain?"

"It isn't the POW stuff. That doesn't qualify him to be president, but I respect him. He doesn't agree with Bush on everything. He's voted against him plenty of times."

That was enough political jabber on such a fine day. The revelers on the banks of the Hocking had realized it long ago.

"Think those white bass might take a fly?" I asked.

"They might. You never know till you try."

I transferred the beer to what Uncle Ned used to call an ice chest. Once I'd assembled my rod, I tied on a big bushy caddis fly known as an attractor pattern, but the bass were too busy gorging on gizzard shad to be attracted. I'd been skunked, as Ned would say.

TWO WEEKS INTO his journey, John Steinbeck took a breather and spent a long weekend with his wife at a Chicago hotel. Imelda was still in Dublin, alas, but I intended to take a similar break at Ball State University in Muncie, Indiana. A professor friend had invited me to meet with some of his students and talk about creative writing, so I deserted U.S. 50 again and started for Columbus on U.S. 33 through Fairfield County.

Athens, where I stopped for lunch, is the home of Ohio University, the oldest in the state. It's also the former site of the Athens Lunatic Asylum, opened in 1874 to treat disturbed veterans of the Civil War. Psychiatric care, still in its infancy, prescribed a lobotomy for intractable cases, and the doctors doled them out like aspirin.

A report from 1876 listed masturbation as the primary cause of insanity in men, while the change of life or menstrual problems were responsible for unhinging the oppposite sex. Ghosts from the asylum frequently stalk the campus, or so the rumors have it.

The Village Bakery and Café, a student hangout, shook me up after all my nostalgic musing. If the bait shop felt like Minnesota in 1953, the café replicated Berkeley in 1969. Americans seem to have a talent for recycling cultural styles of the past, as I'd first noticed at Pistone's. We have enough space, it appears, to let the iterations of different eras coexist.

The young women working at the Village dressed in casual, loose-fitting hippie gear, determined to reject the tyranny of *Vogue*, Hollywood, and the cosmetics industry. They all wore head scarfs, too, as if they belonged to a sacred sisterhood of organic food purveyors. When they took your order, you felt they might be guessing at your astrological sign. It was wonderful to bask in their well-meaning aura, even though I'd begun to suffer flashbacks.

The cooks were guys with beards, earrings, tons of hair, and head scarfs of their own, and they darted from the kitchen at random intervals with a fresh pot of lentil soup or an esmerelda salad of organic lettuces and sprouts, tomato slices, avocado, baked tofu, roasted onion, and whole roasted almonds.

The Village thrummed with happy vibes. I looked forward to my veggie burger after all the garbage I'd been eating. The monster land may be huge, but the chance of finding restaurant food that will do more good than harm is depressingly small. Americans will gobble up anything, it seems, as long as it's either salty, fatty, sugary, or—better yet—all three.

My meal was slow to arrive. Hippies operate in a parallel universe, I remembered, where the clock is merely a device to quantify and keep track of time, something Native Americans did by being in touch with nature, observing the flight of birds, ingesting peyote, and so on.

Twenty minutes went by before a server finally set a plate in front of me. She rippled with enthusiasm, as if the burger represented a sublime moment of creation. And why not? Ah, youth!

ATHENS PROVED TO be unusual for Fairfield County. The university kept it healthy and solvent, but elsewhere people were strapped for cash. There wasn't much farming anymore, except for some dairy cows and orchards. The only jobs were in the service industry. Rocky Boots and Shoes, once the main employer in Nelsonville, had recently moved its factory overseas, and almost one third of the families in town had dropped below the official U.S. poverty line.

Late afternoon found me in Lancaster, a city gradually blending into the Columbus metro area. The local paper consisted primarily of obituaries and ads for foreclosed properties. Ohio had so many foreclosures, in fact, that the secretary of state had instituted measures to assure residents they could vote without a fixed address. Only Mississippi, California, and South Carolina had a higher rate of unemployment that October.

According to a cynical blogger, Lancaster has just three businesses: bars, churches, and tattoo parlors. In the blogger's view, "You go to a bar and become an alcoholic/drug addict, ask God for forgiveness (at Fairfield Christian), then have your excuses tattooed on your body."

At twilight, I sat in Square 13, one of Lancaster's *four* historic districts. Under a blood-red sky, City Hall and the county courthouse were bathed in rosy light, and a carillon rang out to mark the hour. The square looked transcendent, but not a soul was around to appreciate it, while you already had to wait for a table at the Red Lobster and Applebee's on motel row.

Part Three

M‌Y SIDE TRIP to Ball State University did me good. Whenever you feel the Republic is about to perish for lack of imagination, you should surround yourself with students. All the great dreams are still intact and waiting to be born.

In the classroom, I met budding novelists, poets, essayists, and journalists, some of whom would stay the course and actually achieve their goal. For those who'd decide against the arts and take up dentistry or demolition derbies instead, the discipline of trying to express their ideas and emotions clearly would teach them respect for the English language. The act of writing builds character, writers like to think.

I'd be lying if I said I hastened away. I lingered on the leafy campus and shook off the road dust. Youth may be wasted on the young, but college can be, too, as it was in my case. I had the restless gene and couldn't sit still long enough to study, although now I'd gladly spend a year reading at the Ball State library. As the metabolism slows, the scholarly path looks more inviting.

From Muncie, I set off to rejoin U.S. 50 in Chillicothe, Ohio. The mind-numbing drive led through Mount Pleasant, Economy, and Webster to the dread Interstate 70. Around Dayton, the highway was torn up and strewn with construction debris, but I slipped onto a quiet side road that ran through broad fields of corn. Pork bellies were up fifteen cents, the radio informed.

Chillicothe, population twenty-two thousand or so, lies in the Scioto River Valley, once Shawnee territory. Nathaniel Massie, a frontier surveyor, laid out the town in 1796. A mill went up on Kinnikinnick Creek around 1812 and jump-started a papermaking industry.

When the Ohio-Erie Canal opened about twenty years later, farmers were able to ship their pork, turkeys, grain, and other crops to New Orleans. The railroad arrived in 1852, and though that ordinarily spelled the end to any trade by water—trains were faster, cheaper, and more efficient—the canal survived by a quirk of fate. It flowed from north to south, while the rails went from east to west.

There's still a paper mill in Chillicothe, and it colors the air at times with a slightly acrid smell. On Main Street, several people were just hanging out, sitting on benches or slumped on the courthouse steps, a shadowy army of the unemployed. The Crosskeys Tavern was already busy before noon, judging by the throng of smokers on the sidewalk. The original Crosskeys, a two-story log cabin from Massie's day, catered to brawling drovers and stockmen.

Free blacks flocked to Chillicothe during the Civil War, and the city continues to have a large contingent of African Americans, at least by the lily-white standards of the rural Midwest. It also has the Paints, a baseball team named for Paint Creek nearby. The team plays in the Frontier League—or did until it switched to the Prospect League in 2009—and sells its merchandise at a downtown shop, where I bought a Paints cap, sure to be the first in Dublin. "How'd the club do this season?"

"It could have been worse," the clerk shrugged. "Ypsilanti did us a favor."

"How so?"

"They finished last instead of us."

Every state has its idiosyncrasies. Among Ohio's are its drive-through liquor stores, and the fact that you don't pay any tax on take-out food—in Chillicothe, anyway. I discovered this when I bought a deli sandwich to go. A wheelbarrow would have been useful for transporting it to Yoctangee Park for my intended picnic.

In the heartland, portions defy logic. As it happens, Ohioans rank tenth on America's obesity chart, with 28.6 percent of them overweight, but West Virginians are much fatter and hold down third place be-

hind the folks in Mississippi and Alabama, the champions of chub-
biness.

Yoctangee Park is a civic treasure. It covers forty-eight acres and
stretches to a floodwall that retains the Scioto River, as miserably polluted as all the other streams on my route so far. If rivers are the nation's
lifeblood, we're due for a coronary bypass. The ducks didn't seem to mind,
though, and they quickly disposed of half my ham and Swiss on rye.

At Chillicothe's vistor center, I dutifully checked on the local attractions. The staff hadn't greeted many tourists since Labor Day, it appeared, because they fussed over me. The head greeter loaded me up
with brochures and pamphlets, including a flier for *Tecumseh!*, an outdoor historical drama about the extraordinary Shawnee leader that runs
at Sugar Mountain Amphitheater every summer.

"Too bad you missed it. Try the walking tour instead," she advised
me. "That'll get you through the afternoon."

I'd become a sucker for these tours. This one focused on Caldwell
and East Fifth Street, where the city's grandees lived in the nineteenth
century—lawyers, bankers, merchants, and bigwigs from the paper
mills. They raised chickens and kept horses and cows that were shooed
out to pasture daily amid the orchards and vineyards at the end of town.

The Greek Revival mansion at 147 Caldwell was once the residence
of D. K. Jones, an inventor who dabbled in explosives. Jones added a wing
lined with brick and cement to shield his family from any accidents
resulting from his experiments. Captain William Evans, who owned the
Queen Anne at 171 Caldwell, installed side entrances to be spared
the embarrassment of a recently deceased relative being carried out the
front door.

A ne'er-do-well had preyed on the wealthy widow at 174 Caldwell,
bilking her of every last penny. The Reverend H. W. Guthrie taught
reading and arithmetic at 150 Caldwell and charged only fifteen cents
per class, or "less than a 40-cent cigar." And at 80 East Fifth, Aunt Hat
and her sister Lib held séances and communed with the spirit world.

As promised, the afternoon flew by. At the Crosskeys, I toasted the
ongoing ingenuity of Americans. Every town I'd passed through, no matter
how paltry or dreary, had managed to package an aspect of itself for the

possible, although not necessarily guaranteed, entertainment of travelers like me.

The walking tour was small stuff compared to *Tecumseh!*, according to the flyer. Based on a script by Allan W. Eckert, it's been a gold mine for thirty years. I'd never heard of Eckert, but Ohioans love his books. In a library poll conducted in 1999, he tied with Toni Morrison as the Overall Favorite Ohio Writer of All-Time, an honorific that doesn't wear its superlatives lightly. He's not afraid to blow his own horn, either. On his Web site, he bills himself as a historian, a naturalist, a novelist, a poet, a screenwriter, and a playwright.

Eckert's most celebrated novel, *The Frontiersman*, has sold more than a million copies. If you're a particularly ardent fan, you can buy a manuscript from him over the Internet—an unproduced screenplay typed on onionskin paper, say, or a 3,000-word article from *Lapidary Journal*. One fan paid $850 for a copy of his 1,492-page biography of Tecumseh, even though critics had faulted the book for adulterating the facts with fiction.

I knew a little about Tecumseh myself. As a child, I'd seen a terrific action movie about him whose star was Jay Silverheels, *The Lone Ranger*'s Tonto on television. In a nifty bit of serendipity, Silverheels butts heads with Jon Hall, later TV's Ramar of the Jungle, who plays a U.S. government agent. The brutal battle sequences during the War of 1812 were especially effective. Eckert's script works the same angle, it seems, with a "herd of galloping horses and a live military cannon in action."

EDWIN DAVIS IS another eminent Ohioan I'd never heard of. A dedicated amateur archaeologist, he became fascinated with the mounds and earthen structures of the Scioto River Valley in the 1820s, and began collecting artifacts as a boy. While studying at Kenyon College, he read a paper on his findings and received an encouraging pat on the back from Daniel Webster, who belonged to the American Antiquarian Society.

Subsequently, Davis embarked on a medical practice in Chillicothe that granted him ample free time to pursue his hobby. By 1845, when he met Ephraim Squier, the new editor of the *Scioto Gazette*, he'd amassed a museum-quality horde of pendants, pipestone carvings, tools, and other relics.

Squier, only twenty-four, had puzzled over the earthworks on his arrival from New York, but when he inquired about their origins, he drew a blank and had to conduct his own research. Davis's expertise found a match in Squier's skill as a surveyor and a writer, and they collaborated on *Ancient Monuments of the Mississippi Valley* (1848), the first book the Smithsonian Institution ever published.

The book's scientific data, though scrupulously vetted, supported a commonly held belief that Native Americans could not have built the structures. Conjecture dictated that they had to be the work of a superior race instead. One theory credited the Ten Lost Tribes of Israel, while another sided with the Vikings. Even after the first professional digs at Mordecai Hopewell's farm in the 1890s, some diehards insisted in private that highly intelligent alien beings were responsible.

Hopewell's farm is Hopewell Culture National Historical Park now. I visited on another bright blue day under a sky swept clean of clouds. The culture—some prefer to call it a tradition—refers to the widely dispersed set of populations that made up the Hopewell Exchange System, an elaborate, river-based network of trade routes between Lake Ontario in Canada and the southeastern United States.

The Hopewell Culture lasted from 200 B.C. to A.D. 500. Its members farmed as well as hunted, and depended on the river for mussels, fish, turtles, otters, muskrats, beavers, ducks, and geese. They cremated their dead except for very important figures, who were accorded a burial mound. Some experts suggest that the mounds were built over charnel houses, while others believe they have a lunar orientation and were used as observatories and for ritual purposes.

There's no disagreement over the genius of the Native American artisans, though. Digs at Hopewell have turned up more than two hundred pipes carved to represent animals and birds. Carvings in mica have been unearthed, too, and necklaces and earrings. The wealth of materials employed reflects the exchange system's riches—the teeth of grizzly bears and sharks, freshwater pearls, seashells, copper, and even a little silver.

With its bountiful resources, the Scioto River Valley afforded the Native Americans a very special haven. Lalawethika, Tecumseh's younger brother, recognized this and warned the Shawnee that it might be snatched from them if they weren't careful. Ugly, abysmal as a warrior, so clumsy he poked out his own eye with an arrow, and yet unaccountably a braggart, he was a joke to his people at first, who called him One Who Makes Loud Noise.

In his youth, Lalawethika pickled himself in whiskey. He stayed drunk for years until he keeled over by a campfire at age thirty, and entered a trance state so deep everybody assumed he was dead. The Shawnee readied a burial ceremony, but he woke two days later and announced that he'd received a visitation from the Master of Life, who taught him that white men were the children of the Great Serpent and the source of the world's evil.

Thus enlightened, Lalawethika changed his name to Tenskwatawa, or the Open Door, and became a healer and a prophet. He counseled the Shawnee to forsake European dress and influences, and resort to their breechcloths, animal hides, and leathers. They were to shave their heads except for a topknot, swear off any liquor, hunt only with bows and arrows, and rely on rifles strictly for self-defense.

If they engaged in this rite of purification and adopted the old ways again, Tenskwatawa prophesied, the Master of Life would drive the whites from their land, but that, of course, failed to occur.

GREENFIELD, OHIO, IDENTIFIES itself as the home of the country music legend Johnny Paycheck, who once got into a terrible beef at a bar in nearby Hillsboro. When a customer invited Paycheck to his house for some deer and turtle meat soup, the singer supposedly fumed, "Do you see me as some kind of hick? I don't like you," then pulled out a .22 pistol and grazed the fellow's head with a bullet. The caper cost Paycheck almost two years in Chillicothe Correctional Institution before the governor pardoned him.

On Route 28 in Greenfield, I came upon a little market with a row of tanning booths at the back, a first in my experience. You could grab a can of beans and catch a few ultraviolet rays on your way to Leesburg or New Vienna. I was on my way to Wilmington, another change of plan. Governor Sarah Palin would address a rally there the next day, so I'd left U.S. 50 again, to attend.

The Republicans owned Wilmington. George W. Bush had made a whistle stop once, and even Dick Cheney had showed his rarely seen face there. That August, John McCain met with residents and assured them he'd do everything he could to block a proposed merger between the German courier DHL and United Parcel Service. DHL was the chief client of ABX Air, Wilmington's top employer, and the merger would cost the city about six thousand jobs.

In East Monroe, past Rattlesnake Creek, I traveled through farmland planted to corn, soybeans, and wheat, then took Route 73 to Wilmington. The city offered no surprises, configured to specifications now utterly familiar—malls, suburbs, and a historic district. "Localness is not gone but it is going," John Steinbeck had predicted, on the money again.

Wilmington seemed pleasant enough. It has a fine new library and a good small college. The city's median household income was about forty-eight thousand dollars in 2008, slightly higher than the Ohio average and only two thousand or so below the U.S. norm, but bloodsuckers such as Payday Loans and Cashland were everywhere. A typically desperate borrower might accept a 400 percent APR on a two-week "deferred deposit advance" against a future salary check.

As usual, there wasn't much foot traffic downtown. Only Smith's Barber Shop looked jaunty. John Wayne, cut from cardboard and nearly life-size, shared one window with a Georgia O'Keefe cow skull in a desert landscape complete with sand and cacti. A second window featured some antique razors that resembled instruments of torture and made you wonder just how painful a shave might have been in 1879.

Inside the shop, Wayne Smith sat in a corner chair and huddled with a furtive little guy who squirmed at the approach of a stranger, as if he'd been interrupted in the confessional. His voice fell to a whisper, and he cracked his knuckles several times and kept glancing over his shoulder in case another phantom should appear. It was all too much for him in the end, so he vanished like a blue streak.

Smith, who's been holding court for forty-six years, didn't budge. He might even have been mildy intrigued by a head he hadn't barbered. Gracious and slow-moving, he's a big, bulky man, although his son Nick puts him to shame. A framed news clip pictured the young giant being inducted into his high school's Wrestling Hall of Fame. Smith also had hung up a photo of his daughter Erika building a house in Coahoma, Mississippi, as a volunteer with Habitat for Humanity.

Yet the most eye-catching photo was an autographed portrait of President Bush, who'd written, "Wayne, it helps to know people in high places." A friend had scored it as a gift for Smith.

"Very impressive," I said. "Are you happy with Bush?"

"He's made some mistakes," Wayne allowed, suggesting an incredibly forgiving nature.

The shop could have been his den at home. One shelf sagged under the weight of the trophies and medals he'd won with the quarter horses he raises on his 105-acre farm. There were stacks of magazines, of course, and also books. Smith liked Allan W. Eckert and Louis L'Amour— cowboy stuff, tales of the Old West. Videotapes were stacked on a counter next to a miniature flag and a few combs and brushes.

I took the squirmy guy's seat. "How'd you become a barber, Wayne?"

"There was five of us kids, and my mother used to cut our hair," he told me. "One day I complained I could do it better, so she put down the scissors and said, 'Well, go on, then!'"

"You're very proud of your own kids."

"I am. Erika works out at the college. Nick's a farm boy. His mother taught him manners, and she did a good job."

The economy had affected his business, naturally. Customers postponed their cuts and trims as long as possible, waiting for a special occasion such as a big date or a church social. Like almost everyone I'd met, Smith expected things to get worse before they got better.

"You just have to sit tight, grab your ass, and hang on," he recommended. He disapproved of the finger-pointing, all those insincere politicians playing the blame game. "Why don't they just come together and fix the problem instead?"

"I agree." And I did, at least in principle.

"Those Wall Street bankers get me, too. They're capitalists on the way up, and socialists on the way down. When they're making money, they don't want the government around—only when they need to be bailed out." Wayne was on a roll. "What they are to me is wimps. Somebody should spank 'em."

Then Smith began to rip into Barack Obama, criticizing the candidate for his "friendship" with the former terrorist Bill Ayres—proof of how radical the candidate really was—and Obama's attempt to "steal" the election with the help of ACORN, the activist group charged with fraudulently registering voters. He did not seem concerned by the scantiness of the facts, nor chagrined to be repeating Rush Limbaugh's exact words.

I ran into the Limbaugh effect over and over in the heartland. In the midst of a sensible and often enjoyable conversation with someone like Wayne Smith, hardworking, independent, religious, and devoted to his family, the person would veer off on a tangent and parrot Limbaugh's latest proclamations that consciously stoke the fear and paranoia of Americans.

Smith quit talking when Olmy Olmstead came in for a trim. Olmy was the assistant football coach at Wilmington College, currently 1–3 for the season. He studied there as well, and would soon earn a master's degree in special education. Olmy appeared to be less interested in the gridiron than in working with the disadvantaged.

"Coaching's a lot like teaching," he said, hopping into the barber chair.

"Why do they call you Olmy?"

He grinned. "It's my dad's nickname, and the old man stuck me with it."

Olmy's own football career ended at Wabash College in Indiana in 2004, where he ground out the yards as a fullback and handled the placekicking chores.

"I never got any ink for running the ball," he joked, "so I figured I'd better score some points with my foot if I wanted to get my name in the paper."

He felt fortunate to be living in Wilmington after a stint in Columbus, a city too metropolitan for his taste. "It's real friendly here. When you walk down the street, folks say hello even if they don't know you. What brought you to town, anyway?"

"I'm going to the Palin rally tomorrow."

"You might see me out there," Olmy said.

Anyone who hoped to attend the Road to Victory Rally needed to collect a free ticket, so I left Wayne and Olmy and claimed mine at a hastily assembled headquarters in a mall next to Rent-2-Own Furniture. The three women doling out the tickets were new to politics and giddy to be included in the Palin buzz.

When I signed the register with a Dublin address, it created a stir. None of the women had been anywhere in Europe, so they asked countless questions and imbued me with a romantic daring I don't honestly possess.

"What excites you about Governor Palin?" I asked in return.

"She's a woman," they answered, more or less together. They admired her for balancing a career and a home life, and for doing, presumably, the same domestic chores they did. As soccer moms, they identified with a hockey mom. They were kindred spirits. Nobody mentioned John McCain. He'd been shuffled out the back door to cool his heels in the garage.

The ticket was roughly the size of a California ballot. Draped in bunting at the top, it plied the usual red, white, and blue theme. "Country First," the big block letters shouted. The rally would begin at six in the evening at the Roberts Centre, and the women were ecstatic. As volunteers, they might get to shake hands with the candidate.

THE WEATHER GODS cooperated with the Republicans. A gorgeous autumn day awaited the imminent arrival of Sarah Palin, who'd gone for a run that morning before a town meeting in Wisconsin.

"God blessed you with the great outdoors!" she exclaimed to the TV reporters afterward. Palin looked so healthy, radiant, and even sexy one had to entertain the disconcerting thought that if she were the candidate, the GOP would have a far better chance than it did with the experienced, albeit aged and wooden, McCain.

The Roberts Centre is in farm country outside Wilmington, roughly equidistant from Columbus, Dayton, and Cincinnati, and accomodates events both big and small. Conventions, weddings, a cat show, an Art & Pottery Festival, and a gathering of the Ohio Gun Collectors Association were all scheduled for the months ahead. The Holiday Inn next door was booked solid with media types.

When I reached the center at about two o'clock, a security guard waved me into a vast parking lot. Although the doors wouldn't open till four, a couple hundred of the faithful already waited patiently in line.

They'd come prepared for the heat, with bottled water and tubes of sunscreen. The temperature was in the high seventies, but the proliferation of concrete and tarmac made it hotter. If you were fortunate enough to spot a tree, you'd be sharing the shade. There wasn't any wind, either, to relieve the sting.

A dozen or so souvenir vendors were confined to a little island con-course. Unable to circulate and hawk their wares, they were in an ugly mood. "Somebody's gotta buy a hat!" one pleaded. As members of a Gypsy tribe, they adhered to their own code of ethics and had strong ideas about right and wrong. The setup at the Roberts Centre was way wrong. It sucked, as Dexter Zaring put it.

I met Dexter on the concourse. He wore a clean white football jersey bearing the number 17 in bright red. In another life, Dexter might have been a quarterback. He had the size for it, and the blond, square-jawed look. Against his chest he held a placard stuck with many different cam-paign buttons.

"Nice turnout," I offered as an icebreaker. "You should do pretty well."

"Nah, I don't think so." Dexter frowned. "The Republicans are cheaper than the Dems. Too much competition here, plus they've got us pinned down. Are you for McCain?" he asked, and before I could dis-semble a reply, he countered, "I'm a libertarian Republican myself."

"That's a new one on me."

Dexter leaned closer and lowered his voice. "Actually, I'm just a lib-ertarian. I'm for Obama."

Given what I know about America, it's shameful to admit that I na-ïvely assumed the vendors must be GOP stalwarts. They might be dressed in McCain and Palin regalia, but they worked both sides of the street. Dexter's Obama buttons were stowed away for the time being, ready to emerge again at an upcoming Democratic rally in Chillicothe.

At age thirty-eight, Dexter had taken an extended leave of absence from his job as a part-time computer specialist in St. Louis. For the past year and a half he'd been trailing the Gypsy caravan and selling buttons around the country. He'd fallen into the game by accident and had stayed in it because of the whopping profits. He ordered his buttons by the thousands now, and hired a crew of fellow hustlers to help push them.

"It's like a cottage industry," he said merrily. Each hustler kept 30 percent of what he or she sold, and cleared about three hundred dollars on an average day. Dexter surveyed the crowd, almost all white and growing by the minute. "I gave my African American the day off. He didn't fit in here, but he'll make a killing in Chillicothe."

"Will you do this right up to the election?"

"I guess so. It's addictive, like gambling. You invest your money, and you get lucky or you don't."

Dexter had hit the jackpot a while ago in San Antonio. Reduced to his last few buttons, with only forty bucks in his pocket, he maxed out his credit cards to request a new batch from Kansas City, then inveigled a friend to drop him at a hotel where he finessed a room, flicked on the tube, and heard that John McCain would attend a Republican event there the next morning.

At the reception, Dexter managed to thread through the crowd, skip past security, corner McCain, and press a button on him, but a Secret Service agent intervened, and McCain handed it back. Still, it boosted Dexter's notoriety.

"They showed it live on CNN!" He continued to be inordinately gratified by his fifteen seconds of fame.

"Think you'll do this again in 2012?" I asked.

"I won't be able to. The corporations will take over by then. There's a lot of money in this business."

He'd miss the camaraderie, he confessed. He liked shooting the shit about politics, philosophy, and society over drinks. Sadly, it looked as if another tiny sliver of our outlaw culture would soon bite the dust. Dexter's confreres were a band of old-fashioned rogues, close kin to carnies and racetrack touts. If they struck gold, they'd pop for a new nose ring or a suite in an expensive hotel, but they'd all slept in the backseat a time or three.

"They're mostly unemployable, but they're all right," Dexter said, almost sighing.

An elderly fellow in a VFW sash bedecked with medals wandered by. "Got any 'Soldiers for McCain' buttons?" he inquired.

"Sorry," Dexter told him. "Sold out."

"Aw, gee." The old soldier beat a hasty retreat.

"They always want the button you don't have." Dexter brooded for a moment, then got fired up again. "Hey, did you talk to the one-armed guy yet?" I hadn't talked to the one-armed guy. "Well, I'll find him for you. He knows *everything* about the game."

While he conducted his search, I studied the crowd. The line unraveled into the distance now, perhaps a half mile long, but the new arrivals didn't groan or turn away when they saw what they were up against. Instead they smiled wryly and blurted something like "Wow!" or "Holy Cow!," abashed at their own innocence in underestimating the enormity of the rally and less willing than ever to forgo their rightful place in it. Off they marched to the end of the line, meek and unprotesting.

I couldn't fathom it. Even if Elvis had risen from the dead to perform, I'd have avoided the Roberts Centre. Here, raised to the highest power, was Babbitt's desire to belong—to almost anything, really. The fans seemed oblivious of the heat and the sun, glad to chat with their neighbors, make new friends, and sing Palin's praises. They came from all over Ohio and beyond, clutching their cameras, cell phones, and even autograph books.

"She's not just a pretty face," I heard somebody say, and a chorus joined in, "No, she's not just a pretty face!"

"Found him!" Dexter shouted. He summoned me over and introduced me to Daniel Richards, whose card read, "Campaign Accessories, Helping People Get Elected Since 1980."

"Dexter says you're the man," I began.

"I've been at it a while, all right." Richards had a serious demeanor, as befitted the button game's veteran elite. "I started out at fifteen. Reagan and Clinton, those were big years, but this election's shaping up okay, especially since Palin entered the race. She's a novelty item, and that's always good.

"I buy my buttons from N. G. Slater in New York. It's an old firm, one of the oldest. Robert's my contact there. We dream up slogans together. You know 'Read My Lipstick'?"

"Sure."

"That's Robert's. It's going well, and so's the one about the pit bull. I like to recycle the traditional stuff myself. Take 'Country First.' That's from the Reagan era. You can't go wrong with the retro angle. Anything red, white, and blue will sell."

Richards took a cigarette break. I watched the line inch forward—more VFW and American Legion members, two burly bikers in Harley gear, a woman unaccountably wearing a strapless black sheath and stiletto heels. Out on the highway, cars were backed up almost to Wilmington, eight miles away. Every third car was an SUV or a high-end pickup, either brand-new or just a year or two old. There were no junkers anywhere.

"I'm a staunch Democrat myself, but I do the Republican bit," Richards went on. "We all do. I know of a company in Greenville, Ohio, that manufactures Obama merchandise as Tigereye Design, and I think they do some stuff for McCain under another name. Anyway, that's how it goes. When I'm not on the road, I'm a stay-at-home dad."

A toothless old man butted in, tapping my shoulder. "Lot of people," he remarked, indicating the line.

"Quite a scene," I agreed.

He pointed to a much shorter line at a side door. "Those special people?"

"Probably VIPs," I guessed.

"Oh, that wouldn't be me!" he laughed. "That most definitely would not be me."

To escape from the sun, I hid out for a while at the Holiday Inn's bar. Some vendors were doing the same, relishing the air-conditioning and their cold beers. The woman next to me, a stout, soft-spoken government worker from Columbus, wore an "I Love Sarah Palin" button on her blouse. Her husband was holding her place in line. She couldn't stand for very long because of her arthritis.

"Do you really love Sarah Palin?" I asked, half joking.

"You know, I really do."

OFFICIAL SOURCES PUT the Roberts Centre attendance at ten thousand. The first hundred or so people through the door, those who'd stand in the front rows, were given signs to wave for the TV cameras. When the Straight Talk Express, Palin's tour bus, rolled into the arena, the crowd erupted, and the tumult rarely subsided for the next thirty minutes.

The fans cheered her pro-life stance, her promise to lower taxes, and the jab she took at Obama for his alleged ties to Bill Ayers. Indeed, they cheered the simple fact of her, bursting into an incantatory chant of "Sarah, Sarah, Sarah." Like the woman from Columbus, they really did love her.

Palin sounded supremely confident, even full of herself. One sensed that she'd practiced for this moment long ago, maybe as a teenage beauty queen posing before a mirror in Wasilla.

She drank up the adulation, as if it nourished something deep inside her. Her stump speech lacked any note of admonition, nor did it contain much of practical value, but that could be said of most. At an elemental level, she was just having a good time, skating along on the surface of the enthusiasm.

As in Wisconsin, she reminded the crowd that God had richly blessed the nation with natural resources, and they chanted, "Drill, baby, drill." Another allusion to Obama elicited a fearsome "No Bama, No Bama, No Bama." She invoked the deified Reagan more than once, and titanic applause accompanied each mention of his hallowed name.

"America is not the problem!" she bellowed. "America can be part of the solution!" The crowd roared, "U.S.A., U.S.A., U.S.A!"

The faces tilted up to her were as vacant as those of stoned kids at a rock concert, absent of any emotion except surrender. If Palin had asked the faithful to form a conga line and dance to Chillicothe, they'd have complied in an instant. They didn't blink when she glided by the DHL stalemate without any hint of a plan to resolve it.

"We will do everything in our power to help you!" she shouted, and those shopworn words were satisfactory enough. This wasn't a crowd that sought to be elevated or ennobled, merely entertained.

"Palin is a common person," Carla Storer, a twenty-eight-year-old mother of five from Lynchburg told the *Dayton Daily News* later, "and she really connects with the common person."

AFTER THE RALLY, I couldn't face dinner at China Buffet (chow mein, pizza, taco chips, deviled eggs, et cetera) or El Dorado Mexican, where the "Happy Our" was under way, so I knocked around until I found the General Denver Hotel, a four-story Tudor Revival built in 1928 and named for James William Denver, a hero of the Civil War. The hotel still has rooms upstairs and a pub that serves good food at a reasonable price, all cooked to order.

Over a steak sandwich and a glass of red, I deliberated on what I'd seen. The raucous energy at the Roberts Centre, so easily harnessed and steered, scared me a little, as did the wild adulation. A team of twenty-five-year-old sitcom wizards in Los Angeles might have invented Sarah Palin and built a show around her—the tale of a common person thrust into the spotlight by accident, who's weirdly prepared for her destiny.

The Palin cavalcade was pure theater. That's what the audience wanted—no ideas, just some contact with a celebrity. They wanted to believe America had gone astray on its own, too, without any input from them. Absolved from all blame, at least in their own minds, they could hoot, holler, and wave the flag, looking to a former sportscaster from a tiny Alaskan village as their potential savior.

When had Americans gotten so soft? John Steinbeck had caught the scent of decline half a century ago—"the haunting decay," to reprise his words. Americans felt entitled to own a home and a new car or two even if they couldn't afford it, but the materialism didn't bring contentment. Instead it brought more debt, mountains of it, and the abstract longing was still there. Maybe the rally healed the longing for a bit. It bestowed an illusion of meaning.

In spite of Palin's pledge, the merger between DHL and United Parcel Service eventually occurred, and Wilmington did indeed lose those six thousand jobs and became a media symbol for the country's woes.

AN ANGRY HONKING of horns saluted my departure from Wilmington when a big jam at a McDonald's drive-through window stalled the delivery of McMuffins, McGriddles, and caffeine, thereby infuriating the locals.

Highway 68 led toward Fayetteville and U.S. 50. The air had a fine autumn crispness after the previous day's scorcher, and the fields of corn and soybeans were the same rich, gold color as those in Maryland. This was the Ohio of red barns, forests, and streams, quite beautiful in an understated way.

Over the Little Miami River I traveled, then past Vera Cruz and Marathon to Owensville, where I explored a wonderful park and walked a nature trail that identified various species of trees.

Here I learned that hackberry branches are used for witches' brooms, and the white ash for baseball bats, tennis rackets, and polo mallets. From the eastern red cedar comes the juniper for gin. The elm, notorious for its widowmakers, once inspired a forgotten poet to write, "The elum hateth man and waiteth."

Along the trail I saw silver maples and pawpaws, red maples and box elders. There were pin oaks, swamp white oaks, and the black cherries that yield hydrocyanic acid for cough syrup. Daniel Boone fashioned coffins from black cherry and gave them to friends, all but the last.

Beyond Stonelick and Perintown lay the greater metro area of Cincinnati, a city almost half African American. Cleveland has a large black population, too, as does Dayton. The highway climbed to a ridge with an expansive view of the sun-dappled Ohio below, then dipped back to flat ground and hewed to the river's course.

Cleves won the lunchtime lottery. You wouldn't want to mess around there. The police keep close tabs on the town. If somebody goes to a "convenient" store, even late at night, they don't have to worry about criminals or any other major issues. It says so on the Cleves Web site.

Skyline Chili beckoned. I'd been tipped on it, after all. Nicholas Lambrinides from Kastoria, Greece, opened the first Skyline in 1949. It overlooked downtown Cincinnati, hence its name. Located in a Catholic neighborhood, the shop did a booming trade on Thursdays, and on Saturdays after meatless Fridays. Lambrinides' recipe—a secret one, of course—reportedly includes chocolate and cinnamon.

Skyline Chili was bright, clean, and cheerful. The young staff evidenced none of the usual hangdog misery of franchise employees. In seconds, I received a menu and some oyster crackers to nibble. I ordered a regular bowl of five-way—spaghetti, chili, diced white onions, red beans, and shredded cheddar cheese. The dish clocked in at 840 calories, with 45 grams of fat, 2,850 milligrams of sodium, and 150 milligrams of cholesterol.

Once a philosopher, I thought, and twice a pervert, as Voltaire said.

As I waited, I developed a case of nerves and cast a cold eye on the five-way when it landed on the table. No way, I muttered to myself. The chili looked more like a sauce or a gravy, but I gathered my resources and dived in. A few bites later I was a convert, if not precisely an enthusiast. If I lived in Cleves, I'd have to monitor my visits to Skyline carefully, or else invest in some bib overalls.

A GAS STATION SIGN caught my attention in Aurora, Indiana. FREE CHICKEN WITH FILL-UP, it advertised. The offer hadn't sparked a stampede, probably because chicken isn't included in the four main Hoosier food groups. Those would be beef, pork, beer, and Jell-O salad with marshmallows, according to a comic I heard on the radio.

Hoosiers are a self-deprecating bunch, apparently, and not afraid to laugh at themselves. If you carry jumper cables in your truck, have ridden a bus to school an hour or more each way, and know several people who've hit a deer, you're a Hoosier. When you ask Hoosiers if they enjoyed their vacation in an exotic new place, they reply, "It was different."

Nobody's certain about the origins of "Hoosier." An early theory, since discredited, called it a corruption of hussars. John Jacob Lehmanowsky spoke of the light cavalry soldiers in "Wars of Europe," a lecture series he delivered in 1893, but the term was in common parlance before then. Another theory, equally dubious, suggested that settlers on the frontier cried out "Who's there?" whenever someone approached their cabin after dark.

There's more substance to the notion that riverboat men on the Ohio, fierce battlers who "hushed" their rivals in fights, were responsible. The word first cropped up in print in the title of John Finley's poem "The Hoosier's Nest" (1830), a paean to the state that goes in part:

> Blest Indiana! in thy soil
> Are found the sure rewards of toil
> Where honest poverty and worth
> May make a Paradise on earth

Indiana was something of a mystery to me. It isn't a high-profile state that fills you with preconceptions and expectations long before you visit. I knew that it's mostly flat, grows lots of corn and soybeans, runs on coal, and has very devoted sports fans. Wal-Mart is the leading employer. I knew that, too, and also that Hoosiers haven't supported a Democrat for president since Lyndon Johnson in '64.

The landscape between Aurora and Versailles looked much rougher than the sweet Ohio farm country. If anyone had given a thought to zoning, it didn't show. Tangled up on the highway were commuters, gamblers aiming for casinos on the river, and locals on their usual rounds. The snarls can be so vicious that some elderly drivers boycott this strip of U.S. 50 on account of the many suicide lanes that live up to their name.

Forsaking the free chicken, I bought some gas in Versailles. It's pronounced, or mispronounced, Ver-sales, and you wonder if this isn't an unconscious rejection of any foreign connotation since the village considers itself so all-American. That translates into twelve churches for eighteen hundred some residents, plus a Dairy Queen, a McDonald's, a Family Dollar store, and an active American Legion post.

Not a whole lot goes on in Versailles. People were still talking about a big storm in September when trees blew down and some neighborhoods lost their power. One amateur filmmaker had even posted a video of the deadfall on YouTube. Shot through the front window of a pickup, it's called "Storm Debris," and it ends with a montage of splintered branches, a collapsed fence, and a mess of telephone cable ripped free from a pole.

The same amateur contributed a home movie of the annual Versailles Pumpkin Show, when the carnival comes to town and the prom king and queen ride by on a float. Every hamlet in southern Indiana has a similar festival, it seems, and they often reflect a nostalgia for a simpler, more heroic past. North Vernon, once a hub for trains, hosts a Railroad Days Parade, while Seymour reaches way back to the 1940s to inspire its Victory Over Japan Parade.

Life in Versailles may appear wholesome, but it's a hard life. Ripley County is among the state's poorest. On the side roads I saw boarded-up and abandoned properties, with scrawny dogs patrolling them.

Jobs are scarce and usually involve a long commute. Workers are watched closely at most companies and subjected to a constant stream of random drug tests. Even a trace of nicotine can be grounds for dismissal, I was told, because insurers consider smokers a health risk.

The employers, if perhaps overzealous, can't be faulted. Southern Indiana has a huge meth problem and labs by the score. It requires very little money and no special skills to cook up a batch of crank, the poor man's cocaine, from such readily available, over-the-counter ingredients as Sudafed, lantern fuel, ammonia, lye, and brake cleaner.

Each batch of meth produces about five pounds of toxic waste, and the cooks aren't choosy about how or where they dispose of it. Cleaning up a house that's been used as a lab costs a fortune. The tweakers are ordinarily young, white, and out of work.

At Family Dollar, I talked with a restless Versailles native of nineteen, who noticed my New York plates. He wore his ballcap backward and affected a rebellious stance. He was eager to leave town, although not eager enough to join the army, a traditional means of escape that keeps the rolls of the American Legion stocked with former soldiers.

"I read a book by John Steinbeck once," he bragged, pausing to spit.

"Which one?"

"*Of Mice and Men*. They made it into a movie."

"Did you like the book?"

He shrugged "It was all right. Kinda corny. But I wouldn't mind seeing California."

"Long way from Versailles."

"Tell me about it. The farthest I've been is Bloomington."

"What stops you from just taking off?"

"My folks, I guess, and the people around here. They're real decent. Honest, too. If you're in trouble, somebody'll help you out."

This refrain is common. Rural Hoosiers regard themselves as salt of the earth types, whose decency and honesty compensate for their occasional hardships. Each tightly knit community acts as a mutual support system, as well as a shield to ward off any negativity or criticism. To fit in, though, you must pretend to be the person you've always been—or are presumed to be—and that was a challenge the youth at Family Dollar couldn't meet.

IN NORTH VERNON, three times the size of Versailles, there was another revealing sign of the times taped to a café window:

> DUE TO THE UNCERTAINTY OF THE MARKET
> I WILL BE CLOSED NEXT WEEK.
> CALL THE SHOP FOR UPDATES.

The Baltimore & Ohio once propped up North Vernon's finances. As many as seventy trains passed through every day, but that was ages ago, and the town hasn't recovered or invented a new identity for itself. The franchisers rushed into the breach, and now State Street is Any Street, U.S.A. It's demoralizing to take note of the pattern yet again. The repetitiveness robs travel of its essence. There's nothing left to discover.

I stayed in a motel off State Street. An Indian family operated it, members of the vast Patel clan. They were warm and solicitous. Their little son rode a tricycle through the lobby, madly ringing his bell. I smelled a curry cooking somewhere and wished I could invite myself to dinner.

At a park across the way, an astonishing number of people were trying to peddle second-, third-, and probably fourthhand goods without much success. I didn't know whether to attribute this to the economy, or blame eBay for fostering the idea that every cast-off item on earth has an intrinsic value to someone.

For a while I watched a team of Little Leaguers taking cuts in a batting cage nearby. They faced a diabolical pitching machine as tough to hit as Tim Lincecum. The machine must have been broken, because it threw bullets. The frustrated lads banged home plate with their bats and bit their tongues to keep from swearing. Their dads, fireplug guys in shorts, coached and corrected them.

"Don't step in the bucket, Timmy."

"Stop swinging for the fences, Robert. Just try to make contact."

Like the boy on his trike, the enduring baseball clichés lifted my spirits. Even in the gloomiest of times, the world goes about the business of quietly renewing itself.

The railroad tracks downtown, stretching into the distance with no train on the horizon, lent the evening a ghostly aspect. I crossed the tracks, thinking I must be among the last Americans who'd prefer to walk rather than drive. The Hoosier Grill looked promising from afar, but it was closed, and so, too, was Christopher's, possibly forever, judging by the dust.

Miller's Tavern was the only option, so I gave it a whirl. It's still legal to smoke in some public places in Jennings County, and the smokers at Miller's were doing a bang-up job. The bar was like the gin joints of my adolescence, where a pack of Camels and a phlegmy hack were emblems of emerging manhood. My Uncle Ned could clear a room with his cough. The cigarettes he referred to as "coffin nails" proved to be just that.

Once I might have squeezed an ounce of romance from Miller's, but no more. Instead I retreated to the motel, my eyes stinging, and flipped through the weekly *North Vernon Plain Dealer*, whose editors had lately conducted a straw poll on the election. Seven out of ten respondents were dissatisfied enough with the status quo to vote for Barack Obama.

AMERICANS LOVE TO hunt, as John Steinbeck knew. He called it a "natural-born" trait inherited from the pioneers, and the Hoosiers back him up with ardor. They shoot or trap red and gray foxes, coyotes, coons, possums, beavers, weasels, muskrats, minks, skunks, rabbits, crows, ducks, geese, quail, and wild turkeys in addition to the white-tailed deer they covet as trophies.

Deer season hadn't opened yet, but ruffed grouse and squirrels were fair game, so I heard the distant report of firearms at Muscatatuck National Wildlife Refuge in the morning. The refuge covers 7,724 watery acres and provides a superb habitat for more than 280 species of birds, along with an excellent breeding ground for mosquitoes. They attacked the instant I left the car, aggressive little vampires on the wing. I'd have paid ten bucks on the spot for one squirt of insect repellent.

Storm Creek and Mallard Pond were swampy, ringed with bulrushes and thick with lily pads. I spotted an eastern towhee kicking over some dead leaves, and ticked it on my Muscatatuck checklist, still shocked to take such pleasure from birding. The activity made no sense to me as a boy in a denuded suburb, where the only birds, it seemed, were robins, sparrows, and seagulls. Birders were weirdos, too. I'd no more scan the trees back then than get caught with my pants down.

That all changed when I was an aspiring writer, semistarving and living in the vineyards of northern California. The trailer I rented looked out on an old oak hung with Spanish moss, and one morning I noticed some bright yellow flashes high up in the branches. A quick trip to the Healdsburg library taught me they were Bullock's orioles, or small blackbirds. This thrilled but also bothered me. It felt abnormal to be thrilled. I'd fallen into a universe I had previously ignored.

I followed a path along Storm Creek. The mosquitoes followed me, settling on my neck and forearms. I brushed them away, rolled down my sleeves, and kept an eye peeled. Birding requires the same intense concentration as hunting, really, except that no creature dies.

Killing a buck every autumn is still a rite of passage for many Hoosiers, and not only men. They rely on rifles, both standard and muzzle-loaded, and handguns and bows and arrows. Steinbeck had no argument with hunting if it's done cleanly and fairly. He resented, as I do, the "overweight gentlemen primed with whiskey" who'll shoot anything that moves or looks as though it might. An honest hunt should be conducted on foot, not seated on an ATV.

In my two hours around Storm Creek, I added seven more birds to my checklist:

- white-breasted nuthatch (common)
- Carolina wren (common)
- tufted titmouse (abundant)
- purple finch (common)
- belted kingfisher (common)
- house wren, I think (uncommon)
- northern cardinal (abundant, the state bird)

Then I took to the highway again, sorry to leave the reserve. I could still hear the distant reports, a muted preview of the cannonade that would echo through the woods in mid-November. Along the road were support services for hunters—taxidermists, of course, and deer processors, or specialty butchers, and a deer and wild turkey check station for recording any kills.

The check station was part store and part clubhouse, as bleak as a run-down Greyhound bus terminal. Some people drank coffee and solemnly played cards, as if they were doing time. In truth, they were waiting for a carcass to turn up, since deer and turkeys can be harvested on private preserves before the season begins. I could think of better ways to pass an afternoon.

In Hayden, I reentered the realm of earnest commemoration. A plaque there honored Richard Nixon's mother, who grew up in Butlerville, not Hayden. The Junior Historical Society, boosters in training, donated the funds to pay for it. Nixon spoke at the unveiling in 1971, no doubt glad to be invited anywhere after the Kent State massacre and the ongoing calamity in Vietnam.

Hayden also boasts the Center of Gravity, a mystifying force field. In its prime, the field impeded the progress of cars and trains so severely that the railroad tracks and a section of U.S. 50 were rerouted—unbelievable and yet true. You can buy a Center of Gravity T-shirt at the town museum.

Seymour upped the ante as the former abode of the notorious Reno Brothers. They were the progeny of J. Wilkinson Reno, a Kentuckian who wed a Hoosier and farmed twelve hundred acres or so around Rockford. Four of his five boys were rotten apples and a match for the Snopes. In spite of being raised as strict Methodists, they cheated travelers at cards, stole a horse, and burned down so many buildings the whole family fled to St. Louis for a respite in the late 1850s.

The rotten Reno boys were Frank, John, Simeon, and William. The good one, Honest Clint, really wasn't. He never joined his brothers' gang, but he was arrested for assault and operating a gambling den. Honest Clint ultimately lost his marbles and suffered religious delusions in the Topeka asylum where he died. Elvis played him in *Love Me Tender*, loosely based on the Renos' exploits.

During the Civil War, Frank and John salted their pockets as bounty jumpers. They enlisted in the Union Army more than once, snatched up a bonus on each occasion, and never reported for duty. In the course of their chicanery, they met several other psychopaths who formed the nucleus of the gang with Sim and Will.

The Renos started small, robbing general stores and a post office. They were captured once or twice, but they conveniently murdered any witnesses scheduled to testify against them. They bunked at the Radar Hotel in Seymour and intimidated the other guests, beheading one and floating his corpse down the White River. "Be wary of the thieves and assassins that infest the place," went a travel advisory of the period.

In October 1866, the Renos pulled off the first peacetime train robbery. They broke open an Ohio & Mississippi safe and made off with about twelve grand, then held up two more trains and terrorized the Midwest until John was intercepted with his hand in the coffers of a Missouri courthouse. He served ten years in prison and wrote a bestselling autobiography, tales of criminal glory being in vogue then as now.

With the Pinkertons in pursuit, the other gang members lit out for the territories, but the "natural malefactors," as the *Cincinnati Commercial* portrayed them, were rounded up at last. The *Commercial's* account of their final days begins on a note of high drama:

> For a number of years Seymour, a village of perhaps 2500 inhabitants, has been held in terrified subjection by a mere handful of skulking thieves, who have gradually grown courageous from the deplorable lack of resistance, and have perpetrated outrages unparalled in the chronicles of any densely populated city in the country . . .

and swiftly descends into tabloid muck with a grisly account of the brothers' demise.

The Pinkertons nabbed Sim and Will in Indianapolis, and Frank in Windsor, Canada, and transported them to a jail in New Albany by the Ohio border. The boys chilled out until a posse of vigilantes in hoods confronted the sheriff, asked for the keys to their cell, and beat him to a pulp when he refused. His wife, more sensible than brave, complied.

Under the cover of night, the vigilantes escorted the brothers to Hangman's Corner outside Seymour, where they were strung up on a spreading beech tree. Thousands filed past their pine coffins afterward, gaping at their swollen faces and black tongues. John, the last surviving Reno, hadn't gone straight in spite of his bestseller. He got caught dealing in counterfeit bills, and returned to prison for another three years.

The City Cemetery in Seymour is no Père Lachaise. Flat and weedy, it's the sort of neglected spot where teens gather to smoke dope and listen to Metallica. The Renos are the only celebrities in residence.

They don't have proper headstones anymore, because vandals kept stealing them. Instead they're buried behind a fenced enclosure, as if they might yet rise again to rob another train. Some fans had adorned Frank's grave with a vase of plastic geraniums. Americans never met an outlaw they didn't like.

A DRIVE ACROSS southern Indiana teaches one why the Renos appealed to the public's imagination. The region is so placid it begs for some larceny to disrupt the surface calm. It may be no accident that the Midwest has spawned such a trove of gangster idols. Clyde Barrow, Bonnie Parker, John Dillinger, and Pretty Boy Floyd all emerged from the cornbelt to entertain the nation. An overdose of tranquility and harmony, it appears, may result in a life of crime.

Southern Indiana defied interpretation. It just laid its cards on the table, so to speak. Hoosiers were solid, direct, and unaffected. They farmed, hunted, fished, held parades, and went to church on Sunday, rooted for the Pacers and the Colts and could name the star drivers of NASCAR, listened to country music, and ordered personalized licensed plates that read "In God We Trust."

From Seymour I traveled through Brownstown and over the White River's East Fork. Sinclair Lewis came to mind again—his Elmer Gantry this time, not George F. Babbitt. Had churches truly sunk to the level of burger joints by advertising the benefits of redemption on billboards? "Say what you will about the miracle of unquestioning faith," warned the Hoosier sage Kurt Vonnegut, "I consider a capacity for it terrifying and absolutely vile."

There was no surcease to the corn and soybeans on U.S. 50. Wherever you glanced, the view was the same. It taxed the ingenuity of such trade organizations as the Indiana Soybean Alliance, which was charged with promoting new uses for the crops—soy-based candles, for example, cleaner and greener than petroleum-based paraffin. Airplane deicer, crayons, and an additive for jet fuel can be made with soybeans, too. Corn's not just for slathering with butter anymore, either. It turns up as corn-based cups for cold drinks.

Three words were on the lips of Indiana farmers: "biotech," "biodiesel," and "ethanol." Biotech seeds account for 80 percent of the corn and 92 percent of the soybeans grown in America. Corporations such as Monsanto and Dow Chemical develop the genetically modified organisms to tolerate herbicides and combat pests.

The GMOs increase the yield of the crops, their manufacturers assert, but the Union of Concerned Scientists disagreed after a judicious study. Improvements in agriculture could as easily explain the higher yield, the union declared in a 2008 report.

No country in Europe grows GMO corn commercially, because it may damage the soil and reduce biodiversity. Biotech seeds have a drift factor and have already invaded farms in faraway Puebla and Oaxaca, Mexico, endangering the native varieties of maize.

As for biodiesel, it's composed almost entirely of soybean oil. Indiana has four processing plants, the most anywhere in the United States, for blending it with petroleum. Ethanol uses corn in the same way, even though other crops—switchgrass, for one—are more energy-efficient.

The corn and soybeans, so apparently benign, extended all the way to Bedford. Every aspect of modernity is a prisoner to complexity, I thought in the moment. We know too much and also too little. Perhaps this will be the central paradox of the twenty-first century. When Frank Reno was bothered or confused, he just robbed a bank or shot somebody and felt better. While the strategy can't be advocated, one can understand its attraction.

Bedford wasn't merely Bedford, of course. It was the Limestone Capital of the World. Its quarries had supplied the stones for the Pentagon and the Empire State Building. There were lots of quarries around, too, and they had steep cliffs. The standing water ran to a depth of thirty feet, so the locals slipped through holes in fences to go swimming on sultry summer days.

In Oolitic, also a "Stone Belt" town, some punks had bashed a limestone statue of Joe Palooka, the heavyweight champ of DC Comics. Joe's nose was busted, and moss covered the back of his skull like a yarmulke. In Needmore, where boosters had planned to construct a limestone replica of the pyramid at Giza, the dust was doing its triumphal dance.

AFTER AN EXCEPTIONALLY quiet night in Bedford, I took the highway southwest past Bluespring Caverns, watching the corn and soybeans disappear as I entered Hoosier National Forest, where the oaks and hickories were bathed in autumn radiance. The day was another gift, warm and bright, with shafts of sunlight filtering through the leaves. I couldn't remember a better, more forgiving October.

Huron and Willow Valley were tiny and obscure, half hidden in the swirl of color, and Shoals wasn't much bigger. It occupied a junction with U.S. 150, a road that ran through the forest to French Lick.

If you mention French Lick to sports fans, they reply with two words: Larry Bird, not biodiesel and ethanol. Bird, surely among the finest hoopsters ever, first honed his skills on the edge of the forest. You might imagine young Larry, a child of poverty and misfortune, practicing on Dr. Naismith's peach basket, but his hometown and its neighbor West Baden Springs have been sophisticated resorts for more than a century.

From my map, I couldn't tell how long the drive would be, so I inquired at a Shoals grocery store. The clerk, a good old boy in a loose-fitting T-shirt, was suffering from the heat. He mopped his brow with a paper napkin and swigged from a liter of Coke. His voice carried a southern inflection. I might have been in Alabama or Mississippi, except for the absence of black folks.

"French Lick, it's maybe fifteen miles." He balled up his napkin and started on a new one. "'Course, it might be take you an hour on that windy road."

"I won't mind. It's a pretty forest."

"You fixin' to gamble at the casino?"

"I'm going to the Larry Bird Museum," I said, making a bold assumption.

The clerk looked at me funny. "Ain't no Larry Bird Museum that I know of."

I could scarcely believe it. The one museum I might actually want to visit didn't exist. French Lick had missed a golden opportunity. Mitchell, Indiana, had created a museum for the astronaut Gus Grissom, and Lawrence County laid claim to three astronauts. The others were Kenneth Bowersox and Charles Walker, although Bowersox had been born in Portsmouth, Virginia.

"There's a railway museum down there," the clerk added helpfully.

I had a lovely drive. Between Shoals and French Lick, U.S. 150 adheres to the old Buffalo Trace, a path thousands of bison followed as they migrated from the prairies of Illinois and Wisconsin to some salt licks at the falls of the Ohio River. The great herds wore away the earth to a depth of twelve feet in places. Pioneers later used the same route, arriving by riverboat at the falls and heading overland to Indiana, then still a frontier.

Some émigrés from France set up a trading post by a salt lick in the forest, hence French Lick. An itinerant sawbones opened a spa nearby in 1852, subsequently West Baden Springs after Wiesbaden, Germany, renowned for its healing waters. The spa, later acquired by Lee Wiley Sinclair and his partners, burned down in the 1890s, but Sinclair rebuilt it as the Eighth Wonder of the World in 1902.

The new fireproof West Baden Springs Hotel featured a domed atrium larger than St. Peter's or the Pantheon. Guests could avail themselves of such amenities as a church, a bank, a barbershop, a pony track, and a stock ticker, yet it was the sulfur springs that kept the rooms full. A regimen of baths could purportedly cure a laundry list of ailments from arthritis to Zellweger syndrome.

Pluto Water, bottled in French Lick, played a part in the treatments. Billed as America's laxative, its slogan was, "When Nature Won't, Pluto Will." Fast-acting and dependable because of its high content of mineral salts, it supposedly delivered the afflicted from such side effects of constipation as grouchiness, fatigue, and loss of libido. In children, it corrected plain old bad behavior. Many a fraternity used it to haze their pledges, forcing them to drink a bottle before leaving them stranded in the woods far from any facilities.

The hotel fell on hard times during the Depression, and its next two owners—a Jesuit seminary and Northwood Institute, a private college—allowed it to deteriorate. A foundation financed a partial restoration in 1996, but no hotelier would touch West Baden Springs until Indiana licensed casino gambling in Orange County in 2004.

The Cook Group of Bloomington owns West Baden Springs now, where "luxury springs eternal," and French Lick Springs Hotel, where "history meets luxury," two concepts that eluded me since history, though eternal, is seldom luxurious.

West Baden Springs Hotel qualifies as a stately pleasure palace, its ruby-colored dome and four Moorish towers highly visible in an otherwise tumbledown landscape. Visitors are free to wander the hotel's public rooms or pay ten dollars for a guided tour, but some Hoosiers still approach the place with caution. Opulence may be the flip side of decadence, so they creep along the elaborate driveway as if they're about to cross an invisible bridge and be separated from the real Indiana forever.

In the parking lot, I joined a crowd of pilgrims and marched into the hotel. We stepped lightly over the marble floor and craned our necks in the Sistine Chapel position to admire the dome and the atrium. To be honest, I was impressed but also fidgety. I'd been in Indiana long enough for a casino to sound mildly exciting, so I quit West Baden for French Lick Springs.

Hoosiers like to gamble almost as much as they like to hunt. Very few of them live more than fifty miles from a casino, a racetrack, or an off-track betting parlor, and even in the scruffiest of lowlife taverns, they find something to wager on—pull tabs, punch boards, or raffle tickets.

Indiana earns a quarter on every dollar squandered in pursuit of Lady Luck. The state ranks fourth behind Nevada, New Jersey, and Mississippi in total gambling revenue, but it surpasses all the others when it comes to the amount of money it receives in gaming taxes.

French Lick Springs could be West Baden's knock-kneed cousin. The rooms were cheaper, and the décor was flashier. It suited the clientele of bikers in club leathers, skeletal chain smokers, guys with ZZ Top beards, plus-size matrons, and a coterie of small-town players ardently indulging in the vices they kept under wraps at home. Solid citizens so-journed among them, too, various pillars of community who weren't so hidebound by the Bible that they couldn't enjoy a little spin of the rou-lette wheel.

With its vast array of slots, French Lick smacked of the purgatorial. You could feel countless brains being lulled to sleep, switched over to drone mode; small wonder, then, that zombies held such fascination for Americans. Hardly anyone bothered to make conversation even at the bars, where eyes dipped instead to video poker screens.

The farmer I sat next to grew soybeans in Gibson County, about two hours away. He'd just won a nice pot with a full house and let out a modest whoop before he scooped up his coins and popped them into a card-board tub. Almost everyone carried a tub, as they might a votive candle.

"First decent hand all day," he volunteered, as if to excuse the out-burst. "I drew three to a pair of queens, and what do you know?"

"I know you look pretty happy."

"You got that right," he said with a smile.

"Do you play the slots, too?"

He made a disgusted face. "There's no skill to that at all. My wife plays 'em. She's over yonder. She doesn't have a head for math."

"You figure the slots are rigged?"

"It's a known fact."

"What about craps? Or blackjack?"

"Too rich for my blood."

He appeared to be in his early fifties, wrinkly and leathery. Farmers are as taciturn as cowboys, and he'd just about used up all the words he was willing to waste on me.

"Do you come here often?"

"Once or twice a month." He fed the machine some coins. "It helps to pass the time."

FROM FRENCH LICK I drove along the Wabash River to Vincennes, the oldest town in Indiana. Some fur traders, largely of Creole ancestry, built a fort there in 1732 and put François Morgane de Vincennes in command, but he ran afoul of the Chickasaw, who burned him at the stake four years later. The Germans arrived after the French and settled in Dutch Flats, while American Protestants, now the dominant group, lived north of Main Street.

Vincennes is a mecca for train spotters. It has eighty-four railroad crossings over its four square miles, and they can be annoying unless you like waving to engineers. At the first crossing, I spent five minutes counting the boxcars. At the second, I read the whole front page of the *Vincennes Sun Commercial.*

The waiting doesn't bother the locals, or only a little, according to the paper. They're more concerned about what's in the boxcars, often toxic or hazardous materials, and what might happen if there's a train wreck. Vincennes has a terrible meth problem, the paper said, with tweakers and dealers accounting for 70 percent of the caseload in Knox County, the state's second poorest.

Vincennes University, a two-year college that awards some baccalaureates, is the town's pride. It has a good reputation and a residential campus, unusual for such schools. Some townies resent the students, but that's inevitable when you factor in the drugs and the lack of jobs.

One's money does go a long way in Vincennes, though. At the Old Thyme Diner, where a bumper sticker on the wall advocated a Partnership for an Idiot-Free America, a big breakfast of eggs and bacon cost just $4.25.

I remember little else about Vincennes. My curiosity, once boundless, had ground to a halt. A kind of sadness came over me, a dreariness of the spirit, and I couldn't shake it. Even a walk by the Wabash didn't help. The French called the river *Ouabache* after a Miami Indian word that meant "It shines white." The Wabash flows over limestone. Once you could see clear to the bottom, but not anymore.

It's difficult at times for a traveler to separate his emotions from what he perceives. Someone else crossing southern Indiana might find nothing but delight. John Steinbeck understood this. He experienced it himself. On such a night, he'd batten down the camper's hatches, hole up with Charley, and smooth over the rough edges with a couple of drinks. I made do with a double Kopper Kettle.

If Steinbeck were around, I'd tell him a few things. I'm in a quandary about your prophecy, John, I'd begin—about that bleak vision of our future you articulated to Pascal Covici.

One minute I'm convinced of its accuracy, and the next I think you were just angry because the country failed to live up to your romantic image of it. My trip so far, three weeks and counting, involves a host of contradictory impressions. The monster land is in dire conflict with itself—irresolute, panicky about the future, and clinging to a mythical past.

Fifty years ago, you carped about the blandness of American life. It's endemic now, except in the big cities. The debts you worried about are mounting, and people are no less interested in material toys. Your friend Sinclair Lewis's George Babbitt and Elmer Gantry have leaped back to life with a vengeance, the very avatars of real estate bunkum and fundamentalist hokum. Nine percent of our Christians speak in tongues every week, John.

Earlier in my travels, I saw very little poverty, but that's not true of the heartland. I've been shocked at what I've encountered in parts of West Virginia, Ohio, and Indiana. It may not be the grinding, terrifying type—not yet—but it's still a sore point in the so-called land of plenty. The citizens are in distress, and they don't know where to turn. They're galled to watch the government hand out millions to the same bankers, brokers, and insurance agents who walked us off a cliff.

The poverty isn't only economic, but you're aware of that. It's intellectual and cultural, and it creates a vacuum that the pundits of talk radio rush to fill. Count your lucky stars you're not around to endure the pieties and falsities as they encourage a divisiveness that contributes to our problems. If I told you about Sarah Palin, you'd take me for a liar.

Our hope, as ever, lies with individuals. There are still heroes around striving for excellence and hoping to make something better of the nation. Certainly, I'm as blind as the next optimist, but I believe we can solve the problems and go forward. It's our slothfulness that threatens to undo us. Joe Talley's remark, uttered an eternity ago on the Choptank, has stayed with me: "Americans have had it too easy for too long."

Does the name Paul Dreiser ring a bell, John? I'll bet it does. He was

Theodore Dreiser's younger brother, and composed the Indiana state song, "On the Banks of the Wabash, Far Away" while staying at the West Baden Springs Hotel in 1897. The song sold more than half a million copies of sheet music in a single year. It's a melancholy ballad of yearning with a chorus that goes,

> Oh, the moonlight's fair tonight along the Wabash
> From the fields there comes the breath of newmown hay
> Through the sycamores the candle lights are gleaming
> On the banks of the Wabash, far away

Tonight I can't step out from under the sadness, John. I find it hard to believe America ever inspired such sweet sentiments, but tomorrow is another day.

MISO SOUP FOR breakfast. I recommend it as a remedy for too much Kopper Kettle. It came in powdered form in little sachets tucked in among the Lipton Tea and artificial sweeteners at my motel, slipped in there like a secret. Just when I thought the predictable would swallow me whole, the unexpected sounded a grace note.

I dumped the contents into a coffee cup and added hot water. Delicate green shreds of seaweed and scallion swirled around as I inhaled the gingery, head-clearing fumes and studied my road atlas. The Illinois of U.S. 50 amounted to fewer than two hundred miles between Lawrenceville and the suburbs of St. Louis, a drive of two days or a leisurely three.

The miso mystery was solved when I paid my bill. The motel's Japanese owner did a steady trade with Toyota executives who flew over to visit the company's factory in nearby Princeton. Perhaps it was my grogginess, but he seemed hyperalert for so early on a Sunday morning, one of those energetic, probably clean-living types who cause a certain unease in backsliders like me. I asked him for directions to Olney.

"Olney," he remarked genially, tapping at the atlas. "White squirrels."

Had I been given a koan to ponder? I remembered the great poet Basho and the tribulation he faced on his long journey to the far north of Japan. On his return, fed up with others invading his peace of mind, he closed the gate of his hut for a month and wouldn't see a soul, only to emerge with a renewed acceptance of the mundane world. I'd try to do the same.

Lawrence County, on the Illinois side of the Wabash, was farm country writ large, and the look of it differed considerably from southern Indiana. I don't understand why this should be—such a radical alteration in a matter of miles—but everything changed, not only the look of the land but the smell and feel and very texture of life.

The prairie ran flat to the horizon, and the woods had been thinned to make room for crops. Here the autumn color wasn't so ravishing, reduced instead to a few modest flickers of red, yellow, and gold. The air carried a tinge of chemicals and fertilizer. Grain elevators and water towers were fixtures along the highway.

In an age of agribusiness, Lawrence County defied the trend. Individuals or families owned the vast majority of farms, but the impact of GMOs was still immediately apparent. The soybean yield had roughly doubled in the past fifteen years, while the amount of wheat grown had been halved.

There was lots of corn, too—77,429 acres as opposed to 86,971 for soybeans—and hog pens aplenty, but farmers rarely bothered with other vegetables and had planted just 21 acres to orchards.

The clock had not yet struck nine, but Lawrenceville was already wide awake. The IGA supermarket was open and had been since five-thirty A.M. Farmers are early risers, so the place was packed. As I stocked my cooler, I noticed another difference, one of tone. Here the clerk engaged me and chatted readily. The market reverberated with a lively, alert babble of voices.

Lawrenceville looked functional and intact. It belonged to the present, not the past. A grand old courthouse anchored the central square, and the stores around it were still in business. The prices were right, too. For a mere seven dollars, you could devour a catfish platter at Anthony's Towne House. Though flags waved here and there, they didn't overwhelm you. Sometimes the patriotic displays smacked of aggression or defiance, but not in Lawrenceville.

I crossed the Embarras River, pronounced am-brau from the French, and circled in on Olney an hour or so later. It had an aura of solvency as well—a sturdy, rooted quality. Like Lawrenceville, Olney is poor by Illinois standards, but it seemed flourishing compared to Vincennes.

There are indeed white squirrels running around. They're albinos, and two conflicting legends account for their discovery. The legends conclude the same way, with the squirrels in a green box in a window of Jasper Banks's saloon to induce passersby to bend an elbow.

As quiet as Olney must have been, it's still hard to imagine someone blurting, "Wow, check out those squirrels! Let's have a drink!" At any rate, the law ordered Banks to release them. Over the years they became plentiful, but their numbers have dwindled to fewer than a hundred.

East Fork Lake is a hot spot for largemouth bass along with white squirrels, but my fly rod was worthless without a boat. I couldn't cast far enough to reach the fish, so I chose to invest in some spin gear. On Route 130, I found a Wal-Mart Supercenter and almost fainted from the extravagance as usual. Wal-Mart makes you feel paltry for owning so little. It's as if you haven't kept up your part of the bargain.

First I got lost in electronics, then in furniture, and finally in toys, where an unattended child was liberating a G.I. Joe from its package, before I hit sporting goods. For $19.95, I bought a rod and reel combo that included some bass lures. The gear was total crap, and I knew it. For another $20.00, I could have had an outfit that actually worked, but—also as usual—I foolishly talked myself into saving some gas money.

"Going fishing?" the cashier, an upbeat teen, piped.

"How'd you guess?" I replied drily.

"Well, it's pretty obvious!" She, too, was overly bright for the hour.

"I suppose that's true."

"Hope you catch a big one!"

I threw my gear in the trunk and made for East Fork Lake. The morning was hot, already eighty degrees at least. Outside a house on the road, three girls in shorts were gathering up garlands of toilet paper from the shrubs and bushes. They'd been rolled, as the saying goes, either by their boyfriends for an unstated offense or maybe because of the random churlishness that strikes small-town youths on a Saturday night.

At the lake—a reservoir, really—I put on my Paints cap against the bruising sun, set up the rod, and muttered, "What a piece of crap." It's astonishing how tenacious our neuroses can be. You'd think someone my age could outrun them, but you'd be wrong.

The heat was bad news. The bass would lurk in the cooler depths, and that's why so few anglers were around—just two, an old couple drowning worms. My stab at casting was hilarious. With the chintzy rod and reel, I could only lay out about fifteen feet of line. Hopeless, in other words. The white squirrels were just as elusive.

I recouped in Olney, where Daylight Donuts advertised, "A Donut In Each Hand, Now That Is A Balanced Meal." Miso rests lightly on the belly, so I squeezed into Hovey's Diner for a more substantial meal. Churchgoers had flooded in after services, a Sunday ritual, and they hopped from table to table to gossip, generating a kindly warmth.

My waiter was an African American, the first I'd seen since Chillicothe. Considering America's extraordinary diversity, the Caucasian belt that runs from West Virginia to Ohio and beyond is an anomaly indeed, even a country within a country—white, Republican, and conservative.

In contrast to the diner, Olney's Main Street was sobering. All down its length, yellow ribbons were draped on light poles topped with cardboard placards that honored the local men and women enlisted in various branches of the military. Each placard bore a soldier's name—Wayne Sauza, U.S. Army, for instance, or Mark Sauza, U.S. Marines—and below it a brief, prayerful sentence, *Bring Them Safely Home.*

A slick new car was parked across from Hovey's, with Goarmy.com painted on its doors. It looked scintillating against the backdrop of tired old buildings, like a still clipped from a movie. If you grew up on a farm or just dreamed of a more promising future, the sight of it might be enough to propel you to the Army Career Center recruiting office. It's easy to forget our wars in much of America, but not in towns such as Olney. Their families pay the price and make the invisible human cost of the effort achingly visible.

IN THE *Clay County Advocate-Press,* I read a story about Alpesh "Al" Patel and his father Balder "BJ" Patel, who own Midtown Liquors in Flora, Illinois. The story told how the Patels were sick of their customers mistaking them for Iraqis, Israelis, Muslims, or terrorists when they were Swaminarayan Hindus from Gujarat, India, near the Pakistan border, who believed in nonviolence and were even vegetarians.

The plight of the Patels came as no surprise. In Olney, I'd heard Flora was a tough redneck town. Oddly, the rednecks—if that's what they really were—did not fit the stereotype. They had far too much hair. They wore ponytails, mullets, modified Prince Valiants, and flowing Jesus locks, to which they added such au courant touches as piercings and tattoos. Meth was not unknown in these parts, either.

A heady slate of NFL action had started a run on beer in Flora. When I got to Midtown Liquors, BJ Patel stood at the drive-through window patiently explaining to a lumpy, recalcitrant woman in a bathrobe why he couldn't cash her check—because she bounced one last week. She didn't go down without a battle, fighting bitterly and irrationally until succumbing to the irrefutable logic.

"Ah, well," BJ sighed. In a more evolved universe, he'd have the means to solve such problems, or so the sigh implied.

BJ had immigrated to the United States in 1990 to work at his brother-in-law's motel in St. Louis, where his son Al attended a multiethnic school. Al's education in that liberal environment did not prepare him for the abuse he received after 9/11. While he was in college, an angry mob looking for Muslims to harass assaulted him, and only the entreaties of a friend saved his life. There'd been no attacks in Flora, only slurs, curses, and vague accusations.

"We try to tell who we are." Al's sigh duplicated BJ's. "But everybody still says something all the time."

Al sat at a table in a corner, noodling on a laptop. He and his father were about the same size, both short and stocky. They had red dots and a pair of thin lines on their foreheads. The dot wasn't a caste mark. It signified instead that Al and BJ were God's followers, while the lines represented God's feet. Al was comfortable discussing his religion, but BJ kept his own counsel, unwilling to ruffle any feathers.

The Patels had bought the store from a fellow Indian in 2005. Their customers worked on farms and in factories, and every last one of them relied on the drive-through window rather than their legs to make a purchase.

"So you like Flora?" I asked BJ.

"Very peaceful," he said with the hint of a smile. "No bombings. In Gujarat, twenty-four bombs in one day."

Al put it more forcefully. "The bad ones who are doing the bad things, they don't believe in God," he argued. "The ones who destroy, they don't believe in God. Whether they are Muslim, Hindu, or Christian."

BJ claimed he wasn't interested in politics, but I suspected him of diplomacy again. Al hadn't yet decided how he'd cast his vote. He thought the candidates looked silly and unprofessional when they squabbled in debates.

"They act like children," he complained. "Everybody digging up each other's dirt. You can't judge a person on his past."

"What does America need, Al?"

"The president should be a strong leader. Someone to guide the economy."

"Has George Bush been strong?"

"He did what was right for the country." Then Al elaborated an intriguing theory. "If he wasn't good enough, he wouldn't be elected twice."

He cut short our talk to help his dad as the cars and trucks lined up. I might have watched a football game myself, but downtown Flora, less congenial than Olney, was locked up tight. The only weekend activities listed in the *Advocate-Press* were a Kiwanis Club porkburger fest, a talent show and ice cream social at First United Methodist, and Faith Tabernacle's youth ministries annual blowout. An ad for Beltone hearing aids took up the paper's entire back page. Flora had a rapidly aging population, with one fifth of the residents over sixty-five and another fifth between forty-five and sixty.

I nosed around Clay County for a while. The towns named in my atlas sounded enticing, but Bible Grove, Wakefield, and Passport were all of a piece. One saw old dogs asleep in the sun, guys washing their pickups or motorcycles, forlorn parks absent of people, yard sales, and barbecues.

Only Noble had a sense of fun. It rode to prominence on an oil boom in the 1930s, and had the nerve to call itself the Oil Center of the World. Its jail, described as "very popular" in Noble's heyday, used to imprison both bank robbers and drunks. It sat on a side street like a forgotten block of concrete. A latticed window gave inmates a punishing peek at the life they'd been deprived of.

Salem was the Gateway to Little Egypt, a sobriquet bestowed in the 1820s when a drought gripped northern and central Illinois. The settlers hitched up their wagons and went south to search for food, an incident that echoed the biblical story of Israel dispatching his sons to Egypt to buy some grain to prevent starvation.

Halfway to St. Louis, Salem was much more affluent than Olney, Flora, and Noble. It had reaped the benefits of oil, too, pumping ninety-three million barrels in '39, and its fields still produce, although not so lavishly.

When the roustabouts from Texas and Oklahoma first arrived, they knocked the Illinois farmers as "punkin' eaters." They'd never seen such horrendous working conditions. The mud was so deep it could swallow a Caterpillar. You could drive to some fields over corduroy log roads, but if your tires skidded, you were pitched into the ooze.

Among Salem's notables were John T. Scopes, indicted for teaching evolution in Dayton, Tennessee, where William Jennings Bryan, also born in Salem, prosecuted him in the infamous "monkey trial." The G.I. Bill of Rights was drafted in Salem, and Max Crossett, a café owner, sold *his* secret recipe for X-Tra Fine Salad Dressing to Kraft Foods in 1941 for a measly three hundred dollars.

Salem, the ancestral home of Miracle Whip.

ONCE A BUM always a bum, Steinbeck wrote, referring to his incurable urge to be someplace else, and I was just as fickle, leaving the highway again for a look at Carlyle Lake, the biggest in Illinois, where I hoped to put my pitiful angling experience in Olney behind me.

A dam on the Kaskaskia River, built to control floods, impounds 26,000 acres of water to form the lake. It holds almost any freshwater fish you can name—bass, pike, sauger, catfish, crappies, the list goes on. Even an ill-equipped angler ought to catch something, or so ran my wishful thinking.

Henkel's Bait & Tackle was stuffed to the gills, as it were, with gear and clothing. As ever, I felt foolish to be soliciting some advice. It's a character flaw in those who fish. Blindly faithful, we throw ourselves on the mercy of clerks at sporting goods stores, believing they're not as crass or venal as ordinary mortals. Instead we view them as higher beings honor-bound to divulge hot tips to absolute strangers.

The clerk at Henkel's seemed honest, but they all do. There's an element of therapy in the transaction. While you formulate your questions, the clerk folds his arms or scratches an ear and mumbles, "Mmm-hmm." Tackle shops should provide a couch and a box of tissues for their customers, who only crave a kind word and the assurance that they're not as gullible or desperate as they appear to be.

I related the tale of East Fork Lake and my crappy rod, sparing him the neurotic backstory, and when he didn't steer me toward a rack of expensive Fenwicks, I dropped my defenses. The guy was okay. He was on my side.

"They've been doin' real good on the white bass." He paused for effect. "You got a boat?"

"Nope."

"It's tough without a boat. Below the dam by the Kaskaskia, you might do all right in there. Ever fished a curly tail?"

He laid some soft plastic grubs on the counter. They came in psychedelic colors like chartreuse and banana yellow, as if the fish had ingested LSD. I bought a bag of curly tails, but I couldn't fathom his convoluted instructions and refused to further debase myself by asking him to repeat them.

No matter. When I pulled into Mariner's Village and saw Carlyle Lake, I gave up on fishing. The lake looked as broad as an inland ocean, and not one angler was casting from shore. I might have been crestfallen, except the evening was so beautiful. A mild, cool, soothing breeze blew in from the water, and sailboats rocked on the ripples at a marina, their bells lightly clanging.

For the first time in days, a sense of calm washed over me. I hadn't realized how tense I'd become, in fact, until the tension began to abate. The lake and the space around it, eleven thousand acres of lushly landscaped park, worked on me like a massage. My motel stood by itself, not pinched in among clones. Instead of traffic noise, I heard the tide lapping at a sandy beach.

I took a long shower, slept as well as I had in a while, and woke to a gray morning. The clouds sat low over the water, clamped to it like a lid. A storm was brewing if you trusted the gulls' mad cries. I'd had so much sunshine and heat I almost welcomed a change.

After breakfast, I walked along the shore, where a few diehards were camped in folding chairs in hopes that a bottom-feeder would bump into their bait by accident. They were destined to be disappointed, but hope in and of itself is never an entirely bad thing.

At a far end of the lake, I came to a station set aside for cleaning fish. Chester Stogner, deep in thought, stood there with a white bass in hand. He'd landed thirty of them the day before and had stowed them in a plastic bucket. The bass were bright and silvery, and weighed just under a pound apiece.

I watched in envy as Chester worked happily away, a one-man assembly line. He picked up a bass, slit its belly, rinsed out the blood and guts at a sink, and placed it on a wooden board, where he cut off the head and tail, stripped the skin, and removed the filets. Fast and skillful, he finished off a bass per minute. If they held tournaments for cleaning fish, he'd be sure to win a trophy.

"You've got the makings of a fish fry there," I said.

Chester glanced up, startled. It took him a beat to return from wherever he'd been in his head. He had an open, unaffected face, a dimpled chin, and blue eyes behind an oversize pair of specs. His easygoing manner reflected his upbringing in the bayous of Louisiana.

"Uh-uh, no more frying," he told me. "I've got issues with the cholesterol."

"How will you cook them?"

"Brush 'em with olive oil, then put 'em on the grill for fifteen minutes."

He and his wife had just returned from a visit to the Missouri wine country, so they'd split a bottle with their dinner—a sugary wine because Chester has a sweet tooth. They often cross over to drive along Highway 94, the old river road from Augusta to Hermann, and he suggested I try it.

October was a fine time of year for white bass, the angler's last chance before the cold of November put them off the bite. "When it's cold, you can fish all day and never get nothin'," Chester said. "You have to keep an eye out for the duck hunters, too, or else you might get shot."

A stringy fellow in a bolo tie stopped to kibitz. He'd been fishing from shore for three hours without any luck.

"Nice mess of bass," he began, much as I'd done.

"Thank you." Chester kept right at it, never losing his rhythm.

"I didn't have no boat."

"Gotta have a boat, really."

"If I *had* a boat, what would I do?"

"What you'd do is bump a Rapala along the bottom in about seven feet of water. Curly tails are good, too."

"I've got some curly tails you can have," I said. I fetched them from the car and gave them to the man. It might have been the first gift he'd ever been given by the appreciative way he reacted.

"Well, thank *you!*" he repeated several times before he wandered off.

Chester was down to his last three bass. A military lifer, he planned to retire in Carlyle in a year or two. He'd joined up in the midst of the Vietnam War, and soon fell in love with the woman who ultimately became his wife. His buddies warned him not to get married, because the brass would ship him overseas, but Chester went ahead with the wedding anyhow and, sure enough, they dispatched him to Ben Wah two months later.

"I remember thinkin', 'Whoa, this ain't good at all!,'" he laughed.

He served in Cam Ranh Bay and Phuket, too, but he made it home safely, and his subsequent tours of duty abroad were less harrowing and much more fulfilling—three years in Germany, for instance, and a year in the boondocks of Turkey. Soldiers got a raw deal now, he thought, roped into two or even three tours in Iraq or Afghanistan.

"But the army's paying hefty bonuses for some careers," he added. "'Course, they might not be the careers you'd choose for yourself."

"What'll you do when you retire?"

"Enjoy life. Go fishing." Both excellent answers.

"Do you feel secure about your future?"

"Oh, my goodness, I don't!" he exclaimed. "It's kinda scary. We need to do something. Will there be anything left for us down the line?"

"Any thoughts on the election?"

Chester started on his last bass. "My lips are sealed. It's between me and the voting booth. You have a kitchen at your motel?"

"Not even a microwave," I said, recalling Bill Eason's corn.

"That's too bad. I'd like to give you some fish."

"Another time, maybe."

"All right, then. Another time."

I stayed in Carlyle one more night, unable to tear myself away. It was like being retired, really. I understood why Chester had settled on the town, pretty and still built to human scale. I relaxed, read a mystery novel, ate a steak dinner at Schleichers, and let my belt out a notch. In bed by ten o'clock, listening to the lap of the tide, I calculated I'd be in San Francisco to meet Imelda in fewer than three weeks. That was a treat worth hanging on to as I drifted off to sleep.

THE HIGHWAY THROUGH St. Louis terrified me. After all those small, flat country towns, I'd lost my urban edge and struggled to keep up. Drivers whizzed by as I clung to the right lane. Even the city looked intimidating and vaguely threatening, an image borrowed from Ginsberg's *Howl*. The windows were malevolent eyes, the off-ramps led to Hades, and the signs were an exercise in deliberate misdirection.

"A great surf of traffic engulfed me, waves of station wagons, rip tides of roaring trucks . . ." That was Steinbeck battling to stay afloat in Minnesota.

Ahead, a detour—the last thing I needed. U.S. 50 had been broken apart, shuffled, and rejiggered. Quite soon I developed a strong and unpleasant sensation I'd missed a crucial turn and was on my way to Arkansas, maybe to Cave City or Marmaduke. There are worse fates, I told myself, but that was a lie, at least in the moment.

The massive aggression on the interstate contributed to my misery. I wanted to roll down a window and shout, "What's wrong with you people? Count me out of your death wish!" If you consider the aggression an indicator of relative unhappiness, the folks around St. Louis were very, very unhappy. Perhaps it's the old time-equals-money formula in action. The faster you drive, the more quickly you'll get rich, the speeders must believe.

I recalled a pertinent scene from Henry King's *Jesse James*, released in 1939. After looting a bank, Jesse (Tyrone Power) and his gang flee on horseback with a posse on their tail. It looks like curtains until Jesse grabs some stolen money from a saddlebag and scatters the bills to the wind, causing his pursuers to dismount and pick up the cash. If you threw a wad of dollars on the highway, you might achieve the same result.

Outside Ballwin, to my great relief, I connected with Highway 94, Chester Stogner's river road. It's also known as the Weinstrasse because it traverses the Missouri Rhineland, a swath of vineyards and wineries in the river valley where the soil isn't good for growing much except grapes.

Gottfried Duden's *Report of a Journey to the Western States of North America* (1829), a classic of emigrant literature, is responsible for the region's German flavor. Such tales of the New World were immensely popular in Germany, where more than 150 were published in the first half of the nineteenth century.

Duden, a lawyer by trade, cast the book in the form of friendly letters. He heaped praise on the valley and its pioneers, compared the Missouri favorably to the Rhine, and bought a farm for himself in Dutzow. A large number of his fellow Germans soon joined him, and they began making wine in the traditional style in Hermann in about 1837.

The Italians followed the Germans, and Missouri was producing ten thousand gallons of wine per year by the 1850s. The figure increased to two million gallons in the 1880s, second only to California. Prohibition shut off the juice, and the industry didn't revive until the 1960s. The state has almost ninety wineries now, most oriented toward tourists.

The Weinstrasse starts near Defiance, not far from Daniel Boone's last home. He left his beloved Kentucky in 1800, or so I'd read, after losing his shirt as a land speculator. Apparently, he lacked a killer instinct in business. The Spanish still owned the Missouri territory and appointed Boone the commandant of Femme Osage Creek Valley District. He received a grant of 850 acres, but he lost that, too, when Missouri became a state after the Louisiana Purchase.

Boone built a house next on his son Daniel Morgan's spread in Matson. Almost seventy, he continued to hunt regularly and would do so into his eighties. Though often lauded for his survival skills, he counted himself plain lucky to "have miraculously escaped many perils."

The perils didn't stop with old age. In 1802, at age sixty-eight, the Osage captured Boone during a spring hunt on the Niangua River; in

1803 he was injured in a trapping accident and hid in a cave for twenty days to escape from the Indians; in 1808 the Osage robbed him; and in 1814, at age eighty, his canoe capsized on the Missouri and drowned his autobiography, written by hand, and all his family papers.

Boone required no autobiography to cement his fame. Long before Walt Disney introduced Fess Parker, still in the coonskin cap he wore while playing Davy Crockett, as TV's Daniel Boone in 1964—tall as a mountain, brave, fearless, and eagle-eyed, with Ed Ames as his sidekick Mingo, the least credible white redskin ever—he'd already ascended into myth due to John Filson's artfully embellished *The Adventures of Colonel Daniel Boone* (1784).

Filson's was the first of many efforts to capitalize on Boone's celebrity. They ranged from Daniel Bryan's 250-page epic poem *The Mountain Muse* (1813) to Republic Pictures' *Daniel Boone, Trailblazer* starring Lon Chaney Jr. and Faron Young. Lord Byron celebrated Boone, as well, in the eighth canto of *Don Juan*. One stanza goes,

> 'Tis true he shrank from men even of his nation
> When they built up into his darling trees—
> He moved some hundred miles off, for a station
> Where there were fewer houses and more ease;
> The inconvenience of civilization
> Is, that you neither can be pleased nor please;
> But when he met the individual man,
> He showed himself as kind as mortal can

I took Highway F to see Boone's house in St. Charles County, Missouri's wealthiest. The side trip posed several problems. To begin with, the house didn't belong to Boone. It belonged to his son Nathan. He died there, to be fair, but the property did not then include the Hope School House from St. Paul, Missouri, or the Peace Chapel from New Melle, Missouri. They'd been imported in recent years to be part of Boonesfield Village, a little theme park.

The park charged admission. That was another problem. Worse, you had to sit through a video before taking a *guided* tour. Worse still, the guides wore costumes. And worst of all, a fence enclosed Boonesfield Village so completely that you couldn't catch the tiniest glimpse of the house without binoculars—this as a tribute to a heroic frontiersman who capsized on the Missouri at age eighty.

Lord Byron got it right. "The inconvenience of civilization . . ."

ALONG THE WEINSTRASSE I drove, with the river to the south and the woods of Osage Ridge to the north. Some farms hugged the bottomland, but the grapes were usually planted high up in the rich loess soil that glaciers deposited aeons ago. The varietals were different from those I knew in California—Catawba and Seyval, for example, rather than Chardonnay and Cabernet Sauvignon.

In my days as a vineyard dweller, I learned a bit about viticulture and the wine business. Most grape growers thought of themselves as farmers, not impresarios, thirty years ago, and their tasting rooms in Sonoma County were often quite humble, just a barn swept clean of cobwebs. Even in the Napa Valley, already more advanced in terms of promoting itself, the accent was on the product and not the package. Some vintners were testy enough to deny boorish customers a taste of anything.

The industry became afflicted with gigantism, though, and turned into a juggernaut. The wineries got bigger, more corporate and elaborate, and devoted to squeezing a profit from every inch of floor space. Things rarely shrink in America. We equate smallness with death and obsolescence. If you have a chance to expand and refuse it, you're considered a fool. Scale is what counts, the larger the better.

So the wineries expanded. The buildings grew to the size of warehouses, and a fleet of architects were unleashed on them. The architects had a fondness for folly. One saw turrets, moats, drawbridges, and funiculars.

Tasting rooms acquired a suburban patina and were stocked with knickknacks for sale—glassware, coffee mugs, T-shirts, aprons, bad primitive paintings, even Hummel figurines. Gimmicks to attract visitors abounded—llamas, exotic gardens, petting zoos.

With only 1,350 acres bearing grapes, Missouri's output is still modest, so I hoped the wineries would convey a rustic charm. Amazingly, every state in the Union has at least one winery at present. The idea of an Alaskan white or a Florida red sounds far-fetched, but they're available. California remains the kingpin, however, and sells 89 percent of the wine in the United States, trailed very distantly by Washington, Oregon, and New York.

The Weinstrasse, amply bedeviled with twists and hairpin turns, could wreak havoc on an incautious taster. As a veteran, I understood the pitfalls of overimbibing and how to avoid them. Swirl the wine in your mouth, then spit it out—that was a good rule of thumb, albeit impossible to follow. Don't feel you must try every wine they're pouring, another hilarious bromide.

The road to Montelle Winery was very steep. It led to a bluff with a painterly view of the Missouri through the trees. The owners had obviously studied the California model, incorporating a gift shop and a restaurant with a deck overlooking the valley. In temperate weather they offered live music on the weekends.

Inside, a jolly crew of tasters had convened around a long, octagonal bar paneled in wood to work their way through the seven or eight wines to be sampled, all crafted from grapes unfamiliar to me—not only Catawba and Seyval but Chardonel, Concord, Chancellor, and St. Vincent. Montelle also makes wine from fruit—strawberry, raspberry, blackberry— and semisweet reds and whites.

I skipped the sugary stuff—too much like soda pop, plus I lacked Chester Stogner's sweet tooth. As awful as it is to admit, if you've been raised on good California wines, it's difficult to settle for less. Against your will, you become a snob. Only Montelle's Cynthiana, a dry, full-bodied red, impressed me.

In spite of Cynthiana's twenty-dollar price tag, it's the first varietal to sell out. The grape, a native American cultivar, also is called Norton, after Dr. D. N. Norton, the Virginian who developed it. A Norton from Missouri won the gold medal for the Best Wine of All Nations at the Vienna World Exposition of 1873. Often billed as the Cabernet of the Ozarks, Cynthiana ages well.

I visited two more wineries, both similar in style to Montelle, and broke for supper in Hermann, still heavily Teutonic. Browsing in Blanche's on East First Street was like a quick trip to Düsseldorf, what with all the cuckoo clocks, nutcrackers in lederhosen, and beer steins for sale. Hermannhoff Winery, housed in an old stone building, had the sort of simplicity I'd been seeking, so I paid twenty dollars for a Cynthiana, unable to resist temptation the second time around.

"THE NEXT PASSAGE in my journey is a love affair," John Steinbeck swooned over Montana, but it was Jefferson City, Missouri, that stole my heart. Almost everything about Jeff City, as the locals affectionately call it, satisfied me from the moment I laid eyes on it. Clean and orderly, it gripped you like a firm handshake. You can count on me, it seemed to be saying. Nobody here will do you any harm.

Daniel Morgan Boone laid out Jeff City, population forty thousand or so. In spite of its size, it felt neighborly and wanted to befriend you. The streets were wide and light-filled, and the parks were verdant and beautifully kept. Shoppers and government workers, bustling with energy and purpose, crowded the sidewalks. The citizens were particularly well educated, with fully a third in possession of a college degree.

When I checked into a motel, a mirror ambushed me again. It reflected the unsavory fact that I looked like a drifter. One tends to let the grooming basics slide on the road, but I decided I'd better get a haircut before they picked me up for vagrancy. Kenny's on Madison Street was the first barbershop I saw, with a classic barber pole outside and three chairs inside.

The only barber on duty wore a blue nylon jacket and crisp trousers. His shoes were polished to a high gloss, and some combs stuck out of a pocket. He looked to be seventy for certain and possibly seventy-five, but he stood solidly on his own two feet like Jeff City and gave me a practiced, professional smile to put me at ease, as a doctor might.

"I bet you're Kenny," I said.

"Well, you'd be wrong. I'm Larry." He pointed to a wall plaque that read L. L. Horstdaniel. "Larry Horstdaniel."

"What happened to Kenny?"

"He died a long time ago. I bought him out. I used to have two other barbers, but they died, too."

Larry ushered me to the first chair, covered me with a smock, and wrapped a paper collar around my neck. If he'd given me a *Police Gazette* or an *Argosy* next, I wouldn't have been surprised. This was a barbershop from my childhood.

"Just a trim?" he inquired.

"That'll do fine. You've been in business a while, I take it."

"Fifty-five years. I'm eighty years old, and just celebrated my fiftieth wedding anniversary," he said. "I'm not about to hang it up. I might be in a box like Kenny in six months."

Larry began to snip very deliberately and carefully, a master barber of the old school. He wouldn't be rushed into a mistake.

"Where are you from, Larry?" I asked.

"Osage County originally."

"How'd you get into this line of work?"

"Well, that's an interesting story. After high school, I trained to be a mortician. I just thought I'd like it, you know?"

"Sure," I replied, as if everybody dreamed of a mortuary future.

"Then the Korean War came along, and I was sent over there from 1951 to 1953, and when I came back, I changed over to barber college. The college placed me with Kenny. There were thirty-six barbers downtown, but I'm the only one left."

"Where do people go for a cut?"

"The strip malls in the suburbs. I'm just a block from the governor's mansion, you know. The governor used to stroll over here, then go for coffee with his cronies."

"Not anymore?"

"No, sir. Now they pass by with a security detail. I don't think we're that dangerous, do you? What they love is the attention."

A barber who'd dealt with higher-ups should be versed in Missouri politics, I assumed, and that proved true. The state used to be staunchly Democratic, Larry told me, but it switched after the administration of Warren E. Hearnes, its first two-term governor, who served from 1965 to 1973. In Larry's opinion—and the opinion of some others—Hearnes was corrupt, although he was never charged with a crime and insisted he'd been the victim of a Republican witch hunt.

As for the presidential election, Missouri had backed the winner in every year except 1956, although Larry refused to predict how it would go in November.

"I saw an interesting story in the paper the other day," he said, veering onto a tangent. "About a Supreme Court judge. Seems he came to Jeff City for the bar exam as a young man, bought three oranges to eat, sat on a bench to study, and then had a shave. When he passed the exam, he credited the shave. It was lucky." Larry paused to examine a stray follicle. "Later when he had a big case to review, he wanted another lucky shave, but he couldn't get it."

"Why not?"

"Because barbers are afraid of HIV now, just like dentists." He nodded toward the door. "I'm so close to the sidewalk *anybody* could walk in here. I still shave around the ears, of course."

Once it was simple to run a barbershop, Larry went on, but not anymore. It's gotten very complex, with far too many rules and regulations.

"I'll give you an example," he said. "A salesman from a vending company suggested I install a soda machine, so I gave it a whirl. And I did a darn good business, too, until someone from the health department threatened to take me to court if I didn't get rid of it."

"What was the problem?"

"No license to sell food. Did you hear about those two barbers out in California, who got in trouble for coloring someone's hair? It came out all wrong, and they were sued. I carry malpractice insurance now. Costs me $250 a year."

I braced myself when Larry rubbed some shaving cream around my ears and pulled out his straight razor, but his hand was steady. That was it for the haircut. He took off the smock, brushed away the loose hairs, and held up a mirror. I resembled myself as an eight-year-old.

"That'll be ten dollars."

When I gave Larry a ten-spot, he grabbed a poker chip from a tray, opened his cash register, and put it in. "Why'd you do that?"

"Well, the register's broken," he confessed. "I phoned somebody to repair it a while back, but he had a heart attack and died, so I use the chips to keep track. Works just fine, too."

With my new back-to-school look, I felt ready for a stiff drink at Ecco Lounge, an intimate restaurant where the waitress calls you "honey" and the bartender pours the bourbon with a free hand. Booths lined one wall, but I sat at the bar next to an African American chatting with a white pal, the first real interaction between races I'd witnessed since Virginia. It's strange how all those small, entirely white towns consider themselves typically American when they're so utterly atypical.

Diversity was another strong suit for Jeff City. You could see that at Ecco Lounge, an institution since 1945. The customers were young and old, male and female, and both blue- and white-collar. A behemoth farmer in Can't Bust 'Ems and a tractor cap occupied one booth, devouring a pork tenderloin while he discussed the dangers of operating a Bobcat with a hired hand under the influence.

"You can tell with the drink," he said, gesturing with his fork, a chunk of pork impaled on it, "but not with the drugs."

THOUGH I HAVEN'T seen the capitols of all fifty states, I believe few could match Missouri's for sheer grandeur. Built in 1917, it sits on a limestone bluff, and its monumental dome, crowned with a statue of Ceres, the goddess of growing plants and motherly love, rises 262 feet above the basement floor. All around it are heroic bronzes, among them the city's namesake, Thomas Jefferson, the two great rivers in bas-relief, and Lewis and Clark, of course.

A strapping young woman, ultrafit, was re-creating a scene from *Rocky* on the steep flight of steps that lead to the capitol's front door. She dashed to the top, ran back down, rattled off a set of push-ups, checked her pulse rate and probably her body mass index, and repeated the routine, unaware of her astonished audience and attentive only to the churning gears of her own biodynamic.

I mounted the steps at a normal pace and touched the door gingerly, expecting an alarm to go off, but it didn't. No guards were inside waiting to frisk me or check my ID, either. Anyone could just walk into the capitol, apparently, and wander at will. Such access seemed extraordinary in the current climate of fear and paranoia. It represented an old-fashioned populist democracy, where Frank Capra's Mr. Smith fought the scally-wags, and the governor strolled unaccompanied to Larry Horstdaniel's shop for his haircut.

Without any difficulty, I located the House of Representatives lounge and Thomas Hart Benton's overpowering mural *A Social History of Missouri*. Completed in 1935, the mural covers four walls and traces the state's evolution from the pioneer days to the present.

It isn't an unvarnished picture by any means. The artist included images that Missourians would rather forget—the lynching of a slave, say—but Huck Finn and Jim are there, too, along with Jesse James and Boss Tom Pendergast. Hart Benton must have been the opposite of temperamental, because he didn't object to letting the public watch him labor away. His only caveat, posted on a sign, asked that spectators refrain from making any suggestions.

I ascended another flight of stairs to the second floor, still feeling like an interloper about to be grabbed by the ear and tossed out, a sensation heightened by the fact that I had the capitol to myself. Soon I came to a rotunda lined with busts on marble pedestals—the usual assortment of dreary politicians, I assumed, Mayor So-and-So and Senator Whatsizname—but instead Betty Grable, cast in bronze, beguiled me.

The rotunda amounted to a Missouri Hall of Fame, where people one truly respected and admired were enshrined. Among the native sons and daughters on display were Dale Carnegie, Emmett Kelly, Ginger Rogers, Marlin Perkins, Mark Twain, Stan Musial, and Walter Cronkite. Should they all spring into action for a party, Scott Joplin, Charlie Parker, and Josephine Baker could provide the entertainment.

My affection for Jeff City and, by association, America took another giant leap forward. Emboldened, I allowed myself to believe I had a right to be in the capitol, even that it belonged to me, so I climbed to the next floor, where state senators and members of Congress have their offices.

A sign hung on most doorknobs. "Please come in," it read. Imagine a country that granted its citizens such unparalleled freedoms. You could talk to your representatives without bothering to make an appointment. As a test, I chose Senator Jason G. Crowell's office at random—and a splendid office it was, with a grand view of the Missouri and two attractive aides seated at desks. For the first time ever, I understood why someone might opt for a career in politics.

Senator Crowell wasn't in, Angie Plunkett informed me. A first-term Republican up for reelection, he'd hit the campaign trail in Cape Girardeau, a conservative stronghold in the southeastern boot heel, a region that has more in common with Kentucky or Tennessee than the Midwest. Cape Girardeau, the biggest city in Crowell's district, is his hometown and also Rush Limbaugh's.

Here the teenage Rush broke into radio broadcasting under the semiclever alias of Rusty Sharpe. He attended Southeastern Missouri State, as did the senator, but he flunked out, while Crowell graduated and earned a degree in law. A former Eagle Scout, he stood for faith in God, love of family, and the defense of freedom, according to the campaign literature Angie gave me.

She and her husband were from Cape Girardeau as well, and fairly new to Jeff City, still settling in. She was anxious about the election, worried that Bush's unpopularity might hurt her boss's chances and affect her job. She needn't have concerned herself. Crowell trounced his Democratic opponent.

"What about the presidential election?" I asked. "Any favorites?"

She smiled coyly. "No comment."

"No opinion?"

"I'm waiting to see what happens, and then I'll have an opinion."

Pretty cute, Angie. Perhaps she secretly supported Barack Obama. In the media, there'd been lots of twitter lately about the so-called Bradley effect, and how those who praised Obama in public might not vote for him in private. That contradicted what I'd heard on the road. Obama had many fans reluctant to declare themselves openly.

"Do constituents often stop in?" I wondered.

"Not really," Angie said.

I hated to hear it. The lassitude of Americans, again.

"The Silver-Haired Legislature dropped by this summer," Bev, the second aide, chipped in. "It's an organization of senior citizens. They lobby on issues important to them."

"Are seniors a special interest of Senator Crowell's?"

"No, it was just very hot and humid," Bev joked, "and they discovered we had a water cooler."

THE U.S. ARMY'S recruiting center in Jeff City rents some space in a little strip mall on the edge of town. In a splash of late afternoon sunshine, Sergeant First Class Mark A. Smith, the center's commander, was enjoying a smoking break. With his uniform and reflector shades, and his graying crew cut clipped short, he looked tough and resilient and capable of serious persuasion. If you dreamed of being a soldier, Smith could pose as your role model.

As I'd first noticed in Olney, some young people in the heartland take refuge in the military. When work is scarce and all you have is a high school diploma, if that, the army may well look better than the graveyard shift at Taco Bell. The trade-off was familiar, even eternal. If you survived the risk, the payout could set you up for the rest of your life.

Smith gave me his business card. I turned it over and read, "Up to $73,000 for College, Up to $40,000 Enlistment Bonus, Over 200 Career Fields, Jobs are Guaranteed in Contract."

A native of Dexter, Missouri, Smith had been a recruiter for seven years. Though he liked his work, he looked forward to retiring—eight more years and he'd be a civilian again, with a sweet pension in the bargain. He had no firm plans after that. He thought about going back to Colorado, where he'd met his wife while stationed at Fort Carson in Colorado Springs. She'd never been crazy about Jeff City. Selling Harleys, that was one of Smith's fantasies. He really loved those bikes.

At first, Smith was brusque. No good could come of talking to a nosy civilian, he must have felt, plus he was very busy. Harried soldiers ran around the large, sparsely furnished, antiseptic room, or sat at desks tapping into computers under the watchful eye of Uncle Sam, who observed from a poster. All four branches of the military had outlets at the mall, so the competition for recruits could be intense.

"The navy used to beat us pretty bad," Smith admitted. "They sent in a chief petty officer, but he's gone now, so we're even-steven again."

The recruits would be in their late teens, I imagined, callow and easily swayed, but their average age was actually twenty-six. They'd knocked around in the world and had reached a dead end. The bonus scheme, while not dishonest, included clauses and subclauses, and only a rare individual earned the whole forty grand for signing up. The army demanded an eight-year commitment from most recruits, four in uniform and four in the reserves.

A young soldier and his proud dad came in to say hello. The soldier had just completed nine weeks of basic combat training at Fort Riley, Kansas, a program divided into red, white, and blue phases. He'd run the obstacle course, done the fifteen-mile march with a full pack, and learned about hand grenades and machine guns. He'd chosen to be a combat engineer, or sapper, clearing minefields and conducting demolitions.

"Basic wasn't too bad," he bragged. "I ate a ton of sand, though."

"Is that right?" Smith teased, loosening up. "Did you wallow in any mud?"

"Yes, sir, I did. But you *can* get through basic, so long as you don't cheat your body."

Cheating your body involves booze, drugs, and women. "And you didn't cheat, soldier?"

"No, sir. I didn't have a chance to! I never even got an off-base pass. They took away our cell phones, too. That didn't stop us from trying to get them back."

"But you failed in your mission."

"Yes, sir, we did."

"I guess they saw you coming."

"Yes, sir, I guess they did."

For the next hour or so, Smith fielded calls, issued orders, and caught up on his paperwork. One youth, quite tentative, approached to ask for advice and spent about fifteen minutes, then went down the hall to check what the marines, navy, and air force had to offer. Smith applied no pressure. He made it sound as if the youth would have to be a superior individual, indeed, to meet the army's impeccable standards.

Outside, I met a skinny, pimply soldier in fatigues. He'd also just finished his basic, and awaited an overseas assignment. That wasn't necessarily bad news, but he was still nervous. Instead of Iraq or Afghanistan, he could be sent to Germany, Belgium, Japan, or Italy. He'd heard rumors about guys who'd had such luck. Saudi Arabia or Kuwait wouldn't be so awful, either, except for the heat. He didn't know beans about Panama.

The soldier could have added Kosovo, South Korea, Macedonia, and Djibouti to his list of possible posts. Our military presence abroad is massive and very costly. In 2008, the Department of Defense received $554 billion from the U.S. budget, or 60 percent of the government's discretionary spending.

Wherever the soldier landed, he couldn't predict how he'd be received. The American G.I. wasn't universally respected as a defender of the common good anymore. When I was a boy, most fathers on our block had served during World War II and took pride in their commitment, even loaning medals to their sons for our interminable war games. The nature of the sacrifice was crystal clear, but those days are gone forever—gone since Vietnam, if not earlier.

The just cause is frequently compromised now, and our recent wars have not always been fought on the high moral ground. For the skinny soldier, the army was a business decision and a gamble. If he lasted through his tour without incident, he'd return home with a marketable skill—as an information technology specialist, in this case—but there was no guarantee he'd return at all.

HIGHWAY 54 RUNS southwest from Jeff City to the Lake of the Ozarks, an hour's drive or so. On summer weekends, the highway is a parking lot, but I had a free ride through Brazito, Hickory Hill, and Rocky Mount, an appealing stretch of country marred only by a gruesome Church of Christ billboard. It pictured a hand, presumably belonging to Jesus, impaled on an iron spike beneath the legend "Body Piercing Has Been Around For 2,000 Years."

The billboard had me jabbering to myself all the way to Osage Beach, a resort with 110 premium outlet stores, 5 other malls, and 50 antiques shops, enough mercantile overkill to prevent me from leaving the car. Lake of the Ozarks spells recreation with a capital "R," and the numbers keep coming at you—92 miles long, 1,150 acres of shoreline, 17 championship golf courses, untold multitudes of largemouth bass, and 77,000 hotel and motel rooms.

Bagnell Dam, a hydro facility, impounded the Osage River in 1931 to form the lake, once known as Benton Lake, after Thomas Hart. You need a boat to properly explore it, and it was far too cold to swim or sunbathe, so I figured I'd be better off in Jeff City for another night and reversed course on Route 5 through Sunrise Beach and Gravois Mills.

At Versailles, another Ver-sales, I turned onto Route C, quieter and more picturesque. High Point and Russellville were Old Order Amish settlements. If any farm can be described as spotless, theirs deserved to be.

Horses and buggies began to pass by. In the first rode a buoyant teen couple, the lad in a new straw hat and his girlfriend in gingham; a grumpy mother wrestled with two unruly children in the second; and in the third, a sour-looking elder frowned and flicked his switch. I felt as if I'd just sat through a History Channel documentary on the Ages of Man.

Early in the morning, I left for Kansas and beyond, but California, Missouri, west of Jeff City, caught me up short and demanded an inspection. Legend has it that California Wilson bribed the town's officials to name it after him in 1846 with two gallons of whiskey. The famed bandit Cole Younger once delivered a lecture called "Why Crime Does Not Pay" at the Finke Opera House after his release from prison. Lately Hispanics have arrived to take jobs in manufacturing and sometimes indulge in games of eight ball at Charlie's Pool Hall, where the following are forbidden:

NO DRUGS

NO ALCOHOL

NO DRUNKS

NO WAR

Tipton, Otterville, Smithtown, and then Sedalia, elevation 909 feet. I'd embarked on the long, slow ascent of the Great Plains, a gentle grade of five hundred miles or so climbing toward the Rockies. Scott Joplin, born in Texas, landed in Sedalia in 1894 and stayed for six or seven years, playing piano at the bordellos of Lottie Wright and Nellie Hall, and also at the Maple Leaf Club and the Black 400, hangouts for classy African Americans.

The clubs enraged the black clergy. They were "a loafing place for many of our girls and boys, where they drink, play cards, dance, and, we have been informed, carry on other immoral practices too disgraceful to mention," the clergy charged in a letter, begging the town fathers to take some action—unlikely, really, when there were fifteen whorehouses on the main drag.

Joplin studied music at George R. Smith College, boarding with families. He composed "Maple Leaf Rag" in 1899, and cut a deal with John Stark, a local publisher of sheet music. For every copy sold, he earned a one-cent royalty, and when "Maple Leaf Rag" became a big hit, he moved to St. Louis with his new bride, Belle.

George Graham Vest practiced law in Sedalia for a while. A skillful orator, Vest was a Confederate congressman and later a U.S. senator. He displayed his verbal talent most brilliantly when representing the owner of Old Drum, a fox hound shot for trespassing on a sheep ranch in 1870. The owner wanted to be compensated for his loss, and Vest insisted he merited it.

"If I don't win the case, I'll apologize to every dog in Missouri," he swore.

In his closing argument, Vest didn't bother to rebut any testimony or argue over the facts. Instead he waxed poetical about the special bond between man and dog.

"The one unselfish friend that a man can have in this selfish world, the one that never deserts him and the one that never proves ungrateful or treacherous is his dog," he rhapsodized. A dog guards against dangers, fights against enemies, and mourns his master's passing with "his head between his paws, faithful and true even to death."

Vest was spared an apology. He won the case and fifty dollars for the owner, and gave birth, via his speech, to the phrase "man's best friend." A statue of Old Drum stands in front of the Johnson County courthouse, with Vest's immortal words inscribed on a stone below it.

THE GRANDEST BUILDING in Ottawa, Kansas, the seat of Franklin County, is also a courthouse, this one designed by George P. Washburn in 1891. It's another example of the Romanesque Revival style so popular at the time, with semicircular arches and an epic solidarity that suggests the heft of justice itself. A statue called *Buffalo Woman*, probably an Ottawa Indian, stands outside, while the Dietrich log cabin, a relic of the frontier, has been preserved in a nearby park.

My motel clerk, another Patel, guaranteed me a restful night. They rolled up the streets at about nine o'clock, he warned, so I went looking for somewhere to have dinner right away. Sad to say, I'd given up on the illusion that every small town has a mom-and-pop café serving terrific homemade food. Instead of wasting hours on a fruitless search, I made a few exploratory passes and resigned myself to Applebee's Neighborhood Grill—generally the least offensive franchise, to damn it with faint praise.

On the food front, America had taken me prisoner. I wished I could mount a rebellion, but I seemed to be a lone dissenter. Applebee's is a true crowd pleaser. Dine Equity, its parent corporation, owns about thirty-three hundred "casual dining units"—IHOP is its other major brand—and is in the business of treating its loyal customers to the "cravables" that sometimes contribute to their gross obesity.

Applebee's has cornered 95 percent of the world's supply of fatty riblets, for instance, a signature dish basted in various sauces. Its deep-fried mozzarella sticks are a calorific classic, and so, too, is the Three Cheese Chicken Penne—mozzarella, provolone, and Parmesan melted over some chicken and bruschetta, then doused with a creamy Alfredo sauce.

IHOP works the sugary angle. For breakfast, there's Rooty Tooty Fresh 'N Fruity, which consists of eggs, bacon, pork sausages, and two buttermilk pancakes with cool strawberry and whipped topping. For dessert you can indulge in Crispy Banana Caramel Cheesecake quick-fried in a flaky pastry tortilla and crowned with caramel, cinnamon, and more bananas and whipped topping.

"We can't seem to make things sweet enough," a Dine Equity PR man once told the *New York Times*, as if his clientele consisted exclusively of children.

The motel clerk's prediction came true. I enjoyed a restful sleep and woke refreshed. Ottawa looked peppier by day and not so desolate. It had gained a sense of purpose. I did some banking, bought a new notebook, and experienced everywhere the fabled politeness and decency of Kansans. A teenage gas station attendant managed to call me "sir" three times in two minutes.

There was so much space in town nobody jostled for elbow room. The space brought a kind of relief. It created a stillness that encouraged a decorous reticence. Folks were reluctant to disturb it with an unnecessary remark. Their speech had flattened out, too, and the slight southern inflection I still noticed in areas of Missouri was gone.

From Ottawa, I crossed the Marais des Cygnes River on Route 31. It used to flood regularly, cresting as high as forty feet, until the Corps of Engineers stepped in with pumps and levees. Ahead lay Osage City and Council Grove, two Wild West towns frequently invoked in the old cowboy movies. The names conjured up visions of gunfights and saloons with swinging doors, trail drives and a shy but steely lawman who pines for a widow or a schoolmarm.

Osage City was once Indian Territory, the ancestral home of the Osage. "Few [men] are less than six feet in stature," marveled the great painter of Native Americans George Catlin, "and very many of them six and a half, and others seven feet." Though the Osage were excellent buffalo hunters, they also grew squash, maize, and other crops. General Custer employed them as scouts because of their military prowess and knowledge of the terrain.

There aren't any saloons in Osage City now. No general store, either, or ladies in calico. Jimmy Stewart didn't edit the *Osage News*, and Lee Marvin hadn't raised a ruckus the night before. The town could have been an AARP retreat, with its many handy services for seniors. Almost no one between the ages of eighteen and twenty-four lived there anymore. The young fled at the earliest opportunity unless they were tied to a farm or a job.

Religion and prayer figured prominently in the life of Osage City. The Methodists, Presbyterians, and Catholics had substantial, smartly landscaped churches within a one-block radius. It was a quiet, pleasant place, yet it seemed to be fading away, although so unhurriedly and by such tiny increments only an outsider might notice.

Kansas is among the slowest-growing states, in fact, a victim of the exodus that occurs when machines replace men in the fields. It's also riddled with ghost towns, more than six thousand by some estimates. All that space, though a comfort in one sense, has a tendency to undermine any marginal attempt to inhabit it. You'd need the raw grit of a pioneer to survive in such minuscule satellites of Osage City as Vassar or Admire.

I switched to Highway 56 and climbed a gentle rise past enormous cattle ranches. The sky was broad and blue and flocked with pillowy clouds, a harbinger of the West. Rather than a courthouse, the landmark in Council Grove was the Farmers and Drovers Bank. Along yet another Main Street were some old brick buildings and the Ritz Theater, where the marquee declared "Coming Soon." Exactly what might be coming was left to the imagination.

In 1825, the Osage forged a pact with some pioneers at the "council" of Council Grove, agreeing to let them travel through their territory unharmed. The grove itself referred to a copse where the wagons gathered to martial forces, outfit themselves, and do some repairs before they tackled the rest of the Santa Fe Trail, still a dangerous journey, since no other Indians had offered them safe passage.

A path on the Neosho River has signs and plaques that recount the tale, of course. I walked it at a brisk clip and overtook a man and his golden retriever on their evening promenade. The dog was a beauty and so friendly I knelt to pet it, thinking maybe I'd been foolish not to bring along Beanie even if I had to change his clothes twice a day. A fellow could use some company on the prairie.

"Where's a good place to eat around here?" I asked the man, hoping to outfox the franchises for once.

"Depends on what you're in the market for," he replied reasonably.

"Something that wasn't packaged in Wichita."

"There's Mexican. They're local people. Or the Saddlerock Café."

"Where would you go?"

"The Hays House, I 'spose, if I wanted the whole hog."

"That's what I want. The whole hog."

You couldn't miss the Hays House, once the general store of Seth Hays, Council Grove's founder, who was Daniel Boone's great-grandson and a cousin of Kit Carson. Hays first built a log cabin to trade with the pioneers and the Kaw, or Kanza, Indians, close relatives of the Osage for whom the state was named. In 1857 he upgraded to the clapboard building that's now the oldest continuously operating restaurant west of the Mississippi.

At Hays House you can order spicy chili by the cup or bowl. The soup and bread are made from scratch on the premises. Nobody mumbles into a headset, as the floor managers do at Applebee's. On weekends, the restaurant opens at six in the morning to accommodate the ranchers and farmers. The beef is purebred black Angus, but I chose Beaulah's Ham marinated in wine and fruit juice, a steal at $11.95.

America was on the comeback trail.

STRONG CITY, SOUTH of Council Grove, is rodeo country, host to bronc busters, calf ropers, buckle bunnies, and some fifteen thousand fans every June. Otherwise it sleeps through the year. It was taking a nap when I passed by, but I spotted a wonderful mural at the fairgrounds and stopped for a closer look.

The mural featured Technicolor portraits of three beaming cowboys and a sunny cowgirl with daisies in her hair. Rodeo stars, I figured, although one cowboy had a touch of Hollywood glitter. Maybe movie stars, then, of the lesser variety that only video store employees steeped in esoteric film lore can identify.

I got so involved in conjecture and snapping photos I didn't hear the pickup until it braked to a halt five feet away. The rancher at the wheel smiled at me, an elbow poking out a window. He wore a short-sleeved shirt, had a left forearm as dark as mahogany, and tipped back his Stetson in greeting.

"You're a long way from home, New York."

"Don't I know it."

"Any idea who you're taking pictures of?"

I pointed to the cowgirl. "That's not Dale Evans, is it?" A stab in the dark, but she could be a Kansan for all I knew.

The rancher roared. "Roy Rogers' wife? Nah, that's Margie Roberts. She was a champion bronc rider."

"And this guy?"

"Her brother Ken. He rode bulls. Next is Gerald, another brother. All-around cowboy champion a couple of times."

"The older man?"

"E. C. Roberts, their daddy. He started the rodeo here."

"Nice hat," I said, nodding toward E. C.'s, and I meant it.

"You ought to get yourself one."

"I'm more the ballcap kinda guy."

"Don't be so sure." With a wave, the rancher was off to Cottonwood Falls, or maybe Antelope or Bazaar.

Strong City is in the Flint Hills, a residue of limestone, shale, and chert, or flint, left behind when an inland sea that once covered much of Kansas receded. The hills are tough on the plow and not very hospitable to any growing thing except the tallgrasses of the prairie. When the Colorado cattleman Stephen F. Jones rode through the area in 1878, he saw miles of lush bluestem pasture so rich in nutrients that a foraging steer could put on two pounds in a single day.

Jones set about buying up property, first 160 acres along Fox Creek and later a larger parcel from the railroad. Eventually he owned 7,000 acres and enclosed them with 30 miles of 5-foot-high fence, a backbreaking job on account of the rocks. The fence posts were often sunk in chunks of limestone instead of hammered into the ground.

Jones named his spread Spring Hill Farm and Stock Ranch after the many streams that sluiced it, but he was far from finished. In 1880, he undertook construction of a three-story limestone mansion in the Second Empire style, a home for his wife, Louisa, and their five children, one of whom—the unlucky Samuel—died from the bite of a rabid skunk.

On his land, Jones ran Hereford, Polled Angus, Galloway, and Durham cattle. He added a three-story limestone barn to store hay, grain, and equipment, and also shelter his stock. By 1885 he kept two hundred pigs, thirty horses, eight milk cows, and four mules. He built a scratch shed for his chickens and let them range freely in bad weather—it made them more fertile—and a three-holer outhouse, two for adults and one for a child, all of limestone.

As you approach Tallgrass Prairie National Preserve, Jones's mansion is the first thing you see. It still stands where it's always been, on a hill with a view over the valley. The image it presents is romantic, yet disconcerting. Laura Ingalls Wilder comes to mind, as do Willa Cather and John Ford.

The mansion may pose as a bucolic homestead, but it also suggests a fortress and maybe a prison. Probably the Jones family experienced both extremes. They lasted only nine and a half years at Spring Hill.

There's no admission fee at the preserve. You can explore it at your leisure. All the original outbuildings have survived—limestone doesn't crumble readily to time's injunctions. A nature trail winds by the barn and an icehouse, then ascends through some shade trees to an overlook at the edge of the prairie. Once the grasses blanketed 140 million acres of North America and supported the great bison herds that the Osage, Kaw, and others hunted, but only 4 percent of the prairie remains, another diminution.

Cattle still graze at the preserve from May through July. The bluestem, Indiangrass, and switchgrass reach a height of five or six feet, and they sway and quiver and dance—a living, breathing entity. Like the desert, the prairie demands close attention. It doesn't yield its secrets easily. I waited fifteen minutes before a meadowlark decided to show itself.

From the overlook, the trail descends and crosses Fox Creek to a two-acre plot, where Jones built a limestone schoolhouse. His schoolmarm would have been a paragon of virtue. She'd have to avoid men, of

course—some contracts explicitly forbade marriage. A teachers' maga-
zine of 1915 advised schoomarms to wear at least two petticoats in the
classroom, and resist the temptation to dye their hair. Under no circum-
stances should they be caught loitering near an ice-cream parlor, where
unspoken dangers lurked.

AFTER THE GLORIES of the prairie and the fine meal at Hays House, I
began to feel in command again. If my luck held, I could eat anywhere
with alacrity, or so I thought until Florence, Kansas, taught me otherwise. There was no alacrity to be found in Florence.

Along the city's fringes, wheat grew and cattle roamed. At the junction of U.S. 50 and Highway 77 stood an old stone tower erected in 1887
and inscribed with the legend "99.96% Pure Spring Water." The water
comes from a well dug on the east side of the Cottonwood River, and a
pump, once steam-powered, delivers it to the tower, still in use today.

Florence claims the tower as its landmark, but I'd nominate the
monumental flag downtown. It's painted across the entire side of a building, the work of a feverish artist who's seen fit to embellish Old Glory.
From a ragged hole in the Stars and Stripes, a fierce-looking eagle bursts
forth, ready to kick some ass. You wonder what sort of imaginary threat
prompted the belligerent stance. With seven hundred or so residents,
Florence scarcely qualifies as a strategic target for our enemies.

The eagle scared me a little. So did the ramshackle Out Post bar,
thankfully closed at the moment, but the Chuck Wagon appeared innocent enough. Every farmer and rancher in Marion County had squeezed
inside for lunch, it seemed. The room rocked with chatter and suffocated
under clouds of cigarette smoke. I froze in the doorway—the old deer-in-
the-headlights number.

"Sit there at the Liars' Table, why don't you?" a bustling woman suggested, trying to be helpful. She carried hot plates of food in both hands,
carefully maneuvering through the obstacle course. "They won't bite."

But I wasn't so sure about that. I sidled to the only vacant chair, with
a liar on either side of me like bookends. They didn't exactly rise up to
welcome me. Nobody held out a paw and bellowed, "Howdy, partner."
"Ignored" would be the best word to describe it. I buried my nose in the

menu and studied it diligently, as if to bone up for a final exam in diner food that afternoon.

Rural Kansas has two prevailing body types, and Chuck, the older liar, conformed to the first. Well into his seventies, he was a lean, narrow-hipped, stiff-backed wheat farmer, and a model of rectitude. He picked very deliberately at his Mexican Special of ground beef, beans, rice, and cheese, chewing every bite to shreds. He had a dry sense of humor, but he only let little rays of it shine through.

The other liar, middle-aged, represented the second body type, being round, soft, and heavyset. Seated in a wheelchair, he voiced many more opinions than Chuck on lots of different subjects without any hesitation. He wasn't eating, just sipping coffee and opinionating.

The plate-carrying woman—she owned the Chuck Wagon, I think—breezed by and alerted me, "You'll have to speak up. He don't hear too good."

"That's only when you're doing the talking," the fellow in the wheel-chair retorted.

His wisecrack livened things up. A sliver of curiosity came my way, so I parceled out a brief bio, and he reciprocated. He'd intended to settle somewhere warm when he left Nebraska, maybe in the South, but his wife took a liking to Florence, so he bought a motel in town. He'd since sold it.

That seemed to exhaust our interest in each other. We fell quiet for a brief interlude, after which he inquired of his friend, "Chuck, how's that knee doing?"

Chuck looked up from his food. "It's all right. I'm getting the other replaced soon."

"My wife needs one done. But the doctor says she's too young, and she'll have to lose some weight."

Chuck chewed and thought before he spoke. "It's wonderful what they can do now," he said. "I'm grateful for it. Your knee's never really the same, though."

My sandwich arrived, a grilled chicken and Swiss. The chicken turned out to be a hamburgerlike patty—the cook must have pounded it into submission, or maybe ground it up—on a bun with seven or eight potato chips as a garnish. I stared longingly at the last of Chuck's Mexican Special, wishing I'd risked the beans.

"How's your 401(k) going, Chuck?" the second liar started up again.

"It's been better."

"That's for sure. I've been looking into gold and silver myself."

"Silver could do well."

"Wall Street's as slow as molasses. It's still a bear market."

"I don't believe that'll change very soon," Chuck ventured.

The table talk, previously lurching along, gained momentum. Other liars joined in to compare the value of their portfolios and swap investment tips. I hadn't heard anybody mention Wall Street since Maryland. Of all places, I said to myself. What about pork bellies? Shouldn't they be talking about them?

I ate what I could of the sandwich, then pushed it aside. As Chuck got ready to leave, I took a last shot at teasing out some information unrelated to the Dow Jones.

"Have you lived in Florence a long time, Chuck?"

"That's right. A long time."

"A small town like this, there must be plenty of gossip."

"Plenty." He grabbed his check. "But you'd have to sit here for three or four days to hear it all."

A DRIVE ACROSS western Kansas has the shape of a dream. The space and the big sky lull you into a tender complacency, and the affairs of the great world seem very far away. It's simple to lose yourself in the pattern of the landscape—cattle ranches and fields of wheat, corn, and soybeans, then a sprinkling of sorghum and sunflowers. The crops, by and large, wind up as feed for livestock.

For mile after mile, I'd drift along in a bubble and almost forget where I was, but then I'd flip the radio dial and connect with a conservative talk show by accident, and the world returned full force. With the Republicans slipping badly in the polls, the brand-name hosts were apoplectic. Rush Limbaugh practically foamed at the mouth, raising the old questions about his OxyContin habit.

His latest hero was Joe the Plumber, an unlicensed tradesman with a tax problem, who had the "guts" to stand up to Obama and criticize him at an Ohio rally. Such was Limbaugh's influence that John McCain alluded to Joe—regular Joe, a stand-in for the common man—twenty times in the final presidential debate.

In New Orleans, John Steinbeck had listened to the disreputable Cheerleaders spew their bigotry at the black and white children attending an integrated school. Disgusted, he realized "something was wrong and distorted and out of drawing." He had friends in the city who embraced a tradition of kindness and courtesy, but he didn't see their faces in the crowd. Maybe his friends and their ilk felt helpless, he thought, just as he did, but their absence misrepresented New Orleans as a whole.

In the same way, the talk show hosts took up all the oxygen. They drowned out all the other voices and discouraged constructive debate. They seemed, at least to me, linked to the entertainment industry rather than to the political process. Whether they truly conveyed the conservative message or only served to muddy it would be left for their audience to decide.

MY DAY DREW to a close in Hutchinson, once known as Temperance City, where wheat is king. A giant grain elevator in town, almost half a mile long, holds about eighteen million bushels. Hutch's attractions include the Cosmosphere, a museum devoted to the space program and the Apollo astronauts, and the State Fair.

With a population of forty thousand or so, it's got a mild mix of races—a few blacks, a few Hispanics. Often you'd mistake the city for a giant mall, except for the railroad tracks and the train whistles.

"There's something to do here once in a while, anyway," mumbled the clerk at the Grand Prairie Hotel and Convention Center.

Unable to face another motel, I'd upgraded myself to the Grand Prairie at somewhat lavish expense. In my room, I could move around without knocking anything over, and the bed did not depress me with the afterimage of thousands of previous guests. Once I'd cleaned up, I made the rounds of the hotel and ran into a noisy bunch of teenagers in costume, students from Hutchinson High.

They were rehearsing some skits for a review, trying them out on a big stage at the Convention Center. They'd taken to the limelight, too, and had an excellent adrenaline rush going, both boys and girls. Though they were mostly juniors and seniors, they looked a dozen different ages. A little more of life, and they'd even out a bit.

Josh Lightsey and Summer Gajewski were the most outspoken, while the others hung back and functioned like a Greek chorus. They got really excited and animated when I produced a notebook. A grown-up— a writer, no less—was going to record their words and possibly use them in a book. That meant it was time to quit fooling around and be serious, an amusing transformation to watch. Seriousness doesn't come readily to kids who've just spent the past two hours skylarking onstage.

What's Hutchinson like for a young person? That was my first query. They mulled it over and inclined toward "very boring" at first, but it sounded too harsh an assessment, so they revised their opinion and agreed Hutch has many pluses.

"We've got the Cosmosphere," said one.

"And the State Fair," another contributed.

"Hutch isn't too big, and it's not too small," Josh Lightsey concluded, putting a fine point on it—end of topic one. Josh played with Clean Slate, a Christian rock band, and guessed he'd stay in Kansas forever, while Summer was more adventurous and dreamed about visiting Italy someday.

With all the problems in America, how did the future look to them? They were okay with it. No mention of plummeting 401(k)s, no dabbling in gold and silver. No craving for material toys, either. They saw no limits to their prospects.

"A lot of stuff will improve." That was Josh again, very intense and positive, a small boy with spikey blond hair. "There are technologies available we don't know anything about yet."

"Robots," somebody else chimed in. "They'll have a significant role in our lives."

"The Internet," Summer said. "And computers!"

Another voice. "Some diseases will be cured. Maybe even cancer."

"Does anyone ever get afraid?" I asked.

They glanced at one another, then dummied up for nearly a minute.

"I worry about the war," Josh confided at last. "My cousin Cory on my dad's side, he just left for Iraq. If something happens to him, there'll just be two of us men left to carry on the family name."

"Are you all interested in politics?"

"Yes!" they almost shouted.

"All right, let's have a show of hands, then. Who's for John Mc-Cain?"

"Me!" Only Summer's hand went up, and she looked crushed. You could almost hear her thinking, "Damn, that was stupid!"

"And Obama?"

Everybody else. "He'll bring change," Josh insisted. "We need a new leader."

"You don't mind that he's part African American?"

"No, sir!"

Summer was still embarrassed. "It's my parents' fault," she apologized. "They're Republicans."

The school's drama teacher interrupted us, rounding up her charges and herding them back to the stage. Going up to my room, I allowed myself to believe that a lot of stuff would improve in spite of the begrudgers and naysayers. The world truly does go quietly about the business of renewing itself while we're looking the other way.

Before bed, I searched for more info on Hutchinson on my laptop, and came across some poems by William Stafford, who was born there. Of his family home, Stafford wrote, "We sang hymns in the house, and the roof was near to God."

UNENDING KANSAS, IT went on and on and on, and—speaking of fear—I got a scare in Kinsley when I passed a sign with two arrows, one aimed at New York and the other at San Francisco, 1,561 miles in either direction. Could it be possible I'd driven only halfway across the country? My odometer already read 3,567 miles. If the sign was accurate, it seemed a mean trick for the monster land to play.

The wind blew hard as I approached Dodge City. It kicked up dust devils and threw a chill into the air even though the sun blazed. You could sense what a Kansas tornado would be like, the dark funnel visible from afar because of the flat prairie, while jittery people watched it advance, waiting to see if they'd be spared or destroyed.

Dodge City provided the setting for *Gunsmoke*, of course, but Matt Dillon, a fictional character initially created for a radio serial and modeled on Raymond Chandler's hardboiled Lew Archer, never wore a badge there. Wyatt Earp and Bat Masterson did, though, and belonged to a gang that controlled the town through its whiskey trade, a key source of revenue. Everyone drank in Dodge. Its first business, opened after the Civil War, was a humble saloon of boards and sod.

The Kiowa and Cheyenne had been routed by then, and when the U.S. Army built Fort Dodge in 1865 to protect travelers on the Santa Fe Trail, the city began to grow and really took off with the arrival of the railroad in 1872. Soon after, it became known as the Queen of the Cow Towns or, alternately, Hell on the Plains.

A cattleborne tick made Dodge rich, reaching Kansas on the hides of Texas longhorns driven across the state to be transported to the East by rail. The longhorns were immune to the tick, but it caused "Texas fever," a form of anthrax, in other breeds. To halt its spread, the government enacted a quarantine, routing the cattle away from densely populated Abilene and Wichita into the sparsely settled West.

The wild times started in earnest then. Cowboys, drifters, soldiers, railroad workers, hookers, and gunslingers poured into Dodge. Everything in town cost a quarter—a shave, a packet of pins and needles, a shot of liquor. Booze fueled the city's affairs, but drunks paid dearly for their excesses, tossed into a fifteen-foot-deep dry well until they sobered up.

The last of the buffalo hunters were still around, unspeakably filthy with their matted hair, grubby fingernails, and blood-soaked clothes. They smelled to high heaven, and everybody called them "stinkers." They'd decimated the herds—about 1.5 million buffalo hides were shipped from Dodge between 1872 and 1878—and left the prairie strewn with rotting carcasses. Farmers collected the bleached bones and sold them to manufacturers of china and fertilizer for six to eight bucks a ton.

Any pleasure or vice known to humankind was available in Dodge. The villainous Long Branch was just one of nineteen saloons catering to a citizenry of twelve hundred or so. You could buy Russian caviar, fresh anchovies, and opium, and the busy bordellos swiftly filled up with soiled doves. Trainmasters toted the red lanterns from their cabooses when they visited the girls, hence the origins of the "red-light district."

So many corpses piled up after gunfights that new plots were dug almost daily at Boot Hill Cemetery for those who'd given up the ghost with their boots on. No sheriff could do much to curb the violence. Even accepting the position amounted to signing your own death warrant, usually via a bullet in the back, although the lucky ones were just run out of town.

Under siege, Dodge's mayor hired Wyatt Earp, then a part-time lawman in Wichita, to police the city at the enormous salary of $250 a month. Earp used the railroad tracks as a line to divide the city. The north side, where guns were banned, approximated a civilized society, but the killing and the vice continued unabated in the free-fire zone of the south side.

Dr. J. H. Holliday turned up on the south side in 1878. On the lam from murder charges, he promptly hung out his shingle. His dental patients were rare, however, because Doc suffered from tuberculosis, sputtering and coughing while he pulled teeth. He compensated for his financial losses at the card tables, drinking heavily—what that meant on the frontier is unimaginable—and exercising a rapier wit as sharp as the knife he liked to flash.

Doc's prowess with a revolver dazzled even Wyatt Earp, who described Holliday as "the nerviest, speediest, deadliest man with a six-gun I ever knew." Earp's tolerance of a wanted man offended some folks, although it probably just reflected their mutual respect and admiration.

Without question, Doc's friendship paid off when Ed Morrison and his boys tore up Shannsy's saloon after a cattle drive. Earp had once shamed Morrison in Wichita, and the cattleman, bearing a grudge and bent on revenge, was about to plug the sheriff when Holliday snuck up behind him, pressed the cold barrel of a Colt to his neck, and ordered the boys to drop their guns and pray.

The cattle business peaked in Dodge in 1883–1884, but the city had lost its luster before then. The railroad extended all the way to Santa Fe by 1880, making the overland trail obsolete, and the glory days were soon over. Maybe Earp and Doc saw it coming. They'd already ridden into the sunset toward Tombstone, Arizona, and the eternal promise of the West.

DODGE CITY REMAINS a cow town, with a slew of feedlots, slaughterhouses, and meat packing plants. It doesn't take long before a visitor catches a whiff of manure. The livestock industry creates lots of jobs, and many go to Hispanics, who make up almost half of Dodge's population, not counting illegals. A big contingent had recently scooted over from Oklahoma, I was told, after a crackdown there on employers who hadn't been inspecting anyone's papers too closely.

I'd become so accustomed to the sameness of rural Kansas that I blinked when a low rider drove by, blasting *sureno* rap from his stereo. Some gangbangers were on the streets as well, dressed in the latest fashions from East L.A., but most Hispanics wore a T-shirt and jeans and looked sweaty and a little dirty from laboring in the cow pens.

At a Mexican restaurant where I gorged on *carnitas*, a group of workers breezed in on their lunch break, all about the same size and possibly from the same pueblo, flirting with the women at the counter in Spanglish and giving off an aura of contentment. Often I think Mexicans know something I don't. They seem to have an ease of being I envy. I can't remember ever meeting a dour Mexican in California—nasty, yes, and even obnoxious, but never dour.

In Dodge City, Doc Holliday and Wyatt Earp each have a liquor store named after them. The stores aren't far from Gunsmoke RV park or Boot Hill Museum, a string of frame buildings that replicate the originals, including the Long Branch, allowing Dad to slip off for a quick one while the children go for a stagecoach ride or watch a phony shoot-out between actors.

Maybe you can still have a wild time in Dodge if you hunt for it, but I settled for Friday night football. Kansans dote on the sport, so I got to the high school early to be sure of a seat. Two boys were hawking programs at the gate, exactly the sort you'd expect—lanky and unathletic, with the indoor pallor of cyberspace warriors. I asked how the Red Demons were doing this season.

"We're like two and four?" A question, not an answer.

"And the Goddard Lions?"

"They're oh and six."

"So you've got a good chance tonight?"

An emphatic nod. "Most definitely."

If you grew up in Dodge City with a talent for athletics, you'd surely dream of becoming a Red Demon. The quarterback was still a big man on campus and would retain that status forever, his heroic touchdown passes recollected in coffee shops and bars years later. The stadium showed how highly the community valued its team. It was a pro facility in miniature, equipped with a JumboTron scoreboard and a massive sound system loud enough to wake the elderly in the next county.

Dodge's halcyon years were the 1970s and '80s. The school had slumped a bit since then, but their loyal fans hadn't deserted them. More than a hundred, mostly adults attired in Red Demon gear, tucked into a pregame meal of Wendy's burgers and fries at folding tables on the sidelines, while the sun, a dying ember, began its descent and the air got noticeably cooler, making me wish I had a Red Demon warm-up jacket of my own.

The fanfare before the kickoff also imitated the pageantry of the NFL. A pom-pom squad, nine cowboys hoisting red flags, and a brassy marching band converged on the fifty-yard line for the national anthem. The drum major wore a holster and a toy gun on his hip—I think it was a toy, anyway. When the crowd sang "And the rocket's red glare," the darkening sky lit up with fireworks, and the cheerleaders unfurled a huge Stars and Stripes.

The game started. On paper, the contest appeared to be a mismatch. Goddard, the pride of southwestern Kansas, was a little town of about two thousand, or one tenth the size of Dodge. The Lions' porous line only gave their quarterback, Cameron Fisher, about two seconds in the pocket, so he was repeatedly sacked, but the Red Demons were as messy as could be and couldn't run a sequence of plays without incurring a penalty.

"Hey, ref, you suck!" issued a disgusted cry after the tenth penalty, and every Christian head in the Demons' bleachers jerked around to berate the vulgar loudmouth.

The night turned colder, with a hint of frost. The cheerleaders donned track suits before halftime, and when they performed a routine, I could see their breath. In the third quarter, chilled to the bone, I left the stands, and by the fourth quarter, I was reading some more of William Stafford's poems at the motel, only marginally guilty about departing before the game was over.

That proved to be the right decision. I could have turned blue waiting on the final score. The game went into overtime before the Red Demons lost, 33–26, and the defeat did not sit well with Justin Burke, their hyperbolic head coach, who told the *Dodge City Daily Globe*, "It was the worst heartbreaking loss I've ever experienced, that the kids have ever experienced, that this team has ever had."

THE HARD, CLEAR light of western Kansas played out over the shortgrass prairie beyond Dodge City, elevation twenty-five hundred feet. Though still flat, the land continued its gentle rise across the Great Plains, and the air stayed dry and cold. The wind whistled. Along the nearly empty Arkansas River, some cottonwoods yielded a trace of autumn color, but the country looked austere now, rugged and challenging, ancient.

On the fringe of Cimarron, there's a little park on a ridge just off the highway. The ridge provides a good view of a remnant section of the Santa Fe Trail as it follows the river's course toward the montains. The longer you stare at the trail, trying to see it as a pioneer might, the more daunting it becomes. I couldn't wrest an ounce of hope from it myself. It just recedes into the distance, ever the same, without a clue to what lies beyond it.

Some travelers took one look at the trail, and turned back or stayed put, while others gambled on the shorter Cimarron Cutoff nearby. It shaved about 160 miles off the journey to New Mexico, but water was scarce and Indians plentiful. Kit Carson and five other trappers were once pinned down by the Comanches for three days, killing their own mules to use as barricades, before they fought their way to freedom.

The rutted tracks of wooden wheels are worn into the earth of the little park. At the height of overland migration, the wagon trains rattled across the prairie twenty-four hours a day, seven days a week, carrying an untold number of courageous human beings pitting their lives against the unknown. That they so often triumphed seemed an utter miracle.

Had Americans lost their ability to cope with obstacles and surmount difficulties? Steinbeck wondered the same as he pondered the peerless bravery of Lewis and Clark.

"And we get sick if the milk delivery is late and nearly die of heart failure if there is an elevator strike," he wrote.

The age of adventure and exploration brought out the best in us, perhaps, and now the other half of our nature—that gloomy pilgrim soul—had the upper hand again.

GARDEN CITY, KANSAS, the football archrival of the Red Demons, and its neighbor Holcomb are notorious for all the wrong reasons, thanks to Truman Capote. They're cattle and wheat towns on the Plains, as ordinary as salt and pepper, although Garden City, like Dodge, has a burgeoning Hispanic population and isn't quite so calm anymore.

If you drive through Holcomb, you understand why the murder of the Clutter family in 1959, which Capote recounted in *In Cold Blood*, unhinged the place. It's so orderly and single-minded you might correctly assume that nothing significant ever happened there. Though fifty years have gone by, crime still scarcely exists. The police reported no rapes, robberies, assaults, or murders between 2002 and 2006. One could probably interpret that as a corollary to the absence of eventfulness.

Yet Garden City, with almost thirty thousand residents, ten times the size of Holcomb, has a higher incidence of crime than the national average, and it's only 2.6 miles away, leading one to surmise that when someone from Holcomb acts up, they know where to do it.

For my young server at El Rancho Café in Holcomb, the Clutter murders belonged to the Pleistocene. She'd seen *Capote*, shot in Manitoba, Canada, on DVD, but not *Infamous*, filmed mostly in Texas.

"He had such a squeaky voice," she giggled.

"They talk that way in New York. All the smart people do."

"You're making it up."

"I'm not. You'll have to go there and see for yourself."

A pause. "Well, I wouldn't mind," she whispered shyly.

Then the last of Kansas, seventy miles of road with only four towns rooted to it, Lakin and Kendall, Syracuse and Coolidge, population eighty-six. As I approached Colorado, I experienced a fresh wave of optimism, but the West always does that to me.

In Cheyenne, Wyoming, in 1969, I got my first literal taste of the West. On that initial cross-country trip, I'd barreled through Nebraska on Interstate 80, skipping lunch because of my urgent mission and lack of money, but my stomach begged for a snack, so I pulled into a convenience store. A big glass jar of stringy dried meat rested on the front counter.

I pointed at it, a greenhorn. "What's that stuff?"

"Buffalo jerky."

I ate buffalo jerky straight through to Salt Lake City.

Part Four

WHEN OSCAR WILDE visited Colorado on his lecture tour of America in 1882, he took a shine to it. The rest of the country did not impress him so favorably. He found it the noisiest place that ever existed, where everybody seemed in a hurry to catch a train. All the rushing about discouraged poetry and romance, he griped, although he admired our ingenuity and knack for applying science as a shortcut to creating wealth.

As an Irishman, Wilde was unprepared for the scale of the United States. He reacted testily to the inordinate size of everything, and argued that the country tried to bully others into believing in its power by using its magnitude as a club. Not surprisingly, he left his heart in San Francisco, "a really beautiful city," and fell in love with exotic Chinatown.

In Leadville, Colorado, where Wilde spoke at the opera house, miners had discovered some of the world's richest silver deposits, causing the little outpost to blossom into a city of some forty thousand. Rascals and celebrities of every stripe turned up, including Doc Holliday, who rolled through after the gunfight at the O.K. Corral. Doc killed a former lawman over a five-dollar debt, and had the good fortune to pull a jury that refused to convict him.

The miners were not a sophisticated audience. One man had ordered a replica of the Venus de Milo, and sued the railroad company that delivered it because the statue was missing an arm. Wilde read to them from Benvenuto Cellini's autobiography, and when they expressed their sadness that the great sculptor and silversmith hadn't come along, he explained that Cellini had been dead a long time.

"Who shot him?" a miner asked.

Wilde had a look at the silver mines, where a lode was called Oscar after him, and attended a three-course banquet at a saloon. The meal consisted of whiskey, whiskey, and whiskey. He saw a sign there that represented "the only rational art criticism I have ever come across."

PLEASE DO NOT SHOOT THE PIANIST
HE IS DOING HIS BEST

Leadville went bust eventually. It's known as the Two-Mile-High City now, outdoing Denver.

Lamar, Colorado, just beyond the Kansas border, doesn't have a cute nickname and wouldn't want one. The town's farmers and ranchers are no-nonsense types who deal in cattle, corn, wheat, and sunflowers on the High Plains of the Arkansas River Valley.

The land around Lamar once belonged to the cattle baron A. R. Black, who believed the shortgrass prairie was strictly for grazing, not building homesteads. His cows thrived on the abundant grass, hay, and water, and took refuge in groves of cottonwoods and plum trees on the river during the harsh winters. He owned a railroad station as well—Blackwell, on a line that followed the Santa Fe Trail.

A curious breed of hustler connived around the West in those days. The town site platter was an early species of subdivider who relied on a formula of land plus railway to attract settlers.

Reluctantly, Black struck a bargain to sell some land to a platter, but he later reneged, so the platter bought another parcel three miles away. moved the whole Blackwell station to it under cover of night, and advertised lots for sale in Lamar—a tribute to Grover Cleveland's secretary of the interior Lucius Quintius Lamar.

In Lamar I recognized another small town grappling with the future, a child of the railroad waiting for the next big idea to hit home. Its problems started in 2006 when a bus manufacturer shut down. Nearby La Junta lost a prime employer in its pickle factory at the same time, throwing the valley into a recession.

Yet the people in Lamar did not appear bitter or defeated. They seemed happier and more outgoing than similarly affected folks in the deep heartland—a matter of attitude, maybe, or a little spark of the old pioneer spirit. At the supermarket where I grabbed some odds and ends, the checkout clerk almost blew me out the door with his enthusiastic greeting, as strong as a prairie wind.

"How Are *You* Today?" he bellowed, speaking in capital letters as do many Coloradans. All that clean, fresh air must embolden their lungs. Tall and blond, with muscular biceps from lifting boxes, he could have been descended from the German settlers who infuriated A. R. Black.

Cowboys in Stetsons, denim, and boots were walking the streets of Lamar, past a familiar row of vacant storefronts. Their shirts were checkered and sometimes pearl-buttoned. They took dips of Skoal and Copenhagen and squinted quite a bit, slightly blinded by the light. Often the beds of their trucks were piled with hay. From the cab, they could see for miles across the Plains.

I stopped at the old railroad station, now a Colorado Welcome Center. In a corner of the parking lot, a small group of seniors had gathered for coffee under a banner that read "Lamar Democrats for Obama." As a swing state, Colorado had shifted from Clinton to Bush, but the pollsters believed it might be ready to swing the other way.

Dean and Mary were in charge at the Welcome Center. "What Can I Do for You?" Dean inquired pleasantly. He, too, spoke in caps, although with less emphasis than the clerk.

"I'd like to be welcomed, I guess."

"Well, You *Are*! Welcome!"

Being welcomed was no simple matter. It involved a ceremony of sorts. As part of its largesse Colorado, our eleventh-wealthiest state, really lays on the freebies. I received a good-quality map, a 215-page full-color guide to the sights, and a T-shirt that celebrated trout fishing.

Dean and Mary wanted to hear about my trip, so I filled them in and then asked about the Obama supporters outside. The mere mention of the group unnerved Dean, whose face grew flushed.

"They shouldn't be there at all," he protested. His voice sounded normal now, as if to accommodate a serious topic. "They're *supposed* to have a permit. This is city property. We've always been conservative in Lamar. The state used to go about sixty/forty."

Mary endorsed the conservative angle. She was older and calmer, white-haired and grandmotherly. I remarked on what a prize Colorado would be for the Democrats, and how a recent poll I'd seen in the *New York Times* online showed Obama in the lead.

"The *New York Times!*" Dean completely lost his cool. "The media is so biased! I've about had it with the *Denver Post*, too. Every story is from a liberal standpoint!"

I had a sneaky suspicion Dean listened to Rush Limbaugh, but I agreed with him about the media. If anybody still believed in the fallacy of objective journalism, I'd yet to meet the innocent. One could only talk about relative objectivity and trust the sources with the best record for honesty—or for avoiding dishonesty, to lower the bar further.

In the face of Dean's outburst, Mary had gone a trifle fluttery. She wisely changed the subject to Colorado's spectacular natural resources, and soon we were all pals again and sharing appreciative memories of the Rockies.

To complete the welcome ceremony, Dean gave me a pushpin and led me to a contour map on the wall. It was stuck with so many pins it looked like a porcupine. Each represented a visitor to the center, and where the visitor was from. New Mexico was covered with pins, while only a couple of red flags were planted in Maine.

"Well, what do you know?" Dean had regained his composure and professional style. "You're the Second Person from Ireland!"

THERE'S AN OLD joke about La Junta. A motorist, lost, asks for directions to it at a gas station.

"It's pronounced La Hunta," he's told. "How long you plan to stay there?"

"For Hune and Huly," the motorist replies.

La Junta takes pride in its Hispanic community, and so do Las Animas and Rocky Ford. The little towns, each half Latino or more, form a rough triangle on U.S. 50. They're dry, dusty, and agricultural, with distant views of the Front Range. Garlands of dried chilis hang on porches, and you can buy them at *mercados*, too, along with *queso*, epazote, and piñatas.

Rocky Ford farmers brag about their melons. At a roadside stand, I tried a sliver of cantaloupe, the sweetest and ripest I'd tasted since the Eastern Shore. Growing conditions are ideal in the lower Arkansas Valley, but the farmers worry about sprawling cities such as Colorado Springs and Pueblo filching their water, always at a premium. Their semi-arid banana belt gets less snow than the state average and only about fourteen inches of rain annually.

Manzanola, Fowler, Avondale, and then Pueblo, where I quit for the day. As the West dictates, I was traveling longer distances now and had covered 270 miles since leaving Dodge City that morning. The driving was often an exercise in solitude. Between Kendall, Kansas, and Holly, Colorado, I seldom saw another car.

Pueblo looked massive after all the emptiness, four times as large as Dodge and far more congested. The city once earned its money as a saddlemaker, but the industry literally went under when the Arkansas River flooded in 1821 and washed away the downtown. Later Pueblo became known as a tough, pro-labor steel town. Colorado Fuel and Iron was its chief employer until the steel market crashed in the early 1980s.

For Pueblo, like Lamar, the future was a question mark. Some planners think it will rival Denver in twenty years, while others shudder at the idea and oppose any further construction projects. Affordable housing was a bonus for the city's coffers until recently, but the developers couldn't borrow the cash to finance any more subdivisions at present.

In spite of the economic uncertainty, Pueblo's city center is a gracious example of urban renewal done right. That evening, I explored the Arkansas Riverwalk, a path that skirts both sides of the stream. In the renovated Union Avenue District, Don Campbell and Tom Carpenter were holding court outside Campbell's store, a repository for antiques, rare books, and other collectibles.

They sat on straight-backed chairs, regally commanding the sidewalk. Nobody slipped past without a by-your-leave, but they were charming rogues and got away with it. In the court's hierarchy, Campbell was clearly the king, with Carpenter cast as his loyal retainer, still keen and boyish at sixty or so, with his hair in a long white ponytail.

As monarch, Campbell ruled gently and distractedly. There was a ruined magnificence about his rugged, bearded face, as if he'd been trading blows with life for a good half century and had won about as often as he'd lost. He nodded off whenever the conversation bored him, retreating into a private universe.

"Pull up a chair," he offered grandly, and Carpenter jumped up and fetched me one from the store. Our blockade was now almost impassable.

Carpenter hailed from Los Alamitos, New Mexico, but his family had moved to Pueblo when he was ten. Though he had lived elsewhere—Flagstaff, Arizona, for one—he'd returned home to retire. He fancied himself a writer and claimed to be at work on an oral history of the region called "Prairie Walker Chronicles."

"'Prairie Walker Chronicles,'" Campbell muttered with mild disdain.

"Didn't you want to go to Yale, Mr. Campbell?" Carpenter asked, drawing his friend into the mix.

"That is true."

"And didn't a Bush beat you out?"

The joke fell flat. It had a mildly stale aroma.

"I attended Cornell instead," Campbell said, putting things right. I'd never take him for an Ivy Leaguer, but he graduated from Cornell and won distinction as a heavyweight wrestler, although he weighed only 178 pounds. He also threw the discus and held the world's record "for about five minutes" before somebody else broke it.

Campbell's presence in the West was cloaked in mystery. It was a long story he seemed disinclined to relate except in snippets. Iowa figured in the tale somehow, if I remember correctly, and there were some mishaps and wrong turns before Colorado entered the picture. About Pueblo, he was more forthcoming.

"It started bad, and it stayed bad." He sounded facetious, as if the badness suited him. "It's always been a poor town, and it stayed that way."

"Things have been tough here since CF&I closed down," Carpenter reminded him. "That used to be the biggest mill west of the Mississippi. We've got Oregon Steel now, but it's smaller—"

An attractive woman sidled around the blockade, and Campbell snapped to, swiveling his head to appreciate her from behind.

"Good-bye!" He gripped the arms of his chair, as if to rise. "I wanna go where she's going." Then he sat back down.

"Pueblo must be fifty percent Hispanic," Carpenter went on. "There's an underground crime scene, and lots of drugs."

"Mafia," Campbell added. "Can't talk about it."

Carpenter lit a cigarette and smiled at a young couple with a toddler as they stepped off the curb to get around us. He had a sunny disposition in contrast to the occasionally morose Campbell, and decided he'd been giving me an unfair, one-sided view of Pueblo.

"The city has some positives, too," he said, making amends. "There are some good bars and a music scene. Freddy Fender has played gigs around here. Did you know this was Damon Runyon's hometown? The writer of *Guys and Dolls*? He worked for his father's paper. Our repertory theater's named after him. Colorado State University's got a pretty decent football team—"

"I have a blessing in these conversations," Campbell interrupted. "When these sixty-year-old punks come around, I can't hear what they're talking about!"

"They've done a great job downtown," I said. "The Riverwalk's a real plus."

"Private money," Campbell informed me. "Investors."

With its history as a union town, Pueblo usually votes Democratic, so I asked about my hosts' preferences.

"I'm not at liberty to say," Campbell commented, but he was just being sly. After a pause he revealed, "We're both Republicans."

"I might cast a protest vote for Ron Paul myself," Carpenter said.

We shook hands all around, and I carried my chair into the store and fingered the spines of some rare books. The antiques were eclectic, with some fine pieces and some ignoble ones. Through the front window I could see Carpenter and Campbell talking with a heavily tattooed pedestrian, and I felt certain they'd be sitting out there again tomorrow, weather permitting, and the day after that until the first bite of winter drove them indoors.

ON SUNDAY MORNING, the nineteenth of October, I woke to the bluest sky imaginable. Some days are so insistently beautiful that they demand your immediate attention, and this was one. If I wasted another second in bed, even a heathen might construe it as a sin, so I was in the shower and out the door in under fifteen minutes, clutching a Styrofoam cup of tea and a rock-hard motel bagel.

There's a clarity to western light I've rarely seen matched. As it spread across the mesa of Pueblo West, it brought up the pastel colors of the casitas, rose and turquoise and ocher, and the grayish green of the sagebrush. In the arroyos, the cottonwoods and aspens flared in golds and yellows. Though the air was still chilly, I could feel the sun gathering its strength. By noon I'd be stripped down to my Welcome Center T-shirt.

U.S. 50 ran very straight through Pueblo West, tempting drivers to bank some time against what they'd lose later when the highway snaked into the Rockies. I was in no rush myself, not on such a morning, so I turned onto a spur road toward Florence, a hamlet in the shadow of a large complex of faceless buildings—probably a government installation of some kind, or so I assumed.

The road curled downhill and crossed a bridge over the Arkansas, no longer barely a trickle. Instead it flowed briskly through the desert, a classic trout stream of deep pools and riffles. I accepted this as a tip of the hat from the cosmos, my reward for being an early riser and, in general, an affectionate fan of creation.

I assembled my rod and began casting. Only a few activities bring me more contentment than fly fishing for trout. As a novice, I kept a tally of my catches, recording the length and weight of any noteworthy brown or rainbow, but I quit that years ago. I had almost, but not quite, reached the point where just sitting by a river was enough to satisfy me. If that enlightened moment ever occurs, no friend of mine will believe it.

On the Arkansas, I was hampered by the lack of hip boots or chest waders, yet I hooked and released a brace of small trout. That gives the angler a heady, godlike feeling or, better, the sensation of a Roman emperor delivering a thumbs-up rather than a thumbs-down to a gladiator. My trout didn't deserve any bragging, but I thought I'd do some in Florence, anyway.

For such an out-of-the-way spot, Florence defied the economic trend and looked quite healthy, with artsy shops, antiques stores, and the sort of restaurant you'd find in a big city—Sonny's Louisiana Seafood & Steakhouse, where blackened frog legs and fried gator are on the menu. When I remarked on this at a café, eating a plate of toast as a substitute for the bagel I'd fed to the desert, my server shrugged and said, "It's the prison."

Not just any prison, either. Those faceless buildings I'd passed were ADX Florence, one of the nation's four super maximum security facilities. ADX, the Alcatraz of the Rockies, holds some of our most dangerous, violent criminals, many of whom have killed a fellow inmate elsewhere. They're subjected to what critics brand as cruel and unusual punishment, confined for twenty-three hours a day to a cell where the furnishings—a stool, a desk, and a bed—are made of concrete.

The roster at ADX Florence reads like an all-star team of bad guys. It ranges from al-Qaeda operatives to such homegrown terrorists as Terry Nichols, a coconspirator with Timothy McVeigh, and Ted Kaczynski, the Unabomber. ADX also imprisons hit men, serial killers, and the head dudes from the Aryan Brotherhood, Gangster Disciples, and Almighty Latin Kings. Andrew Fastow, Enron's former CEO, does his time in the minimum-security tract.

Colorado is a hotbed of prisons, as it happens. Ever since 1985, when a law doubled the maximum sentence for felonies, the state has been short of cells. Its rate of incarceration, a statistic based on the number of inmates per one hundred thousand of the population, stands at 7 percent, far above the U.S. average. The Department of Corrections, with a budget of $644 billion in 2006, predicted that it would run out of beds for prisoners by the end of 2008.

Women account for much of the increase, but that's true everywhere in America. We jail ten times more women than all of western Europe combined. In Colorado, 86 percent of those incarcerated were convicted of a nonviolent crime, usually for drugs or drug-related theft, and they often leave behind dependent children.

The United States has the world's highest rate of incarceration, in fact, with Russia a laggardly second. About 7.2 million people are behind bars, on parole, or on probation. The astonishing numbers, still rising, do not reflect an upsurge in crime. They're due instead to policy changes, particularly regarding drugs. Our prisons also act as way stations for the mentally ill.

Cañon City, just west of Florence, tops the penology charts in Colorado, with nine state and four federal institutions, and the locals would probably be delighted to squeeze in a few more. They actively sought their first one about ten years ago, when some Benedictine monks decided against selling their abbey to the Bureau of Prisons. The disappointed residents, deprived of the anticipated jobs and income, passed the hat, bought a property of their own, and sold it on good terms to the bureau, a favor since repaid many times over.

Cañon City, founded in 1858, was laid out during the Colorado gold rush. The locus of the strike was Pike's Peak, visible on the horizon that morning and dusted with a postcard sprinkling of snow. Though I expected a fortress mentality in town, with inmates in brightly colored jumpsuits cleaning out gutters and spearing trash, there was no sign of the prisons, only of their positive impact on the economy.

At an old armory in Cañon City, I found a coterie of gun buffs attending a show of firearms and weaponry. These shows are very popular in Colorado. In Denver, there's one on almost any summer weekend. Unlicensed vendors used to be a scourge, exempt from the Brady Act and willing to trade with felons and juveniles, but the voters closed that loophole after Columbine.

The Shriners had sponsored the show. A ticket cost five bucks, available from a wizened gent in a fez. Once through the door, I ran into a rotund dealer in a wheelchair, who held the command post up front.

He wore a cowboy hat and what I can only describe as God Bless America clothing embroidered with flags and plastered with flag pins. He sat like a pasha before a table laden with revolvers, not cheap Saturday night specials but elegant Smith & Wessons that could set you back a grand or more.

The crowd was every bit as eccentric as you might imagine and also very old. I counted four men on respirators. Arthritis appeared to be a common ailment.

Along with rifles, shotguns, and revolvers, the enthusiasts admired Bowie knives, samurai swords, medals, badges, Native American jewelry, bolo ties, and bayonets. The dealers were as frayed as desert pack rats after wandering from show to show. Unable to control their habit, they often squandered any profits by swapping with their peers.

WHEN THE HIGHWAY dipped into the canyon of the Arkansas River beyond Royal Gorge, I began to compose a note of apology to Jefferson City in my head—a "Dear Jeff" letter, I guess you'd call it, because I'd fallen hard for Colorado. Come winter, I'd probably be fickle again and change my mind, but on this perfect autumn day, under a cloudless sky with the sun dappling the water, there was no place else I'd rather be.

The Arkansas wears away a foot of granite about every twenty-five hundred years, so it took many millennia for the canyon to form. If you put a rock under a dripping faucet and checked on it ten years later, you'd have an idea of the infinitesimal pace. The canyon has both a somber antiquity and an austere beauty. Indifferent to the affairs of human beings, it inspires silence and awe, to quote Steinbeck on the redwoods again.

Fly fishing has a fairly severe code of etiquette, and one of its cardinal rules is to give other anglers plenty of space. I usually respect it, but near Texas Creek, while scanning the river from the car, I noticed an expert at work and got out to watch him, creeping closer over the granite to study his technique.

Though I catch my share of trout, I do it by being a good stalker and knowing where the fish lie, but I can't cast for beans. More than once, I've wrapped a line around my neck or hooked a random portion of my anatomy, most memorably when I sunk a barbless but sharp fly into my cheek on California's Truckee River and had to perform some instant self-surgery with a pair of pliers.

The expert on the Arkansas made casting look easy. He could handle forty feet of line with a perfect textbook loop. His fly landed so softly it might have settled on a pillow, but he wasn't having any luck. The sun was too bright, and the trout were too wary. He needed a change of tactics and must have realized it, because he retreated into the shallows to sort through his gear.

He became aware of me then. Some anglers hate to be observed, while others accept it as part of the game, and he fell into the latter category. He had the freshness and newness of Colorado about him, as friendly as a puppy.

"You fishing?" he shouted.

"No waders," I yelled back.

"Hell, I've got an extra pair!"

He scrambled up the bank, a carpenter employed only piecemeal now because of the slowdown. He was still young enough to regard this as a plus. It gave him more free time to fish.

"I've got some money stashed away," he bragged. I knew what that meant. He could cover his rent and still have a little left over for the good times. I'd lived like that myself in what seemed another life and never regretted it.

There's a breed of young men out West who enjoy doing all the handy things bookish types like me spend hours avoiding, and he belonged to it. In his truck, he carried chains, flares, tools, kits to patch a tire or fix a snakebite, a camp stove, packets of freeze-dried food, and virtually every other essential required if nature ambushed him on the way to Cripple Creek. No doubt he could repair whatever broke, too, and build a house from scratch or tear one down if it came to that.

His spare waders fit me not at all. They were much too big. I waddled like a circus clown in a barrel, holding them up with suspenders. Around my waist I cinched a belt to keep the waders from filling up if I tumbled, a real possibility considering the slippery footing. Without any felt-soled boots or a staff for support, I stuck to the slack eddies.

We both fished Pheasant Tail nymphs in various sizes, and my new angling partner caught and released a nice, fat brown. Nymphing can be boring, though, a bit like fishing with bait. The serious fun began around one o'clock, when a hatch of Blue Wing Olives rousted the trout from the depths and enticed them to partake of the banquet.

I'd brought along some BWOs in various sizes and tied on a smallish imitation. On my second cast, the fly provoked a slashing strike, and I landed a fat brown of my own. This day can't get any better, I thought, but I'd underestimated the pleasures of Colorado.

RIDE TOWARD THE radiance. I'd cooked that slogan up on the first day of the trip, but I'd forgotten about it until I cruised into Salida, as radiant a place as I've ever encountered. The highway climbed up from the canyon to a plateau at about seven thousand feet, and the Sangre de Cristo Mountains, lightly capped with snow, created an impossibly romantic, even heavenly backdrop for the town.

The Sawatch Mountains are nearby, too, and so are the Mosquitoes. Salida looks out on a dozen peaks of more than fourteen thousand feet in altitude. The Arkansas runs through it, ideal for kayaking and whitewater rafting. There are outfitters galore to supply gear and lead pack trips. Bikers and hikers have countless trails at their disposal. Salida has fine restaurants, Colorado microbrews, and hot springs. The sun shines almost daily in October, and the air is crystalline

Little wonder, then, that the residents are so fit, absolutely glowing with health. The obesity I'd seen elsewhere doesn't exist in Salida. In general, Coloradans take good care of themselves—fair and square-jawed, with excellent teeth and no sense of irony. They're better-looking for it and less oppressed by circumstance. A taxing hike or a trip over the rapids rids the arteries of sludge.

In various parts of the nation, I'd met with an occasional fearfulness, but the folks in Salida gave the fear a new twist. They were scared their little hideaway would be discovered, worried that someone like me would broadcast its virtues and cause a stampede that would lead to the sort of ruin all Coloradans dread.

The scenario was well established. Outsiders stumble on a jewel of a town and buy second homes, and the price of real estate soon escalates beyond the grasp of the locals. Trustafarians and retirees move in, followed by predatory Californians, a sickening situation. In Colorado, they value a kind of purity and innocence, and they hate to see it compromised. Aspen and Vail were gems until they were discovered, or so the mythology goes.

I heard an earful about this from a ski bum at Benson's Tavern, but he got it only half right. Salida and similarly gorgeous Colorado paradises are great seducers. They encourage those who love the outdoors—especially young people—to scrape by on a menial job to fund their passion, but the years go by, and the young people wake up middle-aged and can't afford a house. That's when the bitching starts. The ski bum blamed all his problems on "invaders."

When I tired of his sorry tale, I dragged myself away and indulged in a healing soak at Salida Hot Springs Pool. The natural mineral water, piped in from a spring in the Rockies, fluctuates in temperature between ninety-five and one hundred degrees. It has no stink of sulfur, and even a half-hour treatment will leave you rosy-cheeked and utterly relaxed.

I'd have gladly spent an extra day in Salida, but I had too much ground to cover, all those challenging western distances to address. First on the next morning's agenda was a drive over Monarch Pass, at 11,312 feet. I'd never crossed a peak that high before. Though I had a phone and a full tank of gas, the what-ifs started to plague me. What if I got a flat? What if a flash blizzard occurs? Is there such a thing as a flash blizzard?

Only a handful of cars and trucks were on the road, and that increased my feeling of isolation. The mountains, so scenic from a distance, grew more foreboding as I approached the pass. The air turned thin, and I shivered and switched on the heater. Above the tree line, patches of dirty snow appeared. A gray cloudiness, dour and steely, replaced the radiance down below.

Yet I made it without a hitch, of course, and pulled over to see the Continental Divide. John Steinbeck crossed it in Montana and grandly called it the "granite backbone of a continent." As he stood astride it facing south, he realized a raindrop falling on his right foot would end up in the Pacific, while the drops that fell on his left were destined for the Atlantic.

WHILE DOC HOLLIDAY was busy shooting up Leadville, Wyatt Earp opted for the quiet life of a faro dealer in Gunnison, a town that evolved through the usual phases of the West, first as a mining camp for gold and silver and next as a railroad hub. Cattle ranches are Gunnison's bread and butter now, and the spreads are sizable and stretch over hundreds of acres.

The sight of tawny pastures and grazing stock warmed me after the chill of Monarch Pass. It would have been different in winter. Gunnison sits in a valley at almost eight thousand feet, where the cold air of the Rockies collects and often drives the mercury below zero for days at a time—thirty-two in a row is supposedly the record—but the constant sunshine takes the edge off the bitterness, the ranchers claim. That's a bonus, because the average temperature in January is minus seven degrees.

It's surely redundant to say that Gunnison is sublimely beautiful. Its namesake river is another blue-ribbon trout stream, and the surrounding mountains arrest the eye at every turn. The rate of unemployment is high for Colorado—the state's overall rate was only 3.2 percent that October—but the landscape nourishes and compensates. More than half the residents are bachelors, perhaps a legacy of the frontier.

WELCOME HUNTERS! cried the signs and banners downtown. Deer season had officially opened, and the men in bright orange caps and camo outfits would be the last tourists until the snow fell. Every merchant around wanted a piece of them.

One gift shop's ad led with the word "Vegetarian," defined as Old Indian for Bad Hunter. W Café took a motherly stance and advised, "Don't Hunt on an Empty Stomach!" The Last Chance Saloon could only muster the lame slogan "Coldest Beer in Town."

The hunters all gravitated to Traders Rendezvous, the largest retailer of big game trophies west of the Missouri. Harold Clark, the store's founder, was behind the front counter when I walked in. He wore a

Stetson, a down vest, and a green neckerchief, as if ready to audition for the Sons of the Pioneers.

"Mind if I look around?" I asked.

"You go right ahead," Harold replied distractedly. "Looking's for free."

The Rendezvous was a little spooky. I hadn't seen so many stuffed animals since my last visit to the Museum of Natural History. The specimens included deer and elk, but also bighorn sheep, bobcats, mountain lions, and a truly scary grizzly bear that stood tall, with its claws ready to maim you and its teeth bared to devour you after you'd been maimed.

The store traded in exotics as well, and they carried impressive price tags. The head of a Cape buffalo cost $1,695, while that of a Rocky Mountain goat would set you back $2,995, but you could bag an ordinary elk's head for your rumpus room for only $495. A buck's sun-bleached skull and antlers were considerably cheaper, although less of a conversation piece.

Harold Clark sat doodling on a pad, oblivious of the dead animals in a way that I was not. He'd come to Colorado about forty years ago from Ohio, where he owned a pawnshop, some furniture stores, and other businesses. Not long ago, he sold the Rendezvous to his son Randy and worked for him now. A recent stroke had hampered his ability to recall some names, he told me, but otherwise he felt as sharp as ever.

"Is Randy a fair boss?"

"Sometimes I don't think so," Harold answered. "But then I realize he's copying the way I did it, so I don't complain."

"Where do you find all these trophies?"

"We have scouts in every western state. Trophies just turn up, you know? Someone dies, or there's a divorce."

"Most couples probably don't fight over who gets the Cape buffalo's head."

"I'd say you're right about that."

Harold wondered what had brought me to Gunnison, so for the umpteenth time I talked about Steinbeck and my trip and how I'd been charting the changes in America since I'd been abroad.

"It's gonna change a whole lot more if Obama's elected," he snorted.

"For good or bad?"

"Bad! You won't be able to own a gun anymore!"

The point wasn't worth arguing. So many gun owners shared Harold's belief that it had acquired a bizarre reality irrespective of the facts. On this particular subject, as with abortion, the possibility of an intelligent discussion had gone by the boards.

Harold made it clear, or tried to, that Obama's ethnicity didn't matter to him. "I'd rather live next door to a black family than white trailer trash," he swore. He spoke next of an African-American comedian he'd seen on TV who distinguished between the words "black"—a positive—and "nigger"—a negative.

"Who was the comedian?"

"Was it Bill Cosby? I don't remember for certain. I'm just guessing."

The country's problems were due to the Fannie Mae scandal, he went on, repeating a line the talk show hosts had been beating to death lately. If people quit running up so much debt on their credit cards and acted like responsible adults, Harold insisted, we wouldn't be in this mess.

"When I get my bill at the post office," he boasted, "I buy a money order right there and then to pay it."

From the Rendezvous, I went directly to the Gunnison Brewery, ordered an ale, and sat across from some hunters, who were decompressing. They were grimy and bedraggled, as if they'd been on an infantry slog, and drank hard liquor with sugary mixers—Jameson and Sprite, Jack Daniels and Coke. The bartender poured doubles for the price of singles. His attitude mirrored the informality of the West. He'd never call you "sir" once, much less three times.

The hunters hadn't roused any deer. "We saw some elk," one said, and then stated a universal truth. "You always see what you're not after."

Later, I checked Gunnison's voting record on my laptop. Harold Clark belonged to a conservative minority, and maybe that accounted for his vehemence. In 2004 the Democrats carried Gunnison County by a wide margin, even with their stance in favor of gun control.

IN OURAY, COLORADO, the self-styled Switzerland of America, I saw the best sign of the trip, a small brass plaque on a nondescript brick building: ON THIS SITE IN 1897, NOTHING HAPPENED.

Ouray was my kind of town, one with a sense of humor. I came to be there for the usual reason, plain old curiosity. When U.S. 50 morphed into a dull, multilane highway in Montrose, I meandered south instead on a less traveled road through Ridgway and over Owl Creek Pass at 10,114 feet, then dropped from the San Juans to the town.

On its outskirts, steam rose in billowy plumes from a hot spring, once the sole province of the nomadic Tabeguache Utes, who visited every summer to hunt and take the waters. Something did happen here in 1879, in fact, when the Ute chief Ouray ceded his territory to some settlers chasing after gold and silver. A modest boom ensued, and the town grew up around it.

The San Juans, sparsely timbered with pines and firs on rocky outcrops, surround Ouray. Tourists love the dramatic alpine setting, and the merchants make no bones about trying to please them, yet they, too, worry about being discovered and ruined like nearby Telluride.

Ouray greeted me with a bruised-looking sky, heralding the chance of snow. The mountains did not beckon, as they do on a bright, clear afternoon. Instead they seemed to draw down and close in, wintry in every aspect. I could feel the town turning inward as it switched over to survival mode, waiting for the ice climbers to arrive and toss around some money.

Bundled in my heavy jacket, I explored the little city center and collected another amusing sign from the battered door of a tavern, this one handwritten:

> It's not that we don't like kids,
> but we don't drink beer at your
> child's daycare, either.

Early voting had begun in Colorado, as it does every year fifteen days before an election. Any resident can show up at the Ouray courthouse and cast a ballot, no excuse necessary. The turnout had been light so far, I heard, although the number of absentee ballots was much bigger than usual.

A trophy elk, sculpted rather than stuffed, stood guard outside the lodge of BPOE 192. The Western Hotel, once a stagecoach stop for those journeying to the high country, had shut down for the season. The sky grew darker and weightier, clamping itself to the top of my head, and a frigid wind blew right through me. The remedy, I knew, was age-old—whiskey and some grub.

The bartender at Buen Tiempo was another casual Coloradan, informal to the point of being rude. He ignored me to discuss a planned trip to Central America with a pal, while I waited and exercised Zen-like control to keep from shouting at him. He'd seen *Cocktail* too many times, and turned a bourbon on the rocks into a performance piece.

The food was good, at least. I ate *carne adovada*, pork in a spicy adobo sauce, and talked with Gail Kelly from Ridgway, who played bass in a bar band and also worked as a massage therapist. Thrice married, she had a son aged twenty-seven, and currently dated a drummer from Grand Junction she'd met on the Internet.

All this I learned in minutes. Along with informality, the West fosters an easy intimacy. People don't seem as defensive, nor as inhibited by their mistakes and defeats. The idea that you can always start over still motivates behavior. If you fail to strike gold, it's time to head on. Westerners seem more adventurous, too, when it comes to embracing new experiences. Gail wouldn't be the last massage therapist I ran into between Ouray and San Francisco.

"I'd like to visit Dublin someday," she confided. "I've got Irish roots."

"Have you voted yet?" I wondered.

"No, I probably won't. I totally lost interest when Hillary quit the race."

The night was brutally cold, and the splendor of the San Juans no consolation. I watched for the first snowflake at my motel window, sure that a flash blizzard, if they existed, would soon bury Ouray and trap me for weeks, but I'd just caved in to loneliness again. Even my traveling library let me down. Thoreau sounded cranky, and Emerson world-weary rather than wise. Miller's rants annoyed me. As for *Travels with Charley*, I couldn't bear to open it.

OURAY LOOKED BETTER in the morning, crisp and clean, though I needed some boiling water, courtesy of Mr. Coffee, to melt the frost from my windshield. Frost covered a pasture at Potter Ranch in Ridgway, too, where Herefords grazed amid the steamy hot springs, an idyllic scene perfect for a cowboy's Christmas card.

Beyond Dallas Divide, Highway 140 was a desolate road through increasingly remote country. Fewer than two thousand people live in the six or seven hamlets between Placerville and the Utah border, a distance of one hundred miles or so.

The Uncompahgre Plateau, composed primarily of granite, shale, and sandstone, provided my first glimpse of desert colors—a subtle palette in a scrappy landscape of rabbitbrush and sagebrush. Higher up in the hills, some piñon and juniper grew.

Insofar as this region ever flourished, its benefactor was the Uravan Mineral Belt, where miners dug the yellowcake uranium used in the Manhattan Project's bombs. You could go to the movies at the Uranium Drive-In or the Radium Theater in Naturita, and play poker for big pots at the saloon. Naturita's poor and tired now, but it isn't a ghost town like Uravan, at least, razed to the ground with superfund money because of its nuclear glow.

Highway 140 could induce one to fall asleep at the wheel, its distractions were so minimal. On occasion, I saw a vacant trailer on an abused-looking lot, somebody's dream homestead come to grief. The plateau might well be the preferred refuge of tax dodgers and aspiring bounty hunters, UFO spotters and adepts of the Rapture.

Bedrock, south of Paradox, has a landmark general store. It's a two-story building of bricks and timber, with a porch sporting a pay phone and an ad for Dad's Old-Fashioned Root Beer. There's also a post office, established in 1883, that operates from a storage shed whose conveniences, such as they are, include an outdoor privy.

A dog indulged in a midmorning nap on the porch. After so much emptiness, I was delighted to see another creature, even a four-legged one. He snapped gently to attention when he heard the car's tires, as sociable as could be. I couldn't identify his breed—maybe he was a mongrel. He was black with a white chest and one white paw. I'd have called him Blackie.

The Bedrock store had an old-fashioned flavor like Dad's and a woodstove, not quite potbellied, that threw a welcome heat. I warmed my hands over it while Blackie nuzzled my ankle. He obviously had the run of the place.

Rose, the store's owner, acted shy initally, and I attributed it to her isolation, but she corrected me. All through the spring and summer, rock climbers and mountain bikers kept her plenty busy. They stayed overnight in a string of huts, and her store was the first they reached in four days. This year, too, the Dolores River, now almost dry, raged with snowmelt and attracted rafters by the score.

"I had no time for anything," Rose told me. She's from Iowa, a slender, direct, well-educated woman. "I've been so busy I just finished reading a book somebody gave me last Christmas."

"What brought you to Bedrock in the first place?"

"After college, I thought about graduate school, but it didn't sound right," she said, "so I joined a tree-planting crew in Minnesota instead. I met some wild and crazy guys from Moab there, and they got me to come out to Utah."

Though she liked Moab, she was restless and moved on. For a time, she lived in Marin County, one of my old California haunts, and worked as a private health caregiver for an invalid. She plays the guitar and writes songs, and still regretted the opportunities she missed while there.

"What's the name of that famous club in Mill Valley?" she asked.

"The Sweetwater?"

"That's it. That's where I wish I'd performed."

She returned to Moab eventually and hooked up with a man who dreamed of owning a country store. They bought the Bedrock place together, but the reality of the situation failed to match her partner's fantasy. He couldn't handle being so far away from civilization, Rose said, so he was back in Moab again, and she had listed the store for sale, although not just to anybody. She'd be picky about the new owner.

"Where will you go when it's sold?"

"Up there." She nodded to a slope behind the store. "I've got a house on two acres. It already has a well dug."

I admitted to being taken aback. "What'll you do with yourself?"

"Play my guitar. Work on my music, and write some more songs."

Blackie escorted me to the car, and I patted his head. He was a terrific dog, really, and probably had no desire to leave Bedrock, either. Home is where the heart is, as the old saw has it, but it wouldn't surprise me if Rose took off for Sacramento or Seattle someday. Lives out West may be more adventurous, but they're also more risky and complicated.

If you mention Sagebrush Jack or Swayback Johnny in La Sal, Utah, you'll surely draw a blank, but they were as gifted as Seabiscuit and Secretariat in their day, two of the fastest cow ponies ever to compete in the match races the valley's ranchers conducted in the 1880s to relieve their boredom.

The ranchers had earned a fortune by selling their steers for thirty-five dollars a head in Colorado rather than ten dollars at home, and in the absence of any fun other than whiskey, they gambled with a passion and sometimes combined to bet as much as seventy-five thousand dollars on a single race.

The Paiutes put an end to the frivolity with their frequent raids, and a gang of rustlers called Robbers Roost later caused so much consternation that the ranchers gave up cattle for sheep and then gave up altogether. As westerners will do, they left town, moved to Coyote, changed the name to La Sal, and started over.

I traveled through La Sal on my way to Moab over Highway 191, skirting Manti-La Sal National Forest, with its rolling ridges of conifers. The red rock country of the Colorado Plateau gradually revealed itself, layers of sandstone and shale compacted over centuries. Though red is the dominant color, you can pick out shades of salmon, pale orange, blue-gray, and even streaks of yellow and purple in the various cliffs and slopes.

Hole N" the Rock, just south of Moab, restored my confidence, all but vanished, in the tenacity of roadside attractions. If you've ever thought about living in a cave, the former home of Albert and Gladys Christensen could be your proving ground. It took Albert twelve years to hollow it out. He carted away fifty thousand cubic feet of sandstone between 1945 and 1957, the year he died of a heart attack.

Albert also considered himself an artist. His masterpiece, they say, is the *Sermon on the Mount*, but his paintings of Jesus are just as masterful. So, too, is the head of FDR he sculpted into a wall. Gladys collected dolls and helped with the rock and cactus garden. The petting zoo came into being after she'd departed, I believe, but I gather she would have approved.

The scruffy fringe of Moab, once the world's uranium capital, soon came into view. A strong wind was blowing again, raising more dust devils that twirled across the desert, but the chill of Bedrock was gone. Instead a relentless sun burned through the thin, clear air.

I'd visited Moab once long ago and remembered it as a gritty town where a chance remark in the wrong bar could cost you a few teeth. The Atlas Uranium Mine was still in business then, but it went bust in 1984 and pitched the city into a deep depression that subsided only when Moab reinvented itself and banked its future on tourism.

The strategy worked almost too well, coinciding by accident with a growing interest in outdoor activities. Moab is nothing if not scenic, and its mild winters coupled with the reliable sunshine drew buyers looking for a second or even a third home, just as in the Colorado Rockies. The city commands top dollar as a destination resort now, so resentful locals have been priced out of the market in the same way.

I've never felt so old as I did in Moab. If Pistone's in Falls Church had fostered the illusion that I was a spring chicken, Moab plucked the feathers and fitted the chicken with thirty-pound weights on its scrawny legs. Everyone in town appeared to be twenty-five or under, and they were fit, tanned, and very attractive in a healthy, granola-fed way, although they refused to preen about it. So much physical superiority was on display it would be absurd to crow about one's own.

In need of sustenance after instantly aging, I doddered, or so it seemed, to the Rio Grill, where Utah's weird liquor laws denied my need. To order a drink, I'd have to pay four dollars to join a private club, even though I'd be leaving Moab tomorrow. Moreover, I couldn't ask for a double, only a single dispensed by a metered device at exactly one ounce per serving. You can't call for your second drink until you finish the first, either. It's illegal.

The bartender, under twenty-five, explained all this. "You could have a beer at the Moab Brewery without becoming a member," he suggested, without specifying the reason why.

The Moab Brewery proved to be a very citadel of youth, and its customers affected a style peculiar to the city, wearing their hair shaggy and their expensive designer shades perched on the crown of a ballcap or a knit cap even indoors. It was the North Face catalog come to life, then given a red rock twist.

Every table in the place was occupied, as were the chairs at the bar. After a brief wait, a pretty young brunette showed me to a seat next to a pretty young blonde. On my other side were a mom and dad trying to ferret out whether their son might be gay.

"We thought you were seeing someone," the dad stated flatly, disappointment coloring his voice.

"I am."

"Why couldn't you bring her along?"

"She's not here." The son sounded annoyed. "She's backpacking."

"By herself?"

"No, with her dog."

He changed the subject to mountain biking, clearly his one true love. Jill, the pretty blonde, was also a biker. She wore a splint on an index finger and an elaborate bandage that ran halfway up her wrist. She held the hand close to her face and inspected the dressing minutely, as if she couldn't figure out how it got there.

"Have an accident?" I asked.

"Yeah!" she chirped, waking up. "It's dislocated!"

"Does it hurt?"

"Not anymore! They gave me some pills at the hospital."

Maybe that accounted for her intense scrutiny. "How did it happen?"

"I fell into a snowbank at Geyser Peak!" Geyser Peak winter trailhead starts at an altitude of about ten thousand feet. If Lewis and Clark were still around, they'd have wanted Jill on their team.

I ordered a Scorpion Ale and some fish tacos, pleased once again to be eating real food. Fish tacos and other "gourmet" dishes were frowned upon as being elitist on talk radio, another aspect of the unstated and perhaps unconscious attempt to convince listeners that America should be the land of lowered expectations.

The evening was mild enough for an after-dinner stroll. When the sun went down, the temperature would take a radical dip toward freezing, though. Autumn in the desert can bring daily swings of fifty degrees or more. I walked by a park where two peewee football clubs were butting heads, then up a path into a canyon, just like that. Ten minutes later, I sat on a ledge and watched the twilight colors spill across Moab. What a marvel is the West.

ANOTHER CLEAR, BRIGHT desert morning. The temperature, as predicted, had dropped severely. It was only in the mid-thirties when I reached Slickrock Trail, high above the city, where the sandstone took on a fiery glow when the sun first struck it. The snow I'd worried about in Ouray had fallen in Grand Junction the night before, in fact.

Despite the early hour, bikers clustered in a parking lot and geared up to tackle the trail, a 10.6-mile loop that attracts more than one hundred thousand visitors a year. Only horses find the rocks slick. Their metal shoes don't offer enough traction, but bike tires grip the stone and let riders careen around at improbable angles, as if freed from gravity's limits. Faith in Friction and Steep Creep, two sections of the trail, accurately describe the riders' maneuvers.

The bikers were all under twenty-five, naturally, except for Mike and Wendy Graham, two middle-aged Californians who own a ranch in Santa Paula. They were Slickrock veterans, having been to Moab a number of times.

"Is the trail as dangerous as they say?" I asked. I'd read some devastating accounts of accidents.

"You can make of it what you will," Mike felt. He meant your chances of a fall are directly related to the amount of care you exercise. An avid outdoorsman, he started as a rock climber and has no use for physical activities that don't entail a challenge. Hiking bores him silly, for instance. He and Wendy came late to mountain biking, taking it up as a family sport with their kids.

"The girls wanted no part of it to begin with." Wendy brushed a lock of hair from her forehead. "But the boys loved it."

"They're eager to go faster and harder," Mike said approvingly. "The more rugged the terrain, the better they like it."

The Grahams can afford to indulge their hobby. Mike had sold his company, a clothing manufacturer, almost ten years ago, and he and Wendy had been coasting along and enjoying themselves ever since, practically an un-American attitude toward being wealthy. People who cash out usually feel compelled to try to repeat their success in a different field. We're not very good at what the Italians call *dolce far niente*—how sweet it is to do nothing, although the "nothing" is really an indefinable something everybody craves.

Because he had owned a small business, Mike said, he'd been a life-long Republican, but not this November.

"I'm voting for Obama," he told me. "He's a smart man. We need to improve ourselves in the eyes of the rest of the world."

Never once in the heartland did I hear that sentiment expressed, precisely the words Nicolas Sarkozy spoke to Condoleezza Rice at their first meeting when she inquired, "What can I do for you?" In the eyes of the world, we'd sunk to a nadir, but that seemed not to matter to those with an insular cast of mind.

"Governments ought to work together," Mike went on, checking his bike a last time. "Not squabble."

Then he and Wendy took off to cycle Slickrock, a round-trip of about four hours at an average pace. I hiked to a ridge for a view of the trail and saw a campsite that would have done Robert Baden-Powell proud. The campers, sequestered in a tiny tent, were prepared for a long stay. They'd laid in propane tanks for cooking, cases of bottled water, reams of toilet paper, a generator for electricity, dirt bikes to escape should Mad Max breeze through, and plenty of food.

A big bearded guy in Jockeys and a sweatshirt lifted the tent flap as I passed by. He'd only just emerged from the cocoon of his sleeping bag and seemed befuddled to see another human being. "Got to pee," he mumbled.

"You go right ahead. I'll look the other way."

" 'Preciate it."

Tim came from Arizona, and I'd guessed his plan correctly. He and his girlfriend intended to stay put for another couple of weeks until the really cold weather drove them away. They'd rented a Jeep in Moab to carry up their provisions and rode to town as necessary to restock the larder.

Every morning, they biked a trail before the sun kindled the sandstone— Hurrah Pass, Negro Bill Canyon, Mill Canyon Dinosaur, they'd done them all and kept a log of their hairiest adventures, such as the time Tim almost lost it on Porcupine Rim.

"Porcupine Rim." The girlfiend shook her head in wonder. "That was awesome."

"Porcupine Rim is deadly, man," Tim agreed.

When I sought a second opinion on Slickrock's dangers, he offered to loan me a bike to ride the practice loop, a mere 2.3 miles. I'd done enough biking in California to accept, especially after I borrowed a helmet from Tim's girl, whose head was considerably smaller than his basketball-size noggin.

I proceeded with caution. I expected the rock to be slippery, regardless of what I'd heard. It *feels* slick to the touch, but the tires did grip it firmly as promised. The practice loop, rumored to be much easier than the main trail, still demanded an effort, at least from me. Twice I dismounted to walk the bike over tricky downhill patches, but I managed to complete the ride and won back some of the years Moab had earlier robbed from me.

ARCHES NATIONAL PARK was a bad idea. I should have skipped it. I'd visited it before and, besides, I was starting to share Steinbeck's aversion to such places. Because Arches is largely about the spectacular scenery, the traffic backs up as it does at Shenandoah, and you're often stuck behind some gapers in an RV or, worse, tailed by a fiend using the park to enact his or her Grand Prix fantasies.

The views are undeniably stunning, as are the geological formations, but they're only rocks in the end. What enlivened the landscape for me and gave it some human resonance was John Wesley Wolfe's old ranch by Delicate Arch.

Wolfe, a Civil War vet with a bad leg, came West from Etna, Ohio, with his son Fred in search of a drier, more salubrious climate, and acquired a one-hundred-acre tract near Salt Wash in the late 1880s. He had enough water and grass for cattle, and lived in a one-room, dirt-floored cabin so hideously filthy and primitive that his married daughter Flora Stanley almost keeled over when she joined him eight years later with her husband and two children.

Flora put down her foot, so the menfolk harvested some cotton-woods along the Colorado River and built a new cabin with a real floor and one little window for light. The cabin looks like the frailest of gestures in the enormity of all that space, and yet there it stands more than a century later. At first glance it suggests an extraordinarily harsh life for its occupants, but then you realize that the simple fact of *being* alive was once enough to satisfy most people.

It satisfied John Wesley Wolfe, anyway, and had the desired effect on his health. He sold the ranch in 1910 and went back to Etna, where he died at age eighty-four.

The wind screamed through the park that afternoon. Hiking up Delicate Arch Trail, I ate so much grit I turned on my heel after a mile or so. My eyes stung, and my cherished Paints cap blew off my head and skittered across the desert. I packed it in then and started north toward U.S. 50 with no real goal in mind, obeying the traveler's eternal injunction—when in doubt, keep moving.

Past Devil's Garden near the far tip of Arches, big swaths of white sand replaced the familiar red rock. At Brendel, I swung west and stopped in Green River, as dead as the proverbial doornail. The river wouldn't float an inner tube in late October, much less a crowd of rafters, and the fabled watermelons had all been picked. An oil rig pecked at the dirt. Green River felt geriatric after Moab, a pensioner limping toward oblivion.

Ray's and Ben's vied for diners in what passed for downtown. Ben's was closed, so I chose Ray's by default, stepping around four Hispanics involved in a make-work project. They were creating something from cement—a curb, maybe, or a square of pavement. The work went slowly, but they didn't seem to care. It was work, after all, and it paid better than farm labor.

Ray's was a classic tavern, with a long bar and booths along a wall. I joined two other customers. The comely woman bartender seized on me the way a thirsty prospector falls on a watering hole and handed over a menu. The burger cost $8.50—Manhattan prices in the middle of nowhere! I settled for peanuts and a beer. The bartender grunted, not quite so comely anymore.

When in doubt, et cetera. Thirty minutes in Green River is quite enough unless the river's running.

U.S. 50 soon blended with Interstate 70, a six-lane highway connecting Cove Fort, Utah, with Baltimore. Between Green River and Salina, a distance of 110 miles, there are no services or towns. When planners first proposed I-70 in 1956, the media dubbed it the "road to nowhere" because it traversed so much uninhabited country. It winds through a dizzying array of land forms so various and striking that one's consciousness of the earth's incredible diversity expands.

The San Rafael Swell, a dome-shaped anticline, initiates the magnificence. Fifty miles long and thirty wide, it's an uplift of buttes and mesas cut through with deep gorges. There are cliffs, too, and canyons and slickrock. Again the colors mesmerize—reds, rusts, shadowy purples. The highway snakes into a tunnel, then erupts into the light with the force of a revelation. You can't think beyond what's happening. Even a dabbler in psychotropics would recognize the sensation.

The yellowish sandstone becomes more pronounced around Fremont Junction. Another ascent begins when you cross the Muddy River, a climb through Fishlake National Forest. Trees appear, the first in ages or so it seems, and look strangely Edenic—firs and spruces higher up, and aspens and cottonwoods along the streams.

On the forest's western edge lies Salina, named for the salt deposits Mormon pioneers discovered in 1861. They found lots of anthracite, too, and coal is still the town's chief source of revenue, trucked to refineries rather than loaded on trains ever since a flood washed away the railroad tracks in the 1980s. Some livestock, a turkey processing plant, a Latter-Day Saints chapel—that's Salina in a nutshell.

Evening caught me out, or I might never have stayed there. Though my motel was almost empty, the owner treated me rudely, as if I had infringed on her privacy by being a guest. She took down every scrap of information as well, including my home phone in Dublin, a foreign entry that increased her suspicion. If I figured a way to act up in Salina, a challenge that would have foiled Led Zeppelin in their prime, she'd have called the sheriff for sure.

I violated a rule of Nelson Algren's that night and ate at Mom's Cafe, the only game in town, but I did not play cards with a man named Doc or sleep with anyone whose troubles were worse than my own, as Algren had advised.

Mom's was not exactly buzzing. The temptation to rest one's head on the table and go to sleep was ever present. The café served no alcohol, of course, so my desire for a drink with dinner, ordinarily in the high normal range, turned acute.

After the meal, I located a state-run liquor store and bought a six-pack to accompany the first game of the World Series between the Phillies and Tampa Bay. The motel's off-brand TV needed some adjusting—a couple of brisk smacks, that is—before it delivered a clear picture.

The patriotic pregame show, virtually required by law, did not surprise me, but I couldn't believe the ugly behavior of the Devil Rays' fans, who hooted and razzed and rang bells and waved banners and sweatshirts to distract the Phils' pitcher and disrupt his rhythm. Maybe I'd been away too long, but the mayhem rattled me in the same way the Palin rally did—the American masses, our face to the world.

IN NEW MEXICO, while camped on the Continental Divide toward the end of his journey, Steinbeck confronted a moment of truth. Beneath the "cut glass stars," he confessed that he'd been pushing himself lately, pounding out the miles without hearing or seeing very much. Each hill he passed looked like the last. He felt helpless to assimilate his impressions, overstuffed with them, and he'd lost interest in talking with strangers and just exchanged monosyllables.

I had a similar experience in Salina. Though I hadn't yet tired of meeting people and being charmed or offended by them, I'd grown weary of long-distance roads, particularly the lonely ones, and there were more to come. From the Sevier Valley, U.S. 50 ran north to Delta and then west across some scrubby desert to Nevada and the Great Basin, where for the next 286 miles the highway is officially known as the "loneliest road in America."

That was one lonely road too many. Moreover, I'd traveled it once and knew what I'd find—defunct mining camps, tumbleweeds, lizards, a house or two of ill repute, and an assortment of cantankerous old dudes far too eager to tell you the stories they've told a thousand times before. On the other hand, the southwestern route to California was new to me, attractively green and timbered in my atlas, with towns all along it to the Arizona border, so I decided to scrap U.S. 50 for good.

The moderately liberal and progressive atmosphere in Moab was the exception rather than the rule in Utah, though, a state almost all white, 70 percent Mormon, and so dyed-in-the-wool Republican that in 2004 not a single county preferred John Kerry to George W. Bush.

This was a troubled Utah, reeling from the economy's collapse. In the Salt Lake City metro area, entire subdivisions were being foreclosed, and many frantic owners were selling short for less than they owed the bank. The ski resorts were singing the blues even before a snowflake had fallen, certain that a vacation on the slopes would be among the first luxuries cash-strapped citizens would sacrifice. On the radio, I heard that the folks in Utah increasingly depended on antidepressants, although—as the talk-show host pointed out—Mormons don't permit themselves the solace of alcohol.

One blogger made light of the report and posted a comment: "I've been in Salt Lake for a year and a half now. Anyone got some Zoloft they can spare?"

Came the reply: "Get it yourself. I don't have the energy."

The towns on my route had little to offer beyond LDS-related activities and the wonders of the great outdoors. Richfield, once a farming community, had become a hospitality center for motorists on the interstate. Elsinore, Joseph, and Fort Cove were links on the Mormon Corridor. Beaver's native sons included Philo T. Farnsworth and Butch Cassidy, but that was scarcely reason enough to spend the night.

Cedar City, larger and yet no less tedious, rested on the fringe of the Mojave Desert beneath a rim of reddish sandstone. By rights it should be called Juniper City. When Brigham Young dispatched the pioneers who founded it in 1851, they mixed up their trees, but they did find some iron, and mining enriched the local coffers into the 1980s.

As I cruised the downtown streets, I passed four police cars in ten minutes, ready to protect me from myself. I checked into a motel, and put a pillow over my head until dinnertime. An uncanny stroke of luck led me to Cafe Orleans, a Cajun place with an excellent jambalaya that lacked only a cold Pearl beer to achieve perfection.

The chef had lived in Louisiana, my server told me, and still made forays there to buy ingredients such as andouille that he couldn't get in Cedar City. She was an affable college student about to embark on an LDS missionary effort in Boston and very anxious about it. She'd never left Utah before, or been separated from her parents.

"I think I'll like it," she said tentatively.

"Oh, you will," I encouraged her, although I had my doubts about such missions, and felt put upon when anyone knocked on my door to try and sell me on a religion. "There are lots of students in Boston. You'll make new friends."

"I hope so."

I uttered a few more words of polite reassurance, then retreated into the drowsiness of the Cedar City night.

WHAT ELDERLY AMERICANS want when they retire, apparently, are sunshine and golf, both of which St. George, Utah, supplies in abundance. It's another Mormon enclave in the high desert, where Brigham Young's followers once grew cotton. The land sprouts subdivisions now, particularly for seniors.

St. George has more golf courses per capita than any other city and receives only eight inches of precipitation a year. Though July and August can be hellish, with an average high of 102 and 100 degrees respectively, that doesn't keep the golden agers away.

In the past decade, St. George has added about twenty-five thousand residents, making it one of the fastest-growing spots in the country along with Las Vegas, 110 miles away. Even Mesquite, Nevada, once a dull patch of sand across the Arizona border, has benefited from the spillover effect. About half of St. George's population is over forty-five, and Mesquite's is probably older based on what I observed during a brief spin.

Mesquite sits above the northern tip of Lake Mead, where a dam impounds the Colorado and also the Virgin River, formerly a scourge that flooded out the town three times. As a planned community, it has an inorganic feel. It's a very strange place, abnormally normal. Its motto goes, "Escape, Momentarily," not much use if you're on the lam.

The architects of Mesquite must have studied Sedona, Arizona, because the resemblance is close, but the real estate isn't nearly as expensive. A tiny condo, slightly bigger than a motel room, costs less than $50,000, while a decent if unfancy house is only $150,000 or so, a mere pittance to the clever Californians who unloaded their overpriced homes before the market crashed.

Everywhere in Mesquite I saw healthy-looking seniors committing exercise. They jogged, power-walked, swam, and whacked golf balls at a driving range. Tanned and attired in colorful leisure wear, they were enveloped in a glow of well-being, suggesting wise investments that had miraculously eluded the shredder. It wouldn't be bad living here, I thought. Just, well, strange.

For the indolent few, the gaming tables beckoned. At the Eureka Hotel and Casino, the front door bore a stenciled warning: NO WEAPONS OR FIREARMS PERMITTED. A small, devoted group of zombies were diddling the slots at ten in the morning, while I took advantage of the air-conditioning. On October 24, the mercury had already zoomed into the low nineties.

The desert between Mesquite and Las Vegas was a "great and mysterious wasteland, a sun-punished place," as John Steinbeck aptly put it when he drove across the Mojave. Signs dotted the raw, unpromising land, crying LOTS FOR SALE!, as if a sucker truly was born every minute.

Like Los Angeles, Las Vegas belonged to the night. By day, the city center was a repellent, smoggy clash of highways and mismatched highrises, where frustrated drivers worked out their pent-up aggression. The tension in Clark County, an epicenter of the subprime crisis, was tangible. Almost all Nevada's foreclosures, the most anywhere in the United States, had occurred there. The banks were slowly taking possession of the county.

Soon I was trapped in traffic and trying to find the Excalibur, not my hotel of choice but the hotel I'd chosen, anyway, because of its bargain deals and my depleted bankroll. It had escaped my notice that the Excalibur deemed itself family-oriented and would be crawling with kids. The Camelot Steakhouse, Roundtable Buffet, and Sherwood Forest Café were among my dining options.

The schlock is inevitable, of course, but once you look past it, the reason for Vegas's popularity even during a recession becomes clear. For the same price as a Moab motel, I rented a room with a marble bath, a forty-two-inch TV, and a splendid view of the city. Access to a first-rate pool and spa were included in the package.

Although I'd been to Las Vegas before, I never really understood it. I'd always been quick to belittle it for the obvious reasons, but on my travels I'd seen how desolate and absent of culture and even simple entertainment so much of America can be. The genius of Vegas was to create a twenty-four-hour playground where bored grow-ups could indulge their childlike impulses, a playground that synthesized all the branding and franchising and brought them to a logical conclusion.

Vegas was a giant suburb posing as a city, or perhaps a city posing as a giant mall. You move about over trams, walkways, and escalators that connect one casino to the next, so that you occupy a kind of rarefied space far above the ordinary cares and woes confined to the wretched pit of existence below.

If you want to live dangerously and try some Thai food, you can give it a go, but almost every hotel features a food court with such staples as McDonald's, Burger King, Krispy Kreme, and so on. Vegas on a budget is just like home except a million times more exciting, alight with neon and vibrating to a recognizable tune. The gambling almost seems beside the point, but that *is* the point, of course, and the drinks are on the house.

At sundown, Las Vegas began to gather its energies, waking from the torpor of the afternoon. The indigo sky masked the smog, and the seductive desert air caressed your skin and made you feel sexy. Everywhere couples were holding hands or locked in an embrace, and I realized how infrequently I'd witnessed any public displays of affection on my journey. The couples lent a sweetness to the night. Imagine the romance of a weekend at the Excalibur for some newlyweds from Olney, Illinois.

I played roulette for a half hour, but my heart wasn't in it, and that killed any chance of winning, as every gambler knows. Gambling demands a purity of intent and a belief that the planets are aligned in your favor or else you're finished, so I circulated instead until a chunky woman from Boise intercepted me. She'd caught the scent of romance and was maniacally pursuing it with a friend in tow.

"We're missing her husband!" she blurted. She'd put a dent in somebody's bottle of scotch. "Have you seen him?"

"What does he look like?"

"Tall, dark, and handsome!" She laughed uproariously and tapped her friend's forearm. "Just kidding!"

"Where's your husband?"

"I don't have one, and I don't want one. I'm in the mood for some fun."

I beat a hasty retreat and escaped into the simulacra of New York-New York where, as serendipity would have it, I found a faux pub called Nine Fine Irishmen. A singer was belting out a passable version of "Galway Girl," and the Guinness, though a pale imitation of the real black stuff in Dublin, went down smoothly enough.

Patrick and Sean Conway were seated at the bar, brothers from Syracuse. They were familiar with Ireland and had visited Easky, near Sligo, where their family had roots. The talk made me lonely for Imelda, and when I expressed this to the Conways and told them about my project, they were sympathetic.

"*On the Road.* What a great book!" Sean exclaimed, skipping so briskly over John Steinbeck I felt slighted on his behalf. "There's something about the way Kerouac writes."

"I've been working on a novel for five years," Patrick confided, although he paid the bills by operating a company with Sean that makes a fingerprint-activated locking device. "I majored in English."

"I did history," Sean said.

"We're proud of our company," Patrick continued. "Syracuse is dead, and we contribute something. We treat our employees well, and they get good benefits."

"Who's older?" I asked Sean.

"Patrick is. We've got a sister in the middle. She's a terrible liberal."

Politics had reared its sneaky head again. The Conways were sick of the presidential campaign and tired of the pundits milking it for profit. They'd already decided what they were going to do, anyway. Patrick would cast a protest vote for Bob Barr, while Sean liked John McCain.

"I'm anti-abortion," he explained.

"Obama's a nonstarter." Patrick drained his pint. "It'll mean higher taxes. He'll redistribute the wealth." I switched the topic to the gaming tables.

"We've been playing blackjack. I'm down five hundred," Sean owned up. "That's it for me. That's the limit I agreed on with my wife." He glanced slyly at his brother. "Of course, Patrick might lend me some money."

I parted with the Conways, two fine Irishmen, and wandered through the casino. In the mood for a nightcap, I found a quieter bar conducive to rumination. Banks of TVs loomed above the rows of bottles, each tuned to a football game or Fox News. It had been the same in almost every restaurant, tavern, motel breakfast room, and convenience store, always the TVs and sports or Fox News.

The balm of the desert air. As I walked into it, I spotted Sean and Patrick at a blackjack table intently studying the hand they'd been dealt.

WHEN DON LAUGHLIN was a teenager, he worked as a fur trapper in Minnesota and used his earnings to buy slot machines and install them in hunting lodges. Soon he was bringing in five hundred bucks a week, enough to encourage any ambitious youth to neglect his studies. That wasn't lost on his school principal, who ordered Laughlin to get busy or take a hike.

Laughlin took a hike. In the late 1950s, he relocated to Las Vegas and bought the 101 Club casino and sold it in 1964, the same year he became attracted to the potential of the desert between Bullhead City and Kingman, Arizona, and Needles, California, a prime stop on Route 66. Subsequently, he acquired a funky, eight-room motel and six-plus acres on the Colorado River. Davis Dam, built in 1951, would supply the water to spur further development, he believed.

In the early days, Laughlin's big draw, aside from gambling, was a ninety-eight-cent chicken dinner. From such humble origins, he created an empire with the Riverside Resort Hotel and Casino as its linchpin. Laughlin, Nevada, is a low-key version of Las Vegas now, laid-back rather than insistently blowing its own horn, and its founder, currently in his late seventies, still likes to shake hands and work the room.

I drove Highway 95 to Laughlin, my last stop before California. ATVs and dirt bikes were carving up the desert, while hang gliders floated above it. This was an ugly stretch of country, ragged and punch-drunk, sizzling under the burning sun and pressed into service as a dumping ground for unmentionable substances. To survive here, you'd need the scaly hide of a reptile.

A late breakfast in Searchlight. The town's gold mines once made it bigger and richer than Vegas, but it had sunk into the bargain basement. At the lightly patronized, infernally smoky casino, a plate of eggs, toast, and hash browns cost less than a fiver, leaving some change for the slots.

Here was the material for a novel by James M. Cain or, better, Jim Thompson. Somewhere on the premises a hot blonde lurked, applying crimson lipstick and fingering her husband's insurance policy as she waited for a drifter to propel the murderous plot into motion.

Laughlin gratified me with its homey style. I hardly gambled at all. Instead I took long walks on a lovely path by the Colorado, where palms grew amid orange and lime trees to create a faint essence of the tropics.

The river, wide and deep here, begins as snowmelt in the Rockies, then flows for 1,140 miles through 3 deserts before emptying into the Sea of Cortez. Without it, there'd be no West as we know it—33 reservoirs, 990 miles of pipes, 345 diversion dams, 50 power plants, and 14,950 miles of canals.

On Sunday I attended Mass in Don's Celebrity Theater at the Riverside. I'd been meaning to go to church all along, mainly because John Steinbeck had put churches on his short list of things to do. He only mentioned a service once, though, in New England, where a John Knox preacher subjected him to a fire-and-brimstone sermon.

"He spoke of hell as an expert, not the mush-mush hell of these soft days," said the chastened traveler, "but a well-stoked, white-hot hell served by technicians of the first order."

The Celebrity Theater, with a bingo parlor and a Mexican restaurant for neighbors, seemed an unlikely venue. Only the night before, the country star Lynn Anderson had entertained there. The aged congregation sat at marble-topped tables at the foot of a stage-cum-altar decorated exactly like Wayne Smith's barbershop—a cardboard John Wayne, a cow skull, wagon wheels, and so on.

Over some loudspeakers, a taped voice recited the rosary ad infinitum until the Mass proper started with a hymn and a pair of readings from the Bible, after which Father Charles Urnick took charge. Round-faced and genial, he belonged to the school of priests who prefer to praise rather than berate. His parishioners clearly loved him. They were silent and respectful, hanging on his every word.

His past week had been blessed, Father Urnick began. Several friends had returned from trips with gifts for him. He'd received maple syrup from Vermont and Gouda cheese from Holland.

The blessings didn't stop there, either. He'd also been treated to a revitalizing massage and invited to dinner seven times, once for a fantastic supper of lobster and portobello mushrooms. Never before had I been hungry in church, but the Lord works in mysterious ways, as my mother used to say.

"I met my friend Billy for breakfast, too," Father Urnick went on, twinkly-eyed. "He has a demanding infant at home, and he was grateful to be out. Billy said to me, 'Father, this is the first meal in a long time where nobody's thrown food at me or pulled on my glasses'"—a pregnant pause—"so I reached out and pulled on his glasses."

That earned some appreciative chortles from the audience, each of whom had no doubt learned a different lesson from the anecdote. It was one of those capacious vignettes that could be interpreted variously. I'd still be pondering its meaning days later in the Mojave.

Father Urnick segued into a mention of the election and alluded to all the laws voters had to decide on. For a moment, I thought he'd endorse a candidate for president, but he was just setting up a routine that let him enumerate some of the strange laws already on the books.

"In Hood River, Oregon," he said, "you can't juggle without a license. In Memphis, you can't share your pie or take it away. In Las Vegas, you can't hock your dentures. In Alabama, you can't wear a fake mustache to church. In Alaska, you can't give any alcohol to a moose. In Minnesota, you're not allowed to tease a skunk. And in Chicago, you can't fish in your pajamas."

The routine sparked as much laughter as might be permissible during a religious ceremony. Father Urnick had done an excellent job of softening us up for his brief sermon. His message was simple and succinct—no fire-and-brimstone. The love of God is never outdated, he reminded us, and if we paid attention to that love, we'd be rewarded, although not necessarily in material terms.

That was a fine Mass, I thought afterward as I walked by the Colorado again. The pope might not approve of Father Urnick's casual style, but his upbeat, tenderhearted manner worked for me. I was far too aware of my own sins and shortcomings to enjoy being chastised for them. If I had to do some penance in the afterlife, should there be one, I'd rather not know in advance. You can't go wrong, really, with a service devoted to love and laughter.

IN CALIFORNIA, YOU learn to expect the unexpected. No sooner had I crossed over from Nevada than two high-pocket cowboys on horseback rode out of a cloud of dust near Needles. They were dressed like movie extras in their chaps and spurs, and when they held up a hand to stop traffic and slipped between cars to a ramshackle bikers' tavern, the younger one smiled and tipped his hat as gracefully as Gene Autry. The time was ten-thirty-eight A.M, and the temperature was ninety-six degrees.

Nobody in Needles bellyached about the heat. You might as well complain about having fingers and toes. People just shrugged and dealt with it as usual. The air conditioners and swamp coolers were already cranked up to the max, issuing a faintly audible hum like a new species of desert insect. The town was notorious as a blast furnace. On TV, the weather forecasters often invoked it as a symbol of the inferno.

"Think it's been hot in Van Nuys?" they'd ask. "Try Needles, where the mercury hit a hundred and twelve degrees today!"

I drove by fruit stands stacked with juicy Valencia oranges from local orchards and listened to a Bob Wills CD appropriate to the terrain. Across the Colorado, the spiky rocks called "needles" stood out against a soiled-looking sky. Cotton grew in tufted patches near irrigation ditches. Nothing much was going on that quiet Monday, so I saw no reason to linger.

Before leaving Laughlin, I'd mapped out a route for my last week. It led across the Mojave to Barstow, then through the San Joaquin Valley and over the Cholame Hills to Paso Robles, where I'd follow Highway 101 north along the Coast Range into the heart of Steinbeck country and go on from there to my own home ground in the San Francisco Bay Area.

John Steinbeck knew the Mojave well. In his youth, the crossing could be so terrifying, he recalled in *Travels*, that one whispered a prayer on departing. There were no gas stations and certainly no cell phones, and if your car broke down, you were out of luck unless an angel of mercy came along.

The desert "tested a man for endurance and constancy to prove whether he was good enough to get to California"—the very test Steinbeck inflicted on the Joads of Oklahoma.

Interstate 40 slashes through the desert now, so I highballed it to Barstow. Along the way I saw boxcars, tumbleweeds, creosote, mesquite, sagebrush, a junked fridge, cattle bones, and enough roadkill to feed a family of eight. I stopped just once at a rest area, where some Native Americans—Mojaves, I believe—were selling bracelets and necklaces of semiprecious stones.

These Native Americans were the most blasé merchants I'd ever met. Half asleep, really, with their eyelids drooping. They didn't seem to care if they sold a single piece of jewelry. Even a compliment elicited no more than a grunt, and when anybody tried to haggle, they merely caved in. Maybe this was just a kind of fatalism, an attitude of resignation that the implacable desert demands.

Barstow was a poor, tired, beaten-down place. Drifters had been filtering into it ever since the railroad first arrived. The streets teemed with lost souls. There were homeless men carrying their possessions in plastic garbage bags, scavengers pushing shopping carts filled with recyclables, drug dealers openly peddling, and winos huddled in alleys. The shame of it could make you weep.

I continued on to Victorville, the hub of the Mojave and the first real city after the 143-mile run from Needles to Barstow. Victorville occupies a minor niche in Hollywood history, having played the fictitious Sand City, Arizona, in *It Came from Outer Space*, a 3-D extravaganza I watched as a boy in 1953, relieved to discover the aliens did not intend to destroy planet Earth. They only wanted to pick up some spare parts for their spaceship.

Supposedly, Victorville has a downtown, but I couldn't find it in the familiar maze of malls and subdivisions, where foreclosures were again common. In one neighborhood, vandals had broken into a vacant house and trashed it, while squatters were living in another. Skateboarders hunted for empty swimming pools, drained by their owners for issues of liability, and used them as skate parks.

All I asked of Victorville in the end was a good night's sleep. The motel clerk assured it by upgrading me to a "junior suite" when she noticed my Dublin address. She was a charming young Latina studying at the local college. Fully a third of the city's occupants are Hispanic, in fact, as are 40 percent of all Californians.

If you wanted a glimpse of America's future, you needed to look no farther than California, where so-called minorities constitute 57 percent of the population. Indeed, one third of all U.S. minorities live in the state, with Asians the largest contingent after Hispanics. According to the projections of the Census Bureau, the country as a whole mimics this trend, so that by 2042, with 1.3 million new immigrants arriving each year, the minorities will become the majority.

The solicitous clerk sent me to Johnny Reb's for dinner, where I tucked into a plate of ribs. The food was okay, but I craved a taste of California, not Alabama—the archetypal California of palm trees and balmy beaches—before I faced the dusty San Joaquin, so I deviated from my recently formulated plan and headed south the next morning to visit a writer pal on the ocean in San Clemente.

I thought of this as a day off—a break from being a stranger. I'd be as lavishly welcomed as Steinbeck and his wife in Texas toward the conclusion of his journey. I kept telling myself this in order to tolerate the sort of ridiculously stressful freeway trip that promotes road rage and random acts of aggression. It was in California, after all, where Jack Nicholson smashed another guy's windshield with a two-iron.

At Corona, I scuttled the freeway for a side road that climbed into Cleveland National Forest, looking out over tinder-dry canyons hungry for the first autumn rain to douse the chance of fires. The air was cooler now and not so heavy with exhaust fumes, and there was a good smell of sun-warmed firs and pines. In ten minutes I'd gone from the clotted suburbs to the habitat of bobcats and mountain lions, another of California's miraculous transformations.

I gradually descended from the heights, rolling through Mission Viejo with its horse ranches and golf courses to San Juan Capistrano, where the cliff swallows, as regular as clockwork, had already flown. Late October marked the conclusion of their tenancy, I heard at a gift shop, but the birds would be back from Argentina on St. Joseph's Day in March. This was said with grave conviction. My leg, I suspect, was being pulled.

The basilica from the old Franciscan mission, built in 1776, is still intact, and so are some adobes of the period. Here the friars planted the state's first vineyard and later added a winery. The Spanish influence was everywhere apparent in the town's architecture, and the same was true in San Clemente, originally a resort modeled on those in coastal Spain, with an identical procession of red tile roofs.

That afternoon, the Pacific was a shimmery blue dream. Even a veteran Californian was inclined to swoon. San Clemente's serious money gravitated to the bluffs above the water, where Richard Nixon used to lift a glass with Bebe Rebozo at La Casa Pacifica, the Western White House. My friend Kem owned a more modest bungalow at Forester Ranch that afforded him a peek at—if not a million-dollar view of—the ocean.

A high-pitched yipping announced my arrival. This was the celebrated Beanie, the canine I'd rejected as Charley's body double. Uli, Kem's partner and Beanie's most ardent admirer, had dressed her little terrier in a fetching camouflage outfit, and I must admit the dog looked fit and ready to join Vin Diesel on a commando raid.

Kem, a native Californian, had grown up in Orange County when it still deserved the name. He remembered the acres of citrus groves, and an ocean so lightly surfed that nobody fought over a wave. He'd bought his place to be close to such surfing hot spots as Trestles and San Onofre Beach, ready to grab his board the instant a southwest swell came up, but on weekends the crowds took over. The water was clean, at least, compared to Malibu and Santa Monica, he said.

He gave me a quick tour of the grounds. His fellow occupants, some retired, were great believers in recreation. They swam in an indoor pool, worked out at a gym, and played shuffleboard, golf, and tennis. When we ran into Hal Book, the ranch foreman, who was supervising a Mexican scouring some grease stains from the concrete in a barbecue area, Kem let it drop that I'd been living in Dublin for a while.

"I was married to an Irish lady for forty-nine years!" Hal piped, embracing me as a kindred spirit. On the odd chance I might be considering a move, he listed the stellar attributes of Forester Ranch. "What do you think, Kem?" he asked. "Isn't this a nice place to live?"

"Yes, it is, Hal," Kem dutifully replied.

"Once a month, we have a pancake breakfast at the community center. Do you like pancakes, Bill?"

"Sure!" I tried to sound punchy and enthusiastic.

"My son loves them. We always hold a contest to see who can eat the most!"

After some more pancake chat, Kem and I drove through rustling palm and eucalyptus trees to the beach, where we watched an incandescent sun sink slowly into the ocean as the gulls squawked and the surf pounded.

Here was a California even a rural Hoosier would recognize, an impossibly seductive land you only half trusted yourself to believe in. It seemed not so much real as invented, scarcely American in its devotion to the purely sensual, yet another country within a country.

FOR MY PLEASURES, I paid a price. To get back on track for the San Joaquin, I faced a battle with Interstate 5 north toward Los Angeles, another freeway of the damned, where you're packed in so tightly among other drivers that you're compelled to eavesdrop on their arguments, often conducted at cross purposes in a fractured English spiced with expletives from many different languages.

Only a mile from San Clemente, I heard a brawny Spanish guy in a plumbing truck shout, "*¡Chinga tu madre!*" at a puzzled Sikh in a Toyota. Of the 37 million Californians, 8 million speak Spanish, 800,000 Chinese, 400,000 Vietnamese, 300,000 Korean, and 150,000 each Japanese, Armenian, and Persian. Add to that a smattering of French, German,

Hebrew, Hindi, Urdu, Navajo, and so on, and the chances of a mis-understanding are incalcuable.

For two hours, I inched forward until the freeway bypassed L.A. and began its climb into the Tehachapi Mountains through the rugged expanse of Los Padres and Angeles national forests. The dry brown foothills were studded with ravines and rocky outcrops, and as the traffic thinned, I reclaimed some of the calm I'd felt by the Pacific.

Cresting Tejon Pass at 4,183 feet, I could see the San Joaquin below me, partially hidden beneath a layer of smog. Along with the Sacramento Valley to the north, it forms the Central Valley, some four hundred miles long and the wealthiest, most productive agricultural region on earth.

California lends itself to statistical analysis, perhaps because of its mind-boggling size. The average U.S. farm or ranch earns about $137,000 in annual commodity sales, while the figure soars to $488,000 in the Central Valley. The state earned $36.6 billion on agriculture in 2008, roughly double the take for Texas and Iowa, the runners up, even though California's 75,000 farms and ranches account for just 4 percent of America's total.

California's farmers supply half the nation's fruits, nuts, and vegetables, and 22 percent of its milk and cream. Grapes are the next most profitable crop after dairying, followed by plants from nurseries and greenhouses, lettuce, and almonds. As amazing as it sounds, every commercially grown almond, artichoke, fig, olive, clingstone peach, persimmon, pomegranate, and walnut in this country has its origins in California

After reading those statistics, one imagines a San Joaquin of hanging gardens and Babylonian splendor, but it's often rawboned, hard-nosed, and just plain unattractive, especially in Kern County.

Oil companies have been tearing up the scrappy, windswept desert since 1864, and the pumpjacks called thirsty birds peck at the wells around the clock. The farm fields are big, broad, industrial-looking, and usually cloaked in a grayish pallor of bad air that's at its most oppressive in Arvin, the smoggiest city in the United States.

At Pumpkin Center, I started east toward Arvin on Route 223, trying to see the land through John Steinbeck's eyes. Some things were still the same—the vineyards and orchards, the cherries, oranges, almonds, carrots, and table grapes—but Arvin has a population of about fourteen thousand now, almost all Hispanic, with Weedpatch as its tiny satellite.

When Steinbeck paid his seminal visit in 1936, driving the old bakery truck that was a forerunner of Rocinante, he recognized a change in the labor force right away. Instead of the Chinese, Japanese, and Filipino men he remembered from his childhood, the farmers were hiring and exploiting the Dust Bowl migrants known pejoratively as Okies, who—unlike their predecessors—brought their families with them and occupied filthy squatters' camps on irrigation ditches or the banks of rivers.

Short of food and lacking any sanitary facilities, the Okies were prey to malnutrition and contagious diseases, and dependent on their undependable jalopies and trucks to carry them from harvest to harvest, a gypsy routine that might last for nine months and win them $400.

Steinbeck, profoundly moved and offended, chronicled their mistreatment in seven articles for the *San Francisco News* in an unvarnished prose he'd later polish to a poetic intensity in *The Grapes of Wrath*.

"The three-year-old child has a gunny sack tied about his middle for clothing," he wrote of one camp. "He has the swollen belly caused by malnutrition. He sits on the ground in the sun in front of the house, and the little black fruit flies buzz in circles and land on his closed eyes and crawl up his nose until he weakly brushes them away.

"They try to get at the mucus in the eye corners. The child seems to have the reactions of a baby much younger. The first year he had a little milk, but he has had none since. He will die in a very short time . . ."

Steinbeck developed a keen ally in the saintly Tom Collins, who ran the Weedpatch camp in Arvin for FDR's Resettlement Administration. Every other week, Collins sent a report to Washington as detailed as an enthnographic bulletin. He recorded oral histories, songs, and snippets of the Okie dialect, and granted his new compatriot access to it all, an invaluable contribution to the novel already brewing.

If any descendants of the Okies still live in Arvin, I saw no trace of them, although I've met people from Bakersfield and Oildale whose ancestors knew the horrors described in *Grapes*. You could easily mistake

the streets in town for Mexico—bodegas, *carnicerias*, and lots of taquerias. There were plenty of children around, too, and young mothers es-
corting broods of two or three little ones, often with another babe in
arms.

Migrants continue to show up for the harvest, some legally and others
on the sly, about six thousand every season. Arvin provides some trailers
for temporary shelter, but most laborers prefer to bunk with relatives or
comrades, flopping at a dumpy apartment and parceling out the rent
among six or eight or twelve men.

A fair number still choose to rough it as the laborers did in the '30s,
sleeping in their cars or even among the oleanders along the highway,
all to save a few more precious dollars to take home when they cross the
border again.

The air was awful that afternoon, almost as thick as the blinding
tule fogs that cling to the valley floor in winter, an amalgam of fumes,
both diesel and gasoline, spewed by farm machinery and the ceaseless
traffic between L.A. and Bakersfield on I-5 and Highway 99. Located
between mountain ranges, Arvin is an ideal trap for the smog. It fails to
meet the federal ozone standard about seventy-five days a year.

The region faced a deadline of 2012 to comply with the federal standard, but the valley's air-quality board had voted in 2007 to extend the
deadline by eleven years in spite of the fact that childhood asthma and
allergies are epidemic in Kern County. Activists accused the board of
not caring about poor Hispanics, a charge with deeper roots than any
orange grove in Arvin.

At a central restaurant—more of a cantina, really, in the hour or so
before dinner—several men were drinking beer and listening to a Flaco
Jimenez CD. I asked for a can of Tecate, probably because a busty babe
in a Tecate T-shirt crooked a finger at me from a poster, and when a
woman brought the can with a basket of tortilla chips and two kinds of
salsa, red and green, I squeezed some lime juice on top and sprinkled it
with salt.

"Hey, you did that right," said a gregarious, dark-skinned Mexican at
an adjacent table. Young and long-haired, he'd already put in a hard
day's work by the look of his clothes.

"Thank you, I guess," I replied with a shrug. "It's not exactly rocket science."

He hadn't heard that old cliche before. He thought it was hilarious and moved over to my table. He'd lived in Arvin for three years and found much to like about it.

"You can make good money, even buy a house sometimes," he said.

"Do you own a house?"

"Nah, it's too early for me. I still spend it on fun."

"Fun in Arvin?" I didn't see much around.

"Some," with a wicked leer. Fun obviously involved muchachas. "But there's more in Bakersfield. Real good nightclubs, man."

"You go there often?"

"Often as I can."

I stared out a window at the bleak sky. "Doesn't the smog bother you?"

He thought that was hilarious, too. "Ever been to Mexico?"

YOU WERE NEVER far from Mexico in the San Joaquin. Lamont, Old River, Valley Acres, Buttonwillow, they all resembled Arvin to a greater or lesser degree. On every side road a little market sold *chicharones, masa harina, queso blanco*, many types of peppers, and always the coldest beer, but the customers shunned such imports as Bohemia and Corona for the novelty and cheaper price of Bud. They wanted to be Americans, although not forever.

Sometimes the markets also sold homemade tamales, the corn husks still warm, and *aqua fresca* and *horchata* that smelled of cinnamon. The salsas were delicious, especially those heaped with cilantro and finely chopped serranos instead of jalapeños. On weekends the restaurants served *menudo*, the tripe stew favored as a hangover cure. I'd seen it in action once, a stuporous man bent over a steaming bowl of offal suddenly jolted back to life.

The Mexico of the San Joaquin stretched all the way from Arvin to Salinas, Steinbeck's birthplace, but I'd stop first in King City, where his grandfather ranched, and Monterey, whose sardine canneries had provided the material for *Cannery Row*.

Route 33 cut between the California Aqueduct and the Temblor

Range—from *temblor de tierra*, Spanish for earthquake. The aqueduct irrigates the valley, and allows crops to flourish in what would otherwise be an unproductive desert. There were fields of cabbages and romaine lettuce, and more vineyards stripped clean of their fruit after the harvest. Stands of eucalyptus formed windbreaks for homesteads down hard-packed, two-track dirt roads.

Outside Lost Hills, I took Route 46 northwest, a lovely ribbon of twists and turns that would foil anybody in a rush. At its junction with Route 41 in Cholame, a sign marked the spot where Donald Turnupseed crashed his 1950 Ford Tudor into James Dean's Little Bastard, the Porsche 550 Spyder that Dean acquired while shooting *Rebel Without a Cause*.

Beyond Cholame, in Whitley Gardens and Estrella, grapevines covered the hills in spritely green rows, the leaves just beginning to wither and die. Paso Robles used to be a buckboard town where the cowhands from Templeton and Santa Margarita whooped it up, but now it's "authentic California," another destination resort with bistros, *enotecas*, and dozens of nearby wineries.

I chose Eberle Winery at random, and met an old friend at the tasting room—a bronze replica of Porcellino, the boar who presides over the straw market in Florence. *Eberle* comes from *eber*, the German for boar. I rubbed Porcellino's snout for luck and tossed a coin into a fountain, then sampled a robust Sangiovese and learned about the harvest. For the third straight year, the yield per acre was smaller than usual, as were the berries and clusters.

"We didn't have much rain this winter." The fellow doing the pouring topped up my glass. "There was a frost in April and another earlier this month. That's how it goes. The grapes came good, anyways."

Late afternoon sunlight flooded the Coast Range as I left, feeling exceedingly mellow after the wine. Chet Baker used to sing a ballad with the refrain "I fall in love too easily, I fall in love too fast," and the lyrics ran through my head just then. Though I'd already forsaken Jeff City for the Colorado Rockies, I was about to transfer my affection once again and surrender to the inescapable allure of an old flame.

For ages, writers have described the Coast Range in autumn as "golden," but the color is more subtle than that, richer and warmer and difficult to pin down exactly. Once you've seen it, it stays with you forever. Almost forty years after my first glimpse of those mountains and foothills, they still spoke to me with the same ardor and directness—"a surge of emotion, a soaring sense of possibility," I scribbled in a notebook as I passed San Lucas.

The Salinas River, almost dry so late in the year, ran on the west side of the highway. Cattle grazed on bunchgrass in Crazy Horse Canyon at the edge of King City, once the domain of Charles King, who bought thirteen thousand acres of Rancho San Lorenzo, a Spanish land grant, in 1884 and planted about half of it to wheat. King raised pigs as well, with such efficiency and in such numbers that his spread was referred to as Hogtown.

Here, too, Sam Hamilton, an Orangeman from Ballykelly in Northern Ireland, bought a farm in the 1870s. Initially, Hamilton had settled in Salinas, but he wasn't cut out for town life. His daughter Olive, ambitious and headstrong, taught school near King City where, at twenty-four, she met John Ernst Steinbeck, who managed a flour mill. They were soon wed and moved to Salinas.

John Ernst hired on at the Sperry Mill there, only to lose his job when Sperry folded in 1910. He lost his savings next on a doomed attempt to open a feed store, but a fellow Mason helped to bail him out and set him up as an accountant at Spreckels Sugar. As fraternally inclined as Babbitt, John Ernst later relied on his Masonic ties to secure a position as the Monterey County treasurer, an office he held until his death in 1936.

He owned a fine Queen Anne Victorian on Central Avenue—"an immaculate and friendly house, grand enough, but not pretentious," his son John would write in *East of Eden*. Yet John Steinbeck's attitude toward Salinas was not entirely positive. The town, never pretty, sucked a darkness from the swamps, he claimed, and it wasn't a "gay," meaning happy, place. The wind beat on your nerve ends every day, and there were months of high, sad, gray fog. A blackness—a feeling of violence—lurked beneath the surface, too, he said.

"I was a stranger in Salinas and always felt alien," he once confided in a letter to Elia Kazan.

As a boy, Steinbeck's true Eden was Sam Hamilton's ranch. His grandfather was a "really great man, a man of sweet speech and sweet courtesy," and John dogged his footsteps and learned many practical skills by doing so—an ability to fix things, for example, and a fondness for tinkering, both evident in *Travels*. The ranch may well have represented the idealized version of America whose disappearance he mourned.

For all his vivid imagination, he couldn't have pictured the changes in King City a half century later. His grandmother used to put out milk for the leprechauns, but the Irish had no purchase in town anymore.

On Broadway, hard by the railroad tracks, the restaurants declared their geographical affinity within Mexico—Sinoloense, Michoacán, Guadalajaran. I ate a big bowl of Siete Mares soup at a cash-only café, where the server's English was confined to the terms on the menu. After dark, King City made me uneasy. Youths loitered on corners, often dressed like gangbangers. Maybe this was an affectation, but I had no desire to find out.

FROM KING CITY, I backtracked to San Lucas and negotiated a series of unmarked roads not much wider than goat trails before going over the San Antonio River and the Santa Lucia Range to hook up with the coast highway just above Prewitt Ridge. Ahead lay Monterey, but first I'd pass through Big Sur, Henry Miller's spiritual home, a haven some three thousand miles away from the dread Holland Tunnel.

"It is a region where extremes meet," he wrote, "a region where one is always conscious of weather, of space, of grandeur, and of eloquent silence."

Miller discovered Big Sur in 1944 on a tip from the artist Jean Varda. I discovered it in 1969 shortly after I began my exotic new life as a hippie. To pay the rent, I worked as a stock boy for a book wholesaler, not a job for the materially inclined, although I was granted library privileges and studied more than I ever did in college.

I read Miller's *Big Sur and the Oranges of Hieronymous Bosch*, and also Kerouac's hallucinatory novel about his stay in Lawrence Ferlinghetti's cabin, so when a friend proposed a road trip, I was quick to accept if only to enhance the measure of cool I'd been trying desperately to master. This friend, steeped in the lore of the Beats, knew an inn where we could stay cheaply—Deetjens, built by its Norwegian owner from scrap redwood salvaged on Cannery Row.

The inn stood in a grove of redwoods directly across from the ocean. It was incredibly rustic, its roof covered with pine needles and smoke issuing from several chimneys. A bearded gnome might well have been sitting by the hearth inside and puffing on a clay pipe. The rooms were dusty but comfortable, and nobody seemed to care how many of us piled into one as long as we kept the noise down.

I slept poorly in those days, troubled by what I hadn't yet accomplished and probably never would, but Deetjens soothed me, at least for a couple of nights. The fog softened all sounds except the steady drip of the mist, and the stoical redwoods created a protective sense of enclosure to keep the dark spirits at bay.

The Pacific was gone in the morning, hidden behind a thick gray barrier, but by ten o'clock a shaft of light shot through, and by noon we sat on the deck at Nepenthe sipping green tea, admiring the ocean view and the waitresses—all blonde, braless, barefoot, and beatific—and listening to recorded koto music. Koto music! I'd actually made it to California.

There was a story behind Nepenthe. In the 1940s, Orson Welles and Rita Hayworth, then married, stopped for a picnic in Big Sur and became so enchanted they bought a log house on a bluff for $167, but they soon split up and never spent so much as a night there, selling the property instead to Bill and Lolly Fassett, who opened a café where Henry Miller sometimes played Ping-Pong.

The Fossetts called it Nepenthe from the Greek. In the *Odyssey*, an Egyptian queen administers a drug called *Nepenthes pharmakon*, possibly an opiate, to Helen to help her forget her sorrows. Certainly, I felt drugged and free of sorrows that afternoon, breaking out of the trance only when my friend remarked, "Maybe we'll see Kim Novak. She lives around here, you know."

Impressed, I kept a close watch for Kim. I imagined her as a more mature and voluptuous incarnation of the ethereal waitresses, but she never showed up. Months went by, in fact, before I saw my first movie stars in action—Ruth Gordon and Bud Cort filming *Harold and Maude* at the old Sutro Baths in San Francisco—and advanced a little farther in my quest to become a true Californian.

At Partington Cove, below the ridge where Miller settled, I communed with the redwoods again. He'd given up on cars and pulled a child's wagon to and from the grocery store. Deetjens, still in business, wasn't such a bargain anymore, nor was the vastly expanded Nepenthe, but I meditated on the Pacific anyway, over a cup of green tea.

AMONG JOHN STEINBECK'S most painful experiences in *Travels* was his return to Monterey. He resented the strangers spoiling what he thought of as his country with their noise, clutter, and "inevitable rings" of junk. Though he understood that his reaction was natural and even predictable, it still upset him, as did the rapidly growing population and its harmful impact on the quality of life.

He visited old haunts like Johnny Garcia's bar on Alvarado Street, lamenting his lost amigos. He quoted Thomas Wolfe and insisted that you can't go home again. The strangers he disliked had taken over the town—rich people with swimming pools, who "plant geraniums in big pots." He and Garcia were ghosts, he argued.

Steinbeck often rendered a harsh opinion only to retract it immediately, and he did it again in Monterey, accusing himself of nostalgic spite for being so critical of "a beautiful place, clean, well run, and progressive." He put forth a freakish theory to account for his unease. By reappearing, he'd interfered with how others remembered him, he suggested, as if he'd risen from the dead to confuse them.

"They fish for tourists now, not pilchards," he commented wryly, bemoaning the demise of the sardine canneries, "and that species they are not likely to wipe out."

In truth, you can still buy the day's catch on Old Fisherman's Wharf in spite of the purveyors of caramel korn and clam chowder in hollowed-out loaves of sourdough bread, but Monterey Bay isn't so bountiful now.

Once it supported each new immigrant group to land on its shore, starting with the Chinese, who harvested salmon and set up camp on China Point in the 1850s.

The Japanese came next. Adept at prying abalone from the rocks, they also fished for mackerel and anchovies, and when some Sicilians muscled in on them, they switched to taking squid by night and burned pine torches in their sampans to attract them. The Sicilians introduced the lampara ring, a round haul net like a purse seine, which significantly increased the sardine yield and led to the establishment of the canneries—a "wetfish" operation because the sardines were processed fresh from the sea.

The canneries, grouped on Ocean View Avenue, finally went under in the 1950s when the pilchards vanished. Ocean View is Cannery Row now, recently renamed, fishless, and another magnet for tourists. It's clean, well run, and progressive, but it leans so heavily on Steinbeck's name and image that he might be angry or embarrassed—or maybe both—to see his life's work appropriated for commercial purposes.

"The only good writer was a dead writer," he remarked of Sinclair Lewis while in Sauk Centre, Minnesota, Lewis's birthplace. "Then he couldn't surprise anyone any more, couldn't hurt anyone any more . . . And now he's good for the town. Brings in some tourists. He's a good writer now."

In a decidedly unscientific, wholly arbitrary survey, I asked around Cannery Row to discover what, if anything, of John Steinbeck's the tourists had read. *Of Mice and Men*, often assigned in California schools, topped the list, with *The Grapes of Wrath* second. Nobody had cracked open *Tortilla Flat*, *Cannery Row*, or *In Dubious Battle*, and only one person mentioned *East of Eden*. The late novels, such as *The Winter of Our Discontent* and *Sweet Thursday*, drew a blank.

Oddly, *Travels* earned just a single mention despite being a bestseller. Readers had forgotten about it, apparently, but they praised it when prompted.

"Oh, yes, the one about the dog!" exclaimed a woman from Lodi. "I absolutely loved it!"

Her response was typical. People loved Charley and the idea of being on the road, but they were blind to the author's acid observations, barely concealed malaise, and outright expressions of disgust.

There's no Palace Flophouse on the new Cannery Row, and no bordello posing as the Bear Flag Restaurant. I combed the downtown for a bar like Johnny Garcia's without success. The wild characters Steinbeck cherished—the paisanos, Jolon Indians, and speakers of *poco* Spanish— had moseyed on or just disappeared. In a sense, it didn't matter. What he really missed was the youthful vitality he associated with Monterey—a loss his rough journey had underscored. In old age, death becomes a fact instead of a pageant, he muttered as he left.

IN ELIA KAZAN's *East of Eden*, James Dean shuttles between Monterey, played by Mendocino, and Salinas by hitching rides on top of boxcars. When I looked at the traffic backed up on Route 68 the next morning, I wished a train would roll through so I could jump on it like Jimmy and reach the National Steinbeck Center in Salinas without any further delay.

Faced with a long wait, I pulled a swift and probably illegal U-turn and headed south toward Carmel, a city Steinbeck demeaned as a "community of the well-to-do and retired." For someone who made a fortune on his books, he showed an odd distaste for the wealthy, but maybe we all cling to a more virtuous image of ourselves than exists in actuality.

Though it's true, as he noted, that Carmel doesn't welcome starveling writers and unwanted painters anymore. I saw no inklings of boho culture on the streets Clint Eastwood once ruled as mayor. I didn't see much of anything, really, because the fog had wrapped up Carmel in several layers of wool and obscured all but the red beacons of stoplights.

Yet when I turned inland the fog began to lift, receding like the last wispy filaments of a dream to reveal more tawny Coast Range foothills interlaced with ranches, resorts, and golf courses. Carmel Valley was so dry you could almost hear the grasses about to crackle and disintegrate. At this time of year, the locals lived in terror of the carelessly discarded cigarette or the shard of glass poised at an angle to start a blaze.

The road, almost deserted, swung into Steinbeck's beloved Salinas Valley eventually. To the west lay the Santa Lucias, and to the east the

Gabilan Range, where buzzards and red-tail hawks glide about on the big winds—*gavilan*, Spanish for sparrow hawk.

Only a snippet of *East of Eden* was shot in the valley, but what Kazan captured in 1955 hasn't altered much. Spring is the prettiest season here, when the bright-orange poppies and purple lupine burst into bloom. The air has a clarity it loses when the heat comes on. By early summer the ground is baked hard, and you breathe dust, dust, and more dust.

In Steinbeck's boyhood, the cattle barons were the valley's gentry, as respected as English royalty, with the Spreckels and their sugar beets next in line, but lettuce is the "green gold" now. Strawberries and artichokes also are valuable, and you'll never hurt for broccoli, tomatoes, Brussels sprouts, carrots, or fennel. The vineyards are rooted along the Salinas River. Some forty thousand acres of Monterey County are planted to wine and table grapes.

My idle loop took me back to Highway 101. From Soledad I barreled straight to Salinas. Steinbeck remembered it as a "little little town" of about two thousand, with a general store and a blacksmith shop, where he sat on a bench listening to the clang of a hammer against an anvil. The new subdivisions and cookie cutter houses, all "clustered like aphids," repelled him, as did a TV relay station that lunged toward the sky from a hill where the coyotes used to sing on moonlit nights.

The population of Salinas in 1960 was about 80,000. It hovers at about 145,000 now and looks like most other western cities, its distinctive qualities stamped out over time and buried under the usual sprawl. Oldtown is the obligatory historic district, with the National Steinbeck Center as its anchor. Some businesses from his time still remain—a card room, the Greyhound station, the Traveler's Hotel, and Sang's Café with its brag, "Steinbeck Ate Here."

Chinese-American cafés were once staples in Salinas, reliably feeding huge meals to field workers at a price they could afford. Sang's menu, nearly as long as my arm, favored traditional blue-plate specials over chop suey and chow mein—meatloaf, short ribs, chicken-fried steak, and a prime rib lunch that Wednesday for $11.95.

"Good choice," my server said, scratching on a pad. "Prime rib will be sold out pretty soon."

I couldn't resist asking, "Did Steinbeck really eat here?"

"Yes, sir. Ed Ricketts, too."

They must have had serious appetites, because Sang's doesn't scrimp on the extras. The soup, a rich blend of beans and ham hock, came in a bowl, not a cup. If the salad failed to do justice to the valley's lettuce, the beef compensated—an inch-thick cut cooked medium rare, with some broccoli and spuds on the side. Dessert was an idea I refused to entertain.

THE STEINBECK CENTER, an imposing glass-fronted museum, is a short stroll from Sang's. No other modern American writer—not Faulkner, not Hemingway—has been accorded such imperial treatment.

In spite of Steinbeck's complaints about Salinas, his patrons there and beyond have made his legacy secure. The multimedia exhibits, arranged in chronological order, lead you through room after room of manuscripts, letters, photos, and first editions until you come to a room devoted to *Travels with Charley*, where a reconditioned Rocinante takes up most of the space.

From my reading, I expected Rocinante to be larger and more cumbersome, the precursor of an RV, but it's an ordinary quarter-ton truck painted forest green and fitted with a custom-built Wolverine camper shell. For a big man with a dog, it must have been confining, Steinbeck's testimony to the contrary. He probably couldn't stand up inside without grazing his head on the ceiling.

Though Steinbeck heaped praise on Rocinante and spoke of it in endearing human terms, just as he did with Charley, he sold it at auction to a Maryland farmer right after he got home, as if to put the trip out of his mind as quickly as possible. His quest had failed, after all. He would not be reborn, nor did his contact with America refresh or replenish his creative juices.

His journey, meant to engage, had turned into a withdrawal, even a defeat. Rocinante became his isolated retreat as Elizabeth Otis had feared it would. Steinbeck's attempt to find the truth about the nation also fell short, at least by his own lights. The only generality he risked was that "an exact and provable" American identity exists.

"This is not patriotic whoop-de-doo; it is carefully observed fact," he asserted. "California Chinese, Boston Irish, Wisconsin German, yes, and Alabama Negroes, have more in common than apart."

The last few pages of *Travels* are harrowing, with Steinbeck so anxious to get back to New York he "collapsed into a jelly of weariness" when a policeman blocked his entry to the Holland Tunnel because he carried a tank of butane. Instead he had to cross the Hudson on the Hoboken Ferry, only to lose his way in lower Manhattan during rush hour. Jittery and laughing uncontrollably, he begged another cop to set him straight.

"And that's how the traveler came home again," he says, slamming the door shut without any further reflection.

The door kept swinging open, though. The fate of America obsessed Steinbeck, and he pursued it until the end of his life. His impressions from the road ultimately coalesced in a series of essays published as *America and Americans* (1966) in company with photographs of the country. This would be his last work, issued two years before his death.

Didactic and often humorless, the essays probed the themes he touched on only obliquely in *Travels*. The final one, "Americans and the Future," began by revisiting the ideas first expressed to Pascal Covici. America suffers from a subtle and deadly illness, Steinbeck said. Immorality doesn't describe it, nor does lack of integrity or dishonesty.

What's been lost, he went on, are the rules—"rules concerning life, limb, and property, rules governing deportment, manners, conduct, and rules defining dishonesty, dishonor, misconduct, and crime."

He compared the behavior of Americans to highly bred, trained, and specialized bird dogs cooped up in a kennel rather than allowed to hunt. In a short time, the dogs become "quarrelsome, fat, lazy, cowardly, dirty, and utterly disreputable and worthless, and all because their purpose is gone and with it the rules and disciplines that made them beautiful and good."

For millions of years, he continued, our purpose was simple survival, but we had all that we needed now, including the terrible hazard of leisure.

"I strongly suspect that our moral and spiritual disintegration grows out of our lack of experience with plenty," Steinbeck wrote, and further, "A dying people tolerates the present, rejects the future, and finds its satisfactions in past greatness and half-remembered glory . . . When the greatness recedes, so does belief in greatness."

Americans were not a dying people, he decided. They hadn't lost their way at all, but the roads of the past had come to an end, and they had not yet discovered a path to the future.

"I think we will find one, but its direction may be unthinkable to us now," he concluded.

Fᴿᴏᴍ ꜱᴀʟɪɴᴀꜱ, ɪ took the scenic coast road to San Francisco. Again the fog was heavy, covering the artichoke fields in Castroville. The ocean looked gray, too, and the little beaches along the strand were deserted except for some wishful surfers in wet suits, waiting for a swell. Around Santa Cruz I drove, then past Swanton and Davenport to Pescadero, where I stopped for coffee at Duarte's Tavern and smelled the crab cioppino simmering in the kitchen.

The date was October 31, Halloween. I'd have known it without a calendar. San Franciscans like to dress up for the occasion, even on the job. At a bank on Market Street, one teller wore a bumblebee costume—yellow cap, waggling antennae, the works. She was cashing a check for a vampire with fake blood dripping from his plastic fangs and his Dracula collar turned up against the chilly breeze outside.

Some critics accuse San Francisco of growing its own eccentrics, but it isn't true. They come from all over America, the misfits and refugees from Vincennes, Indiana, say, or Flora, Kansas, tired of pretending to be somebody else and aspiring to explore their true identity in a city that not only tolerates but encourages self-expression.

I met a private detective friend for lunch. Among his investigative specialties is digging up sensational food at bargain prices. He held his beleaguered head in his hands as he described his ordeal of the night before, a caper worthy of Philip Marlowe that involved huge chunks of beef and gallons of red wine at a Peruvian restaurant he'd recently discovered.

The story sounded tawdry at first, another tale of excess and folly, but it gained momentum with each Singha beer he drank until it began to shimmer and glow. The blood surged back to my Marlowe's face. He was enthused, revivified. We'd all have to share a Peruvian meal before I returned to Dublin, absolutely—a big gang of us! To do otherwise, he implied, would be a crime.

He gave me the keys to a mutual friend's flat. She was traveling in England, so Imelda and I would have the place to ourselves. How odd it felt to unlock the front door, climb the stairs, and enter the living room, a stranger no more. That's how *my* trip ended—abruptly, in a flash. Insofar as anywhere qualified as my home, San Francisco probably was it.

No trick-or-treaters called that evening, no skeletons or fairy princesses. I collapsed into bed early and had no idea where I was when I woke. Take a quick shower, grab some clothes, pack up, and hit the road—that routine was history. Instead I'd gone back to the starting point, lingering over a newspaper. The World Series was over, so there were no box scores in the *Chronicle* and no further mention of Tomoji Tanabe, either.

The Focus begged for a thorough cleaning before I left for the airport to meet Imelda. I filled a garbage bag with flotsam and jetsam—a shard of sandstone, some calcified french fries, a flyer for Luray Caverns. Dust and grit coated the dashboard so thickly I could have inscribed notes to myself with an index finger.

Imelda's flight from Ireland, scheduled to arrive around noon, ran late. I paced and fretted. Six weeks was time enough for a woman to come to her senses, after all. When the plane landed she wasn't the first through the gate, nor the fifteenth or the thirtieth. My anxiety spiked until she emerged from the crowd at last, and my world felt whole again.

Thrilled to be in California for the election, she told how the Irish bookies, certain of a Democratic victory, had already paid off any bets on Obama. That was good news for San Franciscans, who overwhelmingly supported him. In Timberville, they might throw a parade for George W. Bush, but here they'd more likely toss a shoe. Obama posters, banners, and signs decorated every corner. The city that needs no excuse to celebrate prepared to do it again.

Even so, San Francisco—for all its upbeat atmosphere—was not immune to the recession. Here, too, were vacant storefronts and long lines of the unemployed, soup kitchens and flophouses for the homeless. The bedraggled multitude of outcasts around the Civic Center, once a sight so familiar I accepted it as normal, horrified me now. You rarely see such apparent indifference to human misery anywhere in Europe.

If I'd finally set aside *Travels*, I was still reading some Steinbeck, mainly the essays in a book of selected nonfiction I'd bought in Salinas. In "The Golden Handcuff," he carried on about his affection for San Francisco, always the City with a capital "C." As a child, he got too excited to sleep on the eve of a visit, and spent part of his scruffy apprentice years by the bay, fondly recalling the dumps he rented during his "tour of duty as an intellectual bohemian."

The dumps had one thing in common, he wrote. They were small and cheap. He remembered a dark little attic on Powell Street with unsheathed rafters and pigeons walking into and out of a dormer window, and a cave in North Beach "carpeted wall to wall with garlic," but his poverty never compromised his ability or desire to have fun.

"My God! How beautiful it was and I knew then how beautiful," he raved. "Saturday night with five silver dollars laughing and clapping their hands in your pocket. North Beach awakening with lights in a misty evening . . . long tables clad in white oilcloth, the heaped baskets of sour bread, the pots de chambre of beautiful soup du jour, then fish and meat, fruit, cheese, coffee, 40 cents."

I decided to show Imelda some dumps from my own youth, first the abysmal studio apartment on Cole Street where I landed in '69. The neighborhood dope fiends burgled me twice in three months, stripping me of my TV, stereo, records, radio, and only good coat. From there I moved to a railroad flat overlooking Kezar Pavilion, where the vicious Roller Derby matches always ended with bottles breaking and bloody fistfights among the fans.

The pungent aroma of eucalyptus came roaring back to me in Golden Gate Park. I used to buy my records at the New Geology Rock Shop and my marijuana from a fuzzy-haired dealer named Roger. The rack of little magazines at City Lights, martinis at Persian Aub Zam Zam, riding a cable car up Nob Hill, the free love I never got any of—I, too, was poor but dazzled.

Like Steinbeck, I adopted North Beach as my playground. Our evenings often started with dinner at the Gold Spike, Italian fare served family-style—ballast, we called it. What the food lacked in quality it made up for in quantity. There were tureens of minestrone, big bowls of pasta, roast chicken or osso bucco, vegetables, dessert, coffee, and wine—"and that means lots of wine," as Steinbeck put it.

Afterward we raced from bar to bar with an eye out for famous poets, the only type of celebrity that mattered to us, and argued ceaselessly about writing, art, music, politics, and what we knew of life—not much—reveling in the brilliant future destiny had in store for us. I was still riding the zephyr of optimism that had carried me West, and I believed, as we all did in those days, that anything was possible.

One morning, I took Imelda to Sonoma County, where my old trailer, long since scrapped, once stood among the vineyards. Along the Russian River, I regaled her with tales of steelhead glory, and she did her best not to nod off. In a meadow on Chalk Hill Road, the wild mushrooms called "pinkies" still grew, and over there, by a ramshackle barn, was the big oak that had sheltered a pair of Bullock's orioles so many years ago.

THE IRISH BOOKIES seldom get it wrong. At precisely 8:01 P.M. on election night, right after the polls closed in California and the rest of the West, the TV networks declared Barack Obama the new president-elect of the United States. San Francisco predictably erupted with backyard flares and Roman candles, while champagne corks bounced off ceilings and ricocheted off walls.

Obama's sober demeanor was better suited to the occasion. He understood the formidable challenges ahead and the obstacles to be surmounted before the current torpor might lift—and there was no guarantee it *would* lift. Already certain forces were allied to try to prevent his success. I knew this from the road.

I thought about *Travels* during the broadcast, of course. If John Steinbeck had sounded overly dark at times, perhaps because of his failing health, his analysis still contained a large measure of truth. He recognized the need for the country to rise above the ordinary when history demands it. Whether Americans had the capacity and the will to do so would be answered soon enough.

Steinbeck expressed his doubts in 1960, and I shared them to a degree. Almost fifty years later, our citizens were frequently lax, soft, and querulous, and they sometimes capitulated to a childish sense of entitlement that, once thwarted, turned into an equally childish disappointment. So many lived in a bubble, too, especially in isolated rural towns, and found their satisfaction in "past greatness and half-remembered glory." They cared not a whit about the nations beyond Main Street.

Yet I also felt more hopeful than Steinbeck, maybe because I'd done more listening. Whenever my faith wavered, as it often did, I met someone who helped to restore it. The young were particularly useful in that regard, less concerned about the economic freefall and as breezily dreamy as I was in my optimistic prime. All across America, I encountered people who weren't threatened or cowed and still ardently believed in the bright promise of the future.

Steinbeck blamed our debatable "spiritual and moral disintegration" on the lack of experience with plenty, and that's not entirely inaccurate. The older European societies are quieter and gentler, more sophisticated and adult. Americans are friendly, well-intentioned, good-humored, kind, and generous, but also loud, aggressive, clumsy, gullible, and poorly educated on the whole. Poetry matters very little to us, and the same could be said of romance.

Some of the problems that bothered Steinbeck probably can't be fixed. The trashiness of the landscape, the pernicious malls and ugly subdivisions, and the uniform blandness of our mass culture are here to stay barring a cataclysm. At the same time, he missed so many positives—the huge tracts of wilderness we've saved, for example, and the potential rewards of new technologies—that he often comes across as an old fogey stymied by what he failed to comprehend.

America can do that to you. It gave me fits for 5,943 miles, alternately grand and awful, sublime and stomach-turning, both a riddle and a paradox. You could no more capture its quicksilver essence than catch lightning in a jar. The fifty states, each with its own mores and set of priorities, don't cohere except on paper. There's no proper instrument to calculate the real distance between Denton, Maryland, and Gunnison, Colorado. If a common American identity once existed, "exact and provable," it doesn't anymore.

One wants to sing the country's praises, but it isn't easy when we have the highest rate of incarceration anywhere, and spend so much on defense that our schools, the ultimate engine of democracy, go begging. Nobody would shout "Hooray!" over our gross obesity or polluted watersheds. Our unsurpassed talent for living on credit merits no fanfare, either, nor does our indulgence of the divisive talk-show pundits or the way we've devalued—and even become suspicious of—the pursuit of excellence.

Still, Americans had just awakened from their long slumber to cast a vote for change. The previous eight years might yet be looked on as an aberration, as if a strange virus had infected the body politic and caused it to go haywire. Change involves risk, though, and rewards only the noble, heroic gesture. To create a unifying vision, the pioneer spirit must triumph again. That may require an imaginative leap, the ability to believe we can be better than we really are.

MY MARLOWE MADE good on his promise. He rounded up a boisterous group for dinner at Mi Lindo Peru in the Outer Mission, an even dozen celebrants who devoured empanadas and lomo saltado, yucca and plantain, fried potatoes and boiled rice, all washed down with sangria, beer, and that dangerous red wine.

The idea of leaving San Francisco while the air still throbbed with hope and abandon made Imelda and me a little sad. No city accommodates its idlers so readily, or so enthralls them with its beauty. Our last two days in town were treacherously seductive—mild and sunny, light-filled. We tried to do and see everything, stuffing ourselves with California against the cold Dublin winter ahead, walking for miles in any and all directions.

The old Italians had mostly disappeared from North Beach, but you could still get a strong doppio espresso at Mario's Bohemian Cigar Store and a game of boccie on the courts behind the library. Ducks still hung by their feet in the Chinatown markets, and the condemned fish still stared at you bug-eyed from their tanks. Budding writers still ransacked the little magazines at City Lights, palpably aching to be published. The bay did its job and glittered.

Would I ever move back to San Francisco? My friends asked that question. I told them I thought about it all the time. Imelda's sons were young men now, finished with school and living independently, so we had more freedom to roam. We'd enjoyed our stay and the loaner flat and especially the supercharged atmosphere of the moment. Anything could happen, really. I told my friends that, too.

They asked about my trip as well, eager for the details. They weren't surprised that certain aspects of America had displeased me—they had their own laundry list of complaints—but they knew nothing about the Virginia Gold apples of Flint Hill or the heavenly setting of Salida, the big trout in the Arkansas River or the juicy melons of the Eastern Shore.

There's still a lot to love about America, I counseled my Marlowe, bequeathing him my copy of *Travels*, fallen apart now and split down the middle at page 123.

The world is what we make of it, although John Steinbeck phrased it differently. External reality has a way of being not so external after all, he suggested. It's tied more closely to our feelings than we care to admit. As the hardships of the road began to fade, I dwelled instead on the incidents to be cherished—a ten-buck haircut in Jeff City, say, or Father Urnick's uplifting sermon in Laughlin. Often I recalled Clifford Dewey's belief in the long view and kept my fingers crossed.

Acknowledgments

My thanks to David Shipley and George Kalogerakis at the *New York Times*, who published a bit of this material in a different form; Dr. Joseph Trimmer of the Virginia Ball Center at Ball State University, for his kind invitation and some much-appreciated gas money; David Milch, whose generous spirit made life easier once I sat down to write; Jacqueline Johnson, for her helpful editorial comments; and George Gibson, a first-rate publisher if ever there was one.

Author's Note

In order to understand John Steinbeck's decision to make the trip that resulted in *Travels with Charley*, I relied on Jay Parini's *John Steinbeck: A Biography* (New York: Henry Holt, 1996), and *Steinbeck: A Life in Letters*, edited by Elaine Steinbeck and Robert Wallsten (New York: Penguin, 1989). The essays collected as "America and Americans" are included in *Of Men and Their Making: The Selected Nonfiction of John Steinbeck*, edited by Susan Shillinglaw and Jackson J. Benson (London: Penguin, Allen Lane, 2002). I am indebted to Theodore H. White's incisive *The Making of the President 1960* (New York: Atheneum, 1961) for the background information on that election.

A Note on the Author

Bill Barich has written extensively for the *New Yorker*, and his work has also appeared in such diverse publications as *Sports Illustrated*, *American Poetry Review*, *Best American Short Stories*, and *The Literary Journalists*. His racetrack classic *Laughing in the Hills* has never been out of print, and he is the author as well of *A Pint of Plain*, *Crazy for Rivers*, the novel *Carson Valley*, and *A Fine Place to Daydream*. He has been a Guggenheim Fellow and a Literary Laureate of the San Francisco Public Library, and currently lives in Dublin and California.